DESCENT

D1626183

```
                              FRANCES
    HON. FRANCIS            WILHELMINA
  HELY-HUTCHINSON  =  NIXON        WILLIAM WRIGHTSON = HARRIOT HEBER
          |                                   |
COL. THE HON. HENRY HELY-HUTCHINSON   =   HARRIOT NORTH DOUGLAS
                                  |            (née WRIGHTSON)
        |
 JISA HELY-HUTCHINSON


 ERESBY SITWELL


 TWELL      SACHEVERELL SITWELL


 JGUSTA DENISON


 ADY EDITH SOMERSET
          |
  GEORGINA FITZROY = HENRY, 7TH DUKE OF BEAUFORT = EMILY CULLING SMITH

                        LADY
  6TH DUKE    | CHARLOTTE SOPHIA                              LADY ANNE
 OF BEAUFORT = LEVESON GOWER    CHARLES CULLING-SMITH = WELLESLEY
```

LEFT HAND, RIGHT HAND!

THE AUTHOR, AGED 3

LEFT HAND
RIGHT HAND!

An Autobiography by
OSBERT SITWELL

THE REPRINT SOCIETY
LONDON

THIS EDITION PUBLISHED BY THE REPRINT SOCIETY LTD.
BY ARRANGEMENT WITH MACMILLAN AND CO. LTD.
1946

TO

MY BROTHER AND SISTER

Printed in Great Britain by
The Camelot Press Ltd., London and Southampton

INTRODUCTION

ALL works of art that are purely imaginative—poems, novels, stories—are pulled out of the future as you may pluck a roasted chestnut out of the fire, scorching your hand in the process. But in this cruel and meaningless epoch, behind the bars of which I now write, neither past nor future seems to have any existence; only the present which contains the dead ashes of the past. Since the whole of life and its background is being dissolved to chaos before our eyes, it is impossible—because our balance from day to day remains too precarious—to wrest a book from the future. In consequence, I have resolved to start the story of my life, to describe some of it, and some of those who have figured in it.

Already the borders of the pages from which I take my notes are stained by the cold fingers of Time and the hot fingers of the sun; the sun of hot countries, China and Guatemala, Indo-China and the West Indies, Sicily and Malta and Morocco, reminding me how long these books have been in my possession, and that the hour has now struck for me to start on this journey to recapture the past. Already I am nearing fifty and the grey hairs are beginning to show. I have reached the watershed and can see the stream which I must follow downhill toward the limitless ocean, cold and featureless. It is indeed time to begin.

No biography is easy to write and, because we know more of ourselves than of others, autobiographies are the most delicate of approach. . . . Of the kind of book that I want to write, I will treat in a moment. But first it is necessary to explain that I had the fortune to be born toward the sunset hour of one of the great periodic calms of history. So placid was this brief golden halt that often as a small child, passionately addicted to reading books of history, I used to wonder whether its stream had not altogether dried up. The Diamond Jubilee, the Boer War, the Edwardian Decade, none of these, viewed separately, was history—indeed the Jubilee was a sort of official celebration of its death. Nothing had happened for so long, and nothing would happen again: nothing. (But life seems static to all children, even those of the present day. Such is their innate confidence in parents, that it is only necessary for the father to dismiss an aircraft, in the very act of dropping bombs, as "one of ours", for the children immediately to believe him and regain their sense of security.) Everything was calm and still and kindly. Yet as I listened sometimes to the complacent chatter of my nurse, while she sewed new ribbons on to a new lace cap and, in my presence, talked about me to my mother's maid over the hum of the sewing-machine (I can smell the warm, oily smell of it as I write), saying how lucky I was to be an elder son of such parents, and therefore of assured prospects, growing up in a world which had improved, owing to Queen Victoria and the benevolence of all members of the British race, beyond what anyone could have expected, and held in it no possibility of deterioration even though the general progress was occasionally impeded by the spite of foreigners such as Kruger, how lucky to be born exactly then and thus, and not in any other age; at such moments a very strong doubt, arising from the wisdom of the blood, that fragile scarlet tree we carry within us, used to assail me, and I would wonder, "But am I; is it true?", prompted by a precocious spirit of contradiction which has its good as well as its bad side, being the fount of such wit as I can show.

Notwithstanding, it is to that halcyon age in which I grew up that now I turn; years in which human life had a value set upon it, inalterable as it seemed then, and when the ape, so cleverly fitted in just under the skin of each human being, was a secret taint of which to be ashamed, a shadow, the mere glimpse of which would frighten the bravest man, and not, as now, an ideal to be extolled and after which to struggle. Vaguely people still talked with horror of the Siege of Paris; the only thing, real thing, that had happened within memory. But that, after all, was an incident in *French* history, and, as such, perhaps should have been looked for: it had not affected us except to make rich English merchants and hotel proprietors yet, and still more justifiably, richer. It had been *dreadful*, though, everyone admitted that, and out of keeping with the times. And my Aunt Florence[1] kept, I remember, as a reminder of the depths to which human beings can come, a kind of *memento mori*, a piece—given her by a former French governess—of the bread that the people ate in the beleaguered city. Straw-coloured and apparently petrified, it stood as granite, and in those days constituted the sole evidence of human cruelty. It was, I want to emphasise, necessary to remind oneself. . . . But in the years that have followed I have watched the endless massing of the apes for conflict.

Everywhere men have unlocked the prisoners within, and from under the disguising skins the apes have leapt joyfully out. Yet perhaps we wrong them, for they love new tricks, new ways, else would they still be monkeys: whereas the only new ideas, new things which men have proved themselves ready to regard and use without fear, are horrible methods of slaughter, ever more horrible. A new development in art, a new conception in politics, a new invention for saving human life, and hysterical fright seizes upon them; a new manner of killing, on the other hand, and an uncontrollable impulse to set it in motion descends upon them. The bomb-auction to which this leads is now upon us. Tit for Tat, pinch for smack, kick for pinch; "Blitz on London!", "R.A.F. bomb Berlin!", "Wops bomb Malta!"; "R.A.F. Raid on Syracuse!", "Japs bomb Manila!", "U.S.A. bomb Tokyo!", so the captions run. "If Athens is bombed," writes a correspondent, suffering from an overdose of logic, to a London paper, "why spare Rome?" Why indeed? And, so that we may in other times remember the putting of this question—for other times *will* come—let me now, in hot blood, reproduce a letter that appeared, toward the end of November, 1940, in the pages of the *Spectator*. It ought not to be forgotten.

SIR,

On reading the article by Janus against the bombing of Rome by reason of its various antiquities, I feel that I must disagree with him. Who cares whether the Forum or the Colosseum is razed to the ground? At least 90 per cent of the British working population have never seen, and have no wish to see, these two objects which are, as like as not, an eyesore. They are just there for large-stomached capitalists who go because they think it is high class. There was also

[1] Her diary appeared as the second part of *Two Generations*. (Macmillan & Co., 1940.)

a letter which advocated the bombing of Rome, but not the Vatican City. Why not? The Vatican City has done nothing to stop the war. All this blather about the Holy City, etc., is absolute trash, and it with all the rest of Rome should be visited nightly by our bombers in the same way as London is by theirs.[1]

But I recall with love and pride when London and Rome were sacred shrines: and as such they will rank again. One is as indestructible as the other; both are flowers of the human spirit. No night is eternal, though every night seems long.

> I saw a cloud upon a hill
>   Anchor its shadow on a grave;
> I saw a vulture, O! how still,
>   Upon a broken architrave.
>
> I saw a hill within a cloud,
>   I saw a grave within its shade,
> I saw a phoenix from its shroud
>   Soar upward to a fiery glade.
>
> I saw a man with broken heart
>   And angels drooping broken wings,
> I heard the rumble of a cart
>   Piled up with bodies of dead kings.
>
> And then I saw a cloud ope wide
>   And out of it a white dove come,
> Alighting in sweet, cooing pride
>   Upon the branch that rocked its home.
>
> And then I heard a human voice
>   Far off, in laughter loud and free;
> The phoenix cried "Rejoice! Rejoice!"
>   And all my soul burned inwardly.
>
> For as she cried, the west wind blew
>   With force gigantic that space gives
> And deep within my heart I knew
>   That tyrants die, but freedom lives.
>
>   . . . . .
>
> I saw the cloud lift, drift along
>   To shelter all the sweltering plains
> Where rose the loud triumphant song
>   Of broken hearts that break their chains.

[1] T. Fairless, 10 Saltwell Place, Gateshead-on-Tyne, Co. Durham.

I saw the vulture's scaly face;
I saw it quit the architrave;
I saw the phoenix give it chase
And blossoms burst forth from the grave.

Men die, even the most evil, and stupidity perishes as much as grace. By its nature, the triumph can be but temporary of ape over man. Between them Art is, and always has been, the dividing line. And for this reason, if for no other, and to show, after the manner of Disraeli, that I, too, am "on the side of the angels", I want my biography, no less than a novel or a book of travel—and, indeed, it must partake of the essence of both—to be a work of art, upon which I can expend not only such gifts as I possess, but the skill acquired through many years of labour at my task. I plan, if I am allowed to finish it, a book of several volumes to cover a longer span of time than is usual. The first portion will deal with many people who died before I was born, but who still influence me, perhaps, in ways I do not know as well as in ways to be recognised, for past and future both work upon the present; but the chief interest of the earlier chapters must derive from the circumstances surrounding, and the events befalling, a family which has produced three writers in a single generation—writers who are, I should say, in spite of a family likeness apparent at first sight, very dissimilar—and in the description, too, of the characters in the foreground of their young lives.

Not even the beginning of the book, however, do I wish to be written with childhood's innocent eye: for nothing can alter the fact that it is impossible again to travel into that lost kingdom. (And, as for that, just *how* innocent is the eye of childhood? My sister says, indeed, that since the publication of my novel, *Before the Bombardment*, she has never been able to look a child of between three and twelve straight in the eye again, for, to her knowledge, all the material for it, all the full characterisation and detail, was gathered by myself at that age from my surroundings when at Scarborough, or from what I divined to be behind them.) Moreover, a great deal of my young life was no doubt dull, a great deal sad, but I need not inflict a repetition of these emotions, when they are trivial, upon others. Only the crucial sadness need I reproduce; for, by temperament, though not sanguine, I am—or was—high-spirited. I will not, therefore, concern the reader with those parts from which I want, myself, to escape, for the aim of this book is to beguile, and not to improve, the mind. I do not pretend to tell the reader everything, only to paint for him in a setting, a portrait, of which, as in a surrealist picture, many diverse incidents compose the features. I leave the skeletons in their cupboards, and the flesh in its clothing, and walk where I will. I claim the right, moreover, to jump forwards and look backwards as I choose.

In addition I should like to emphasise that I *want* my memories to be old-fashioned and extravagant—as they are; —I *want* this work to be as full of detail, massed or individual, as my last book, of short stories, was shorn of it—had to be shorn of it because of its form; I *want* this to be gothic, complicated in surface and crowned with turrets and with pinnacles, for that is its nature. I mean it to be full of others besides myself and my brother and sister, giving scenes and *divertissements*, crowded with people of every sort; for I have always found friends and, perhaps because of my origin, coming of a family that has lived within three miles of the room wherein I now write, for at least seven hundred years, I have never experienced that sensation of being separate from the working classes, in the way in which the city-bred, middle-class poets of the proletarian movement continually proclaim themselves to feel cut off, deploring in foot-sore metre, often very justly, their own stiff collars and priggish, coy, self-conscious silence. . . . No, we all here draw our strength from the same soil, and my friends recognise it. I do not acknowledge the barrier of the white collar. The only fence I admit is that which exists between those who create—whatever may be the form of their creation—and those who do not, who absorb: (and I must remind the reader that, even as children, the *creators* tend by their nature to be set apart). Though I have loved the companionship of the clever, the beautiful, the sensitive, yet the pretentious have never pleased me, and with the simple have I often found refuge.

I have seen many people in many countries, and will write of some of them. In descriptions of persons, it is often difficult

not to give offence, but I shall try for the most part to avoid it.
In a former book I showed new people in lands new to me, and
endeavoured to evoke the age-old life of the Chinese against the
threadbare golden expanse of their country: now I am setting
myself to the task of bringing out the equal fantasy and beauty
that are to be found in people and objects familiar to us from
birth, these qualities being only obscured for us by their vicinity
or the custom of many centuries, and to prove that English life,
today and yesterday, often contains as much power and
character as when Chaucer first presented it in a new language.
In the book to which allusion has just been made,[1] I offered, in
illustration of the genius for the grotesque of the Chinese,
various catalogues of the names of birds, insects and flowers.[2]
One such list—I choose it because it is the shortest, not because
it is the best—applies to the various types of goldfish bred in
Peking: Red Dragon Eye, Five Colour Stripes, Blue Dragon
Eye, Tiger's Head, Celestial Telescope and Toad Head. . . .
But are these heraldic titles more imaginative and characteristic,
more exotic, even, than Spotted Elephant, Black Arches,
Purple Shades, Ground Lackey, Green Forester, Belted Beauty,
White Admiral, Rosy Rustic and Light-Feathered Rustic,
Crimson-Speckled Footman, Black Chestnut, November
Dagger, Long-Legged Pearl, Ringed China Mark, Beautiful
Pug and Beautiful Snout; these being the names of English
butterflies and recently instanced for their national flavour by
that most talented writer, Mr. H. E. Bates,[3] in the columns of
the *Spectator*? Full of local genius, too, are other names he
gives us: Glory of Kent, Lulworth Skipper, Dover Belle,
Emerald Essex, Brixton Beauty and Cambridge Veneer; while,
though less fabulous, a vein of poetic fire runs, too, through the
homeliness of the following names of apples and pears that I
have found in *Pomona Herefordiensis*:[4] Forest Stire, Loan

[1] *Escape With Me!* (Macmillan & Co., 1939.)

[2] These lists were mostly culled from an enchanting book, entitled *Annual
Customs and Festivals in Peking*, by Tun Lich'en, translated by Derk Bodde
(Henri Vetch, Peking, 1936), and from Arlington and Lewisohn's *In Search
of Old Peking* (ibid., 1935).

[3] Mr. Bates kindly informs me that these names occur in Curtis's *Ento-
mology*. He attributes to them an eighteenth-century origin.

[4] Published in London, 1811.

Pearmain, the Red Must, Golden Pippin, Hagloe Crab, Foxwhelp, the Best Bache, Teinton Squash, Redstreak, Old Quining, the Huffcap Pear, the Garter Apple, the Brandy or Golden Harvey, the Siberian Harvey, Cowarne Red, the Friar, Woodcock and Yellow Elliott. These words, as I have said, are less strange in their music than the lists of butterflies, yet their sound exhales the crude, fresh scents of farm and orchard; the scent of moss rose and bedstraw and milk and blossoming fruit trees and, even, of the midden.

Again, what strange customs and ceremonies we have been privileged to see; never before, for example, has there been a period when the style in which the women of the richer classes dressed, changed completely every year and, latterly, in the two decades between the wars, every three months. What fantastic, what beautiful people have been provided for us to see and know. Though Shelley and Pope and Shakespeare have long been dust, we have all of us been given the chance of passing in our own streets Yeats, than whom no human being could look more noble, with his sweeping grey-white mane, that appeared to be almost blue, and his fine and enrapt features, or of seeing the octogenarian Bernard Shaw striding down Piccadilly in all the vigour and sparkle of his unending youth. Though Cézanne and Seurat, though Schubert and Brahms, lived before we were born, we have been able to sit in the same room as Picasso and Matisse and Tchelicheff, as Ravel, Stravinsky and Debussy. (Indeed so overcome was I as a very young man, at meeting Debussy—for whom I entertained an immense reverence and admiration—when he came to London in the summer of 1914, that I was never able afterwards even to recall what he looked like. I have no recollection of him. The intensity of the emotion killed memory.) On the stage, too, we have watched Chaliapin and Nijinsky, Karsavina and Duse; artists whose merits those of my generation must sing, whose memory they must make an effort to preserve for posterity. How often lately have I not been asked by those half my age in what manner Nijinsky could have surpassed the dancers of the present day, and, although I also in my youth had not believed in the superior skill of, let us say, Taglioni over Karsavina when extolled by my elders, and had been irritated at the idea of such a presumption, have yet found myself lost before these depths of tragic ignorance. . . . But these artists, or most of them, must be left to a later volume. . . .

First I must essay, in order to effect a portrait of an age and person, to show how a child of such a family as mine *should* have developed, what his background was, as well as how he *did*, in fact, evolve.

Before I begin, and all the trumpets blow, only one point remains; I must explain the title I have chosen. The whole work is called *Left Hand, Right Hand!* because, according to the palmists, the lines of the left hand are incised inalterably at birth, while those of the right hand are modified by our actions and environment, and the life we lead. But, because I phrase it after this manner—the name so perfectly expressing the purport of the book, and the sense I wish to convey—, and although I believe all men, including myself, to be superstitious, do not, gentle reader, conclude that, except in so far as any attempt at divination is more apt to catch the glint of the future than if none at all were made, I accept the childish boundaries of chiromancy.

ACKNOWLEDGEMENTS

IN the first place I would wish to thank the Duke and Duchess of Beaufort for their kindness in arranging for the portrait by Winterhalter of the 7th Duke of Beaufort to be photographed, and in allowing me to reproduce it in these pages, and to make similar acknowledgements to Mr. and Mrs. Sacheverell Sitwell for like favours regarding the portrait by John Phillip of Colonel the Hon. Henry Hely-Hutchinson with his daughter, Louisa Lucy, afterwards Lady Sitwell. Further, may I express my gratitude to the Mayor and Corporation of Scarborough for permitting the delightful mid-Victorian group, by Barker, in their possession to be photographed and reproduced, and to the Town Clerk for the trouble he has taken in this matter.

To my friend Madame Guéritte I am particularly indebted for the facts with which she has furnished me concerning the Duchesse de Plaisance. My thanks are also due to Messrs. George Bell and Sons for allowing me to republish the account of life at Badminton in the time of the 1st Duke of Beaufort, which appears in Roger North's *Lives of the Norths*; to Messrs. Gerald Duckworth & Co. who have granted me leave to reprint various poems by Miss Edith Sitwell, Mr. Sacheverell Sitwell and myself; and to the proprietors and editors of the *Evening Standard*, the *Daily Telegraph* and *The Times*, for allowing me to reprint from their columns the passages occurring in Appendices A and C. I should like, too, to express my obligation to my friend Mr. Thomas Mark for his help in seeing this book through the press.

Last, but not least, I must thank my friend Dame Ethel Smyth for writing and allowing me to publish the letter from her included as Appendix D.

OSBERT SITWELL.

CONTENTS

Book I

THE CRUEL MONTH

Book II

LET THERE BE LIGHT!

LIST OF PLATES

Between pages 176 *and* 177:

Book One

THE CRUEL MONTH

CHAPTER ONE
Roots of the Tree

THE garden would be beautiful—and is beautiful—with no flower blooming there. Though this lovely country teems with industry, every prospect is idyllic, and chimneys in the distance become tall obelisks. Its architecture does not consist so much in stone walls and paved walks, as in green walls of yew and box. If you stand with your back to the large old house and face due south, on your left, behind and below the formal arrangements of beds and statues and fountains and yew hedges, lies the Wilderness, part of a wild garden surviving from the eighteenth century, with dark, mysterious cut glades, and at the end of them, far away, a golden cornfield in which in August and September you can just descry the turreted sheaves. Here in spring, when the trees are burgeoning, the ground is covered for three weeks at a time with the azure snow of bluebells, and later, in the summer, you find the tall, over-weighted spires of wild Canterbury bells, no doubt descended from flowers escaped long ago from older enclosed gardens of monasteries and manors. On your right hand towers up the Avenue, a piece of formal planting, old elms alternating with limes, surviving, it is said, from 1680. To the south, in front of you, the garden descends by level terraced lawns and green platforms, each with its piece of water, pool or fountain, to the outer green terrace, which commands a wide view of the lake, lying far below, and of a sweep of beautiful country rising up beyond it.

The gimcrack, tangled battlements of Barlborough, that have yet stood so long, show near at hand among the green mounds of the fat-leafed tree-tops, while, on the horizon, you can distinguish the lofty stone keep of Bolsover, jutting like a cliff, its windows burnished every evening by the setting sun, and, upon a clear day, the three tall towers of Hardwick, perhaps the most beautiful Elizabethan house in England, a skyscraper of glass and golden stone. A little to the right, the view ascends towards the Peak, so that in the distance are the shimmering faint outlines of what, for England, are mountains. On each side of flights of steps, stone statues of Neptune and Diana, and of two giants, gaze outward from the house towards this superb and romantic prospect bound together by the glint of water,—pool and lake and fountain.

Often you would wonder which is the most beautiful moment in this garden; at noon, on a hot summer day, when the light reflected from the water quivers in dazzling patterns upon statues and walls, and upon the warm velvet of the lawns, or on spring mornings when in their mist the trees are towers of crystal, each twig a glittering vein in it, or later, when whole rival choirs of birds practise within them, and every twig is unfurling a golden and transparent pennon; on summer nights when you feel its mystery as at other times you feel its joy,— for in the manner of all gardens it is a little haunted, with the mystery of stillness and space and silence, a rustling sense of expectancy that, though alarming, is not disagreeable,—and then, a miracle that can only occur in this neighbourhood, the whole sky flames out from the furnaces, and the sighing, tall summer trees and the dark walls of the hedges smoulder in the fierceness of this light until, after a minute or two, the flares subside and the world settles to darkness again, the white owl snores once more in her moated grange, the hollow tree upon an island, and the startled bats fly home in arching, segmented flight; or in the early mornings of October, when the mists and cobwebs natural to a Derbyshire fine morning at that season are being brushed away by the sun, which, nevertheless, all day long, seems a little tarnished, so that everything, every stone and trunk and dying, gilded leaf, takes on a hue of deeper and decaying gold.

But this is the pompous month of August—a month of an unnatural length ordained by the pride and caprice of an Emperor eighteen centuries ago—and the early, the very early, morning. Already, however, the light summer mists have evaporated, the distances are visible, and at the end of the long, sombre aisles of the trees, upon the sides of the hills at

which they are pointing, the pale yellow glint of cornfields
twists in and out of the nearer pattern of green leaves like the
Arabesque by Schumann. And already, too, a tall man, fair
and with a curious air of isolation, is out there upon the terraces.

My father is very fond of walking, extremely rapidly, in
these gardens he has made. All day long he can be found in
them: and this year, into which I lead you, he is there for a
longer time than ever, because to him the Middle Ages are
the model for all life to follow—hence the isolation you noticed,
for he lives behind invisible barriers of pedigrees and tourneys
and charters and coats-of-arms, and all round him hang its
shields and banners, all round him sound its discordant
trumpets and the battle-cries of armoured men—and since
every medieval romance opens in a garden at the hour of
sunrise, he has, this summer, chosen to be called every morning
at five. But, though he has his share of the proselytising spirit
and is anxious that others should benefit from the same experience, he is still alone. But this, in itself, in no way irks him.

He walks up and down, surveying his work, which will
never be finished, his head full of new projects of sun and shade,
but never of flowers, measuring the various views with a stick
to his eye or a pair of binoculars. Sometimes he is planning a
boat of stone upon the lake, or a dragon in lead, writhing for a
quarter of a mile through its level waters, or a colonnaded
pavilion upon another island, or a Roman aqueduct in counter-
feit to frame the prospect with its elongated arches, or a cascade
to fall down a stone channel for a hundred and fifty feet, from
the water to the garden below: and, for projects such as these,
though most of them never materialised, he would cause
wooden towers, built up of planks and joists and beams—like
an early machine for siege warfare or a drawing by Piranesi—
to be erected here and there at the right points of vantage. In
the summer he would spend many hours aloft on these platforms, with a large grey hat or grey umbrella to shield his
light-coloured skin and eyes from the sun, and with a telescope
to his eye, enjoying the air and also, perhaps, the feeling of
command which such an altitude above the ground affords.
Then he descends, preoccupied, recognising, if it is by now the
hour of social activity, no one whom he passes, and walks up

and down the terraces again, pausing occasionally to contemplate a vista lately cut. If it is past eight-thirty in the morning —for to his sorrow he "cannot induce the fellow to follow the right plan and be here by six"—, he will stop occasionally to talk to his agent, ever and again asking, after surveying the model for some new box-edged, formal beds or the possibility of a new perspective, "How much can we twist this, without being found out?" . . . All my life, these have been his ways, in one place or another. He made the great garden lay-out at Renishaw just before I was born, and I grew up, year by year, with its yew hedges. I never remember a time between the ages of three and seventeen when we were not the same height, though now they overtop me, and this is a privilege and rare experience for which I have him to thank. Indeed, though he has written many books—of which, perhaps, the best and best-known is, happily enough, a volume of essays entitled *On the Making of Gardens*—it is as an artist in levels and lawns and vistas and lakes that he lives and will survive.

At any rate, one fine summer morning, when the yew hedges were about four feet high, and I was about nine years of age, he raced me at a tremendous pace up and down the Avenue, telling me of various relations of his in the past. I can see now the wide expanse of lake and woodland—nowhere else in England can you find such contrasts in the sky, such dramatic effects of cloud and sun and smoke—, high over which flew the proud streamers from the mines. Suddenly he stopped talking of these dead lives, and said, as though to himself—and, indeed, I had not been paying much attention:

"It's quite evident, if you read the family letters, that we've been working up towards something for a long time, for well over a century."

He did not, I think, realise fully the implications of what he said—though as he said it, I experienced a slight lifting of the heart—, for his mind, though in many directions so very unconventional and gothic, displayed certain strata of intense conventionality, and he did not think of writers when he made this pronouncement—because writing was to him only an incidental accomplishment, part of the general make-up of a cultured man—and doubtless in his heart he dreamt of colonial governors and proconsuls, supreme over the wastes and teeming cities of an empire, shining somewhere among his descendants, among his great-grandchildren—since he was interested more in ancestors and descendants than in fathers and sons.

Mothers and daughters were worse still. Thus when he talked of the "family", he was indicating, of course, his own, and not his mother's, or my mother's; for the English tradition regards every child born in wedlock—just as it considers a bastard as having no father, only a mother, and, therefore, no ancestors—as being solely his father's, descended from *his* father and his father's father. The mother's family do not enter in, bear no responsibility, and derive no credit. My father, however, frequently noticed, and never failed at the time to mention with distaste, traits, physical and otherwise, occurring in me which he had observed in members of my mother's family, directing attention to them, too, with a sour look, as though I had in some way broken all the rules of the game of heredity and as though they were evidence, also, of original sin. And, as time went on, this unfortunate embodying of other characteristics besides those belonging to himself and his own family, was to be one of the great troubles existing between us in our relationship.

Yet it may well be that some qualities vital for achievement in the arts were transmitted through my mother, though herself set so little value on this side of life. Artistic creation, like any other form of creation, is born of energy, is connected with the body and the backbone and the blood, being in no way merely cerebral. Thus it is important for the creator to have sources of energy that have not been tapped, to come of blood, at any rate in part, that has not been obliged to endure too great a strain upon it; an artist—not a cultivated lover of the arts—flowers best when the blood flows most freely in the veins, from stock that has not, intellectually, been overworked. To generalise, governesses are the friends of culture, but the foes of the artist; and, to particularise, were Mrs. Humphry Ward *my* aunt, as she is my friend Mr. Aldous Huxley's, and Matthew Arnold *my* great-uncle, and Dr. Arnold *my* great-grandfather, and Thomas Huxley *my* grandfather, I should find the joys of artistic creation attenuated and not easy to capture; but I should be more cultivated.

My mother's acuteness of the senses was much stronger than my father's. Her love of pleasure, her sensual delight in driving through summer woods at night, catching their scent and feeling their cool air, had much of a child's, and perhaps of an artist's, feeling in them, as, too, had her swift seizing on the peculiarities of people and places and her vivid gift of instantaneous mimicry, keen and acute imitations which she could do once but never again. The kindness and cruelty in her seemed without reason or basis. She was so impulsive. . . . Only yesterday, I found some letters of hers written to me nearly thirty years ago, when I was a young officer in the Brigade of Guards. In one of them she wrote, "I must have a large bunch of white Parma violets", stressing it as though it were a point of the utmost importance to her, causing me no doubt to search all over London for them. Her love of flowers, especially if they were strong-scented, was overwhelming: the rooms, summer and winter, were crowded with lilies and tuberoses and stephanotis, and, from the time I can first remember her, she always wore at her waist gardenias or tuberoses, with sweet geranium leaf, so that I always associate her with their scent, and if I were to smell them now, would expect to hear her footstep or see her come into the room; and this strong physical emphasis of the senses, may not this, too, be connected with the perceptions of the artist? . . . Certainly it was hereditary, for my mother would tell me how, when she and my aunts used to drive in Hyde Park with their mother, my grandmother would say, suddenly, "Oh dear, there's a Chinaman somewhere near!" . . . And sure enough, after a few minutes, they would see a figure in long robes and a pigtail—for Chinamen then really wore pigtails—approaching beneath the trees.

Such slight but curious characteristics, altered and exaggerated, may play a much more important part than one would imagine in the make-up of descendants, and be transmitted in one family, or from one family to another, for many generations. But "form" may only be studied now in horses, not in men. (If racing were truly democratic, the race would go to the tortoise.) I recollect a visit a few years ago to Haddon; which

—for it is situated about twelve miles from Renishaw—I had known, when a child, as an immense grey, deserted house, one of the most beautiful shells in the world; everything in it then was bone-coloured, or the colour of ivory or wood-ash, but, though it was the oldest unfortified residence in the country, no one, I think, expected to see life come back to it, apart from the uncongenial, invading hordes of tourists who at that time trampled through its panelled galleries to the accompaniment of a custodian's whistle, as she marched her gaping army in rough formation from room to room. But life returned to it after more than two hundred years, for its owner perhaps felt in his own blood the same call which had moved his ancestors to dwell there. . . . It looked no less lovely when lived in again, and at dinner I asked the sister of the owner, my old friend Lady Diana Cooper, next to whom I was sitting, if she was not very attached to it, and she said yes, adding "But roots are out of fashion now." . . . So they were, and so, more than ever, they are: but though hidden, they can still strengthen, just as they can on occasion enfeeble the character.

Who knows whence come the various traits of sensibility? Ancestors stretch behind a man and his nature like a fan, or the spread tail of a peacock. At every turn, in every gesture and look, in every decision he takes, he draws on the reserves or deficits of the past. Every human being, the first man marching ahead of the endless ape armies of prehistoric times, you and I, no less than our descendants, are the heirs of all the ages, poised on the perilous brink of time. Every single human being, the criminal or mentally weak, no less than the great poet or the great soldier, is the culminating point of some experiment, worked out by life forces beyond our knowledge and control over a span of a million—but the figure is arbitrary, it may be a thousand million—years. Thus, though a man may be negligible as an individual, he is, notwithstanding, of a certain experimental interest.

Countless radiations from our descent help us to modify our environment. Whatever position in life by chance we occupy, all these diverse rays of lineage centre in every human being. Our ancestors, whether we know who they were or not, roll away at gathering speed into the past, at times taking us with them. From our summits, turning to look back, we can see them fading into the distance, the perspective diminishing, head by head, individuals merging in the crowd, and beyond that into the misty ramifications of history.

Thus each of us, when the English freedom concerning a choice in marriage is taken into account—and though this choice was formerly, until the end of the eighteenth century, more limited, it was always wide when compared with foreign, class-bound nations—, is a synthesis of his race. Even if in reality the romantic marriage is no more conducive to happiness than the Continental marriage of convenience, it does at least afford us that fascinating mixture of blood which in England constitutes the aristocratic tradition.

Let us, therefore, stop to look back and scan the mist out of which three writers have emerged—or, rather, let us survey those figures that, though they still stand out clearly in the foreground, have attained something of heroic exaggeration. The mist of oblivion drifts up at them, it is true, obscuring them a little already, yet it makes what we can see of them loom out at us with an unnatural and overwhelming immensity. Let us glance rapidly at collateral, as well as direct ancestors, so long as they stand near the main line of descent, since a man often resembles his uncle more strongly than his father. And let us first, before examining more intently the faces that are still almost close to us and easily recognisable, survey, too, for the instant, the various gleaming points, high or low, in the haze behind us, the eyes of the peacock tail of which I have spoken and which each of us carries.

Here, for example, if I look back three hundred years, I can identify the now forgotten features of Dr. John Wallis, the most remarkable of the mathematicians who preceded Newton, and a man for whom Newton entertained a profound veneration. He is an interesting character, and so we will stop for a moment to regard him. The son of a clergyman, as a boy of fourteen he spoke and wrote Latin with facility, knew Greek, Hebrew, French, logic and music, and, at the same age, took during his holidays to poring over arithmetic, "not as a formal study, but as a pleasing diversion at spare hours". When older, it was his habit, if sleepless at night, to while away the time in mathematical exercises. On one occasion "he extracted the square root of a number expressed by fifty-three figures, and dictated the result to twenty-seven places next morning to a stranger. It proved exact."[1] Vicar of St. Gabriel's in Fenchurch Street, and then of St. Martin's in Ironmonger Lane, he published a famous book which contained the germ of the differential calculus, introduced into science, we are told, the principles of analogy and continuity, and invented the symbol for infinity. In his spare time he was a great cryptographer, deciphering during the Civil Wars documents of unimaginable difficulty at exceptional speed, exposed in a pamphlet Thomas Hobbes' ignorance of mathematics, and also invented, and experimented with, a new method of helping deaf mutes. "I am now upon another work," he wrote to Richard Boyle on 31st December 1661, "as hard almost as to make Mr. Hobbes understand a demonstration. It is to teach a person deaf and dumb to speak." Two years later he triumphantly exhibited his living experiment—a youth named Daniel Whaley—cured and chattering, before Charles II, Prince Rupert and the Royal Society. . . . This great mathematician lived to the age of eighty-six, but two years before his death, he wrote a pathetic letter to his old acquaintance, Pepys,[2] saying, "Till I was past four score years of age, I could pretty well bear up under the weight of those years; but since that time, it hath been too late to dissemble my being an old man. My sight, my hearing, my strength, are not as they were wont to be. . . ." From him, though directly descended, how little I find in my own temper: to add up twice two would keep me awake at night, rather than make me sleep. . . . On the other hand, though I have never taught the dumb to speak, and, indeed, had my advice been sought on the subject, would have enjoined them to keep silence, I have sometimes tried to help the blind to see.

But we cannot spend so long on other distant ancestors, no less well known in their own day, if not equally deserving. . . . Almost level with Dr. Wallis in her century is Arabella Churchill, sister of the Great Captain, mother of James Fitz-James, Duke of Berwick and Marshal of France, and, legitimately, the grandmother of my great-great-grandmother; and,

[1] See the *D.N.B.*   [2] *Pepys's Diary* (ed. Braybrooke), v. 399.

in another direction, and at the same date, we see William Sacheverell, the now neglected founder of the Whig party and leader of it in the House of Commons; then, in the next century, Admiral Boscawen and his charming blue-stocking wife, and the Marquess of Granby, the celebrated general, after whom so many public-houses were named in his time. Further back can be distinguished the Bacons, on one side, on another Dorothy Vernon, and, on a third, Henry Wriothesley, 3rd Earl of Southampton; that intimate friend and patron to whom Shakespeare dedicated *Venus and Adonis*, beginning his address with the sentence, "*I know not how I shall offend in dedicating my unpolisht lines to your Lordship, nor how the world will censure me for choosing so strong a prop to support so weak a burthen: only if your Honour seem but pleased, I account myself highly praised, and vow to take advantage of all idle hours, till I have honour'd you with some graver labour . . .*", and, a year later, inscribing *Lucrece* also to him, beginning with the words "*The love I dedicate to your Lordship is without end. . . .*" Near him, is the romantic and ill-requited Cavalier Earl of Glamorgan, Marquess of Worcester, who lent two million pounds (which were never paid back) to King Charles I, and who, after being imprisoned for two years, was subsequently obliged to exist on a pension of three pounds a week, gave all his time during that period to mechanical experiments and, the H. G. Wells of his epoch, published in 1663 his *Century of Inventions*, wherein he adumbrated many inventions of future times, outlining his idea for a calculating machine and an engine "for driving up water by fire"; a book that was burnt as a work of witchcraft. There is, nearer at hand, the eagle profile of the Duke of Wellington—features I knew so well, for they were repeated, with modification, in the appearance of my grandmother, his great-niece. We can discern, though we know little of them, various worthy Scots of the eighteenth century, a stonemason and his father, who was a gardener, and the romantic Flora Macdonald, who helped the Young Pretender to escape to Skye after the battle of Culloden. Then we notice, too, a poor youth setting out from Leeds, in an effort to raise himself above the poverty line, and saying goodbye to his family—and they to him—as though another meeting was out of the question, so distant then seemed London, and so costly the journey, even if undertaken in the most humble manner; his daughter, for the ten years of his reign the favourite of George IV; several Irish statesmen and generals, and many English squires. In the distance can just be discerned Robert Bruce, King of Scotland, Wallace the Patriot, the gleaming golden armour of Plantagenet Kings of England and of the Kings of France, their plumes flowing from helms that almost mask their strong profiles, the sturdy figures of numberless yeomen upon their farms, and beyond again, various squires of adventurous disposition, leaving their homes, acquired not so long before, in Normandy, to follow their Duke across the Channel, while on the horizon, on the border between history and legend, stand out the immortal figures of the Macbeths.

They stretch behind one, these ancestors, as I have said, at a gathering speed; two parents, four grandparents, eight great-grandparents, sixteen great-great-grandparents, until already, in the tenth generation, a man possesses one thousand and twenty-four of them. These figures form a cloud of witnesses in us, by whom they survive, testifying to our physical and mental heredity—even though the number is less than at first it seems, since the marriage of cousins, from time to time, affords the same ancestors. In the palaces of Germany and Austria and Italy we may often see sets of portraits of ancestors ordered by the ruling princes of small states; these usually begin, at some period during the eighteenth century, with real faces, recognisable faces, human and self-indulgent, but beyond the third generation, become just a pack of royal portraits, painted obviously from a single model, like the kings and queens on playing-cards, with all the attributes of their sovereignty, sceptres and robes and crowns, with different-coloured hair and eyes given them, but otherwise with nothing individual about them except their names on the canvas; so it is in life. Beyond our grandparents, whom most children have known, have stared at and talked to, these men and women enter the realm of personal reminiscence (and how little, even of that, we remember, how much, afterwards, when it is too late, we wish we had tried to impress it more deeply upon the memory). Beyond our great-grandparents, about whom their sons and daughters have told us, so that we know their manner of speech and dress, their peculiarities, and in their children have heard their voices reflected, and have even, perhaps, lived in the rooms in which they lived; beyond them, then, our relatives enter the realm of myth, their faces lose their identity and no longer connect with those round us. They have become ancestors. The point at which this disintegrating but formalising process begins is with our great-great-grandfathers: they and their sons are the crucial generations, and about them I propose to tell the reader the little I know. . . . First let me enumerate my team.

Great-grandparents—

On my father's side:

Sir George and Lady Sitwell.
Colonel the Hon. Henry Hely-Hutchinson and Mrs. Hely-Hutchinson.

On my mother's side:

Lord Albert Conyngham (after his wife's death created Lord Londesborough) and Lady Albert Conyngham.
The 7th Duke of Beaufort and the Duchess of Beaufort.

Great-great-grandparents—

On my father's side:

Sitwell Sitwell, Esq., created, after his wife's death, Sir Sitwell Sitwell, Bart., and Mrs. Sitwell.
Craufurd Tait, Esq., and Mrs. Craufurd Tait.
The Hon. Francis Hely-Hutchinson, son of Lady Donoughmore, and Mrs. Hely-Hutchinson.
William Wrightson, Esq., of Cusworth, and Mrs. Wrightson.

On my mother's side:

The 1st Marquess of Conyngham and the Marchioness of Conyngham.
The 1st Lord Forester and Lady Forester.
The 6th Duke of Beaufort and the Duchess of Beaufort.
Charles Culling Smith, Esq., and Lady Anne Culling Smith.

Fortunately these men and women possessed plenty of character of one sort and another, and, for my illustration of it, I have at my disposal an unusual amount of authentic personal material, in many cases diaries and journals, upon which to draw. . . . So now, gentle reader, let us approach them more nearly, seeing who they were and what currents of life run in them, and thus, perhaps, in me, thereby coming to understand what I might have been and what I am: Left Hand, as we are born, Right Hand, as we make it.

CHAPTER TWO

My Father's Side

SIMON CYTEWEL, son of Walter, was settled like his father before him,—so the summary of a lawsuit of the time, concerning the ownership of land, reveals—in Ridgeway, on the hillside opposite Renishaw, and about three miles distant from it, in 1301. It was not until 1625 that a George Sitwell came to live at Renishaw; a site which he had inherited from a great-uncle, Robert Sytwell, who, although an adherent of the old faith, had contributed to the fund for the defence of the country against the Most Catholic King's Armada.[1] On the tableland in question, George Sitwell built a tall stone house of three storeys, crowned with gables and battlements, and surrounded with garden courts, full of intricate designs in box and of stone obelisks; a house that was as typical of its period and district as was its situation, for elsewhere houses were still more generally built for shelter in the valley. When I was a boy old men would point out to me the marks of cannon-balls upon the stone of the upper storeys (their fathers had shown them these traces of former poundings), and though I found it difficult to identify them, George Sitwell had been, certainly, a staunch royalist—indeed, in the Commonwealth, he was called upon to give up being Sheriff of Derbyshire because of his opinions—and the house had been garrisoned for the King in the Civil Wars.

It is, though, my great-great-grandfather with whom we are concerned. When, at the age of twenty-two, in 1793 he inherited from his father the house together with a large estate and fortune, one room had been added to it, and a gothic appearance had been imposed by the removal of gables and by the substitution everywhere of battlements, and an emphasis upon them where they already existed. The old gardens, too, had been levelled to the idyllic landscape taste of the time. But the interior, apart from the furniture and pictures deposited

---

[1] He subscribed the sum of £25 on the 27th of March 1588.

there by successive generations, remained much the same as when the house had been erected.

As the proud repetition of his name suggests, Sir Sitwell Sitwell seems to have been a very typical figure of the Regency. . . . How he had met her I do not know, but he had as a boy fallen in love with Alice Parke, the beautiful daughter of a Liverpool merchant of yeoman stock. Because he was heir to many thousands of acres and an old name, his family did not approve of the proposed match. In order to render him forgetful of the girl he loved, the young man—then nineteen—was sent on a Grand Tour designed to be even more extensive than usual, and, of course, with a tutor to guard him. When he arrived at Constantinople, the furthest point in his travels, a letter reached him from his old aunt, Miss Warneford, breaking the news that Alice was dead; a cruel stratagem to aid oblivion. But it produced the opposite effect; distracted, he at once set off for home and, arrived there, found her alive! Touched by the devotion he had shown, his father gave consent for the young couple to be married. His wife, as two portraits of her —and especially the exquisite painting by Sir William Beechey —show, was a very beautiful and graceful woman. From the point of view then prevalent, the marriage turned out better than his family had expected, for Alice's brother rose to fame as a lawyer and judge, becoming Lord Wensleydale, his grandchildren numbering among them the 1st Viscount Ridley, the present Viscount Ullswater and the 9th Earl of Carlisle.

Apart from her portraits, we know little of Alice. She died six years after her marriage and, alas for constancy, her husband married again within fourteen months of her death. His new bride was Caroline Stovin, the celebrated blue-stocking Lady Sitwell, the friend of every literary man from Byron to Longfellow.

The best likeness of Sir Sitwell is that contained in *The Sitwell Children*, by Copley, which portrays him at the age of sixteen with his sister and his two younger brothers. Tall and well-built, his high colour and full lips, his very attitude, indicate his characteristics, as they have reached us from more distant sources; impulsiveness, high spirit, taste, audacity and temperament. He was a friend of Pitt's and represented for a time the Cornish rotten borough of West Looe in Parliament. But, typical of the age in which he lived, his existence, as I have said, was chiefly divided between sport and building, the two curses of my family, though as a rule not to be found united in a single person, but ruining alternate generations. He kept two packs of hounds, one at Renishaw and the other across the Yorkshire border, and the blood of his mares and stallions still runs in the veins of the best racehorses of today. His colours were known on all the chief courses in England, and his private racecourse stood at the end of the park, its situation being now occupied by a coal-mine. (As a boy, I was given the huge gold stop-watch with which he there timed the pace of horses, but I have long ago lost it.)

His hunting exploits, like those of his youngest brother, Frank Sitwell of Barmoor Castle, were many and famous. The most fantastic incident at Renishaw—only to be matched, indeed, by the even more exotic episode in the time of his son, which I shall relate shortly—occurred early in November 1798, when a "Royal Bengal Tiger" escaped from a menagerie in Sheffield. On hearing of its jaunt, and that it had killed a child, Sir Sitwell "generously went in person, with a few of his domestics, and with much trouble, as well as exposing himself to imminent danger",[1] subdued and killed the animal with his pack of hounds, as it flashed its cruel tropical streaks through the cool mountain foliage of the Eckington Woods; those hanging woods and deep valleys that were once part of Sherwood Forest, full as they always are at that season of bracken and rowanberries, mingling their gold and scarlet, and of pheasants hurtling through the golden and misty air.

Such tales of Sir Sitwell still haunted the popular memory when I was a boy.

> Do you remember Mr. Goodbeare,
> Mr. Goodbeare, who never touched a cup?
> Do you remember Mr. Goodbeare,
>   Who remembered a lot?
>   Mr. Goodbeare could remember
>   When "things were properly kept up":
>   Mr. Goodbeare could remember
>   The christening and the coming-of-age:

[1] *Sporting Magazine*, November 1798.

Plate II

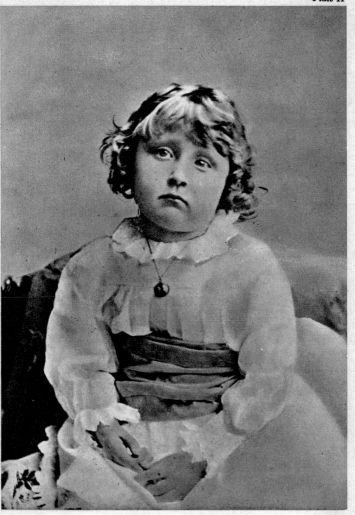

EDITH SITWELL, AGED 3

Plate III

DAVIS, WITH THE AUTHOR, EDITH AND SACHEVERELL
SITWELL, 1898

Mr. Goodbeare could remember
 The entire and roasted ox:
Mr. Goodbeare could remember
 When the horses filled the stable,
And the port-wine-coloured gentry rode after the tawny fox.
Mr. Goodbeare could remember
 The old lady in her eagle rage
 Which knew no bounds:
Mr. Goodbeare could remember
 When the escaped and hungering tiger
Flicked lithe and fierce through Foxton Wood,
When young Sir Nigel took his red-tongued, clamouring
 hounds,
And hunted it then and there,
 As a Gentleman should.[1]

Popular with everyone, even with those with whom he tempestuously quarrelled upon occasions, stories of his wilfulness and high spirit are rife, for he had impressed his personality upon the imagination of the countryside no less by his continual building. He added very largely to Renishaw: and, for example, specially erected the ballroom for a rout he gave to the Prince of Wales in 1806. Its ceiling has an ornament in the manner of the brothers Adam, which displays in the centre the Prince of Wales's Feathers, and is said to be the first work upon which Chantrey[2] the sculptor—who came from the village of Norton near by—was employed. He built, in addition, stables and paddocks and gates and triumphal arches: (himself sketched out upon a piece of paper the design for the gothic entrance arch to the park). In everything he touched, he showed an individual taste. For many generations past, the Sitwells had been extravagant in matters of pictures and furniture—and a letter from a friend and neighbour exists written a hundred years before Sir Sitwell inherited the estate,

[1] Part of a poem entitled "Elegy for Mr. Goodbeare", from *England Reclaimed*, by Osbert Sitwell (Duckworth & Co., 1927).
[2] Sir Francis Legatt Chantrey (1781-1841), the son of a carpenter, a grocer's boy, and subsequently apprenticed to a wood-carver in Sheffield. The neighbouring country houses used to contain a good deal of his work. At Renishaw, in addition to the ceiling, we possess a marble bust of Princess Charlotte presented by her father, the Prince Regent, to Sir Sitwell. An obelisk at Norton marks the fact of its being Chantrey's birthplace, and in addition the terrace at Oaks, the residence there of Mrs. Bagshaw, is said to have been designed by him.

B

expostulating with the owner of Renishaw upon his "unhear
of" expenditure on such kickshaws. In Sir Sitwell this tendenc
found its culmination. The marble chimney-pieces, which h
put in the drawing-room and ballroom, are superb. (The
were bought by auction from the Duke of York, and had bee
designed for the former Melbourne House, later York Hous
by Sir William Chambers: but the heading on certain bill
beginning "For taking down from the Duke of York's"
induced some of the elder members of the family to think for
long while that they must have been removed from the public
house of that name in the village!) The famous Perugin
perhaps the finest example of that master, which Sir Sitwe
bought—I believe at the sale of the Orleans Collection[1] i
London after the French Revolution—was sold by my fathe
a century later to Pierpont Morgan, but the five huge panel
of Brussels tapestry designed by Urbain Leyniers and execute
by Louis de Vos which Sir Sitwell hung in the ballroom an
great drawing-room still, at the moment of writing, haur
those rooms with a plumy exoticism of pearls and elephant
garden vistas and trophies that burn in a livid light. Th
figures within them, clad in sombre, rich brocades, golden o
crimson, live in a sullen glow such as has never lit earthl
beings; just as salamanders were said to be creatures of th
flames, so do these exist in their own element, the same t
which, in their cold burning, all jewels belong. These panel
must influence the imagination of all who see them, still mor
of all who have lived beneath them: and so, perhaps, Si
Sitwell to this day influences his descendants indirectly
besides by the folly of his expenditure. For the strain which Si
Sitwell placed upon the family fortune, though that was s
large, proved too much for it to bear, and when he died of gou
in the head at the early age of forty-two, he left his son a poorer
though certainly not a wiser, man.

Mrs. Swinton, in *Two Generations*,[2] describes how Sir Sitwel
was twice seen after his death, once in the streets of Sheffield

[1] If this is the case, it was the only picture treated separately; for the res
was divided into three parts, and each third formed, respectively, the
foundation of the great galleries by the 3rd Duke of Bridgewater, the 1s
Marquess of Stafford and the 5th Earl of Carlisle.

[2] Edited by Osbert Sitwell. (Macmillan & Co., 1940.)

and once—on the same night—at Renishaw, while his body was still lying in the library. It was a very silent evening, after dark, and a relative of his widow's was sitting in the hall, next the room in which was the coffin. She heard a ring at the front-door bell, and, the servants being at supper, opened the door herself. Sir Sitwell, his face illuminated by the lamp she held up, looked steadily at her from the darkness beyond and then disappeared. . . . The same incident, or something akin to it, has happened on more than one occasion; the face of a man for example, was seen looking through the door at the time of the funeral of Sir George, Sir Sitwell's son, some forty years later. . . . These singular stories possess for me an especial interest, because on the evening of the day on which I first heard of my mother's fatal illness, I entered the house, having returned from an expedition to Bolsover, to find two friends, who were staying with me at the time, much puzzled because a tall, rather indistinct figure had mounted the steps from the park and stared at them through the identical glass panels of the door; but when they opened it, he was no longer there, nor anywhere to be seen.

The next owner of Renishaw, Sir George, was of a less gay and ebullient disposition, and appears in himself to have anticipated by a decade or two the sentiment of the Victorian Age, into which he survived. Like his father before him, he stood for Parliament, though in this case with some semblance of an election; and for a local constituency, Chesterfield. Indeed his candidature took place during the great Reform controversy. It was a brief episode, but left its own memorial behind it, in a book called *Figaro in Chesterfield*,[1] a rare volume entirely devoted to abuse of Sir George and his chief sup-porters; an unusual honour, even in those times of which Dickens, in his account of the Eatanswill Election, gives so unexaggerated a picture. For the rest, like his father before him, again, he was that contradiction in terms, a "great sports-man", and though only half his father's fortune had come to him, liked to spend as much money. Memorials to his love of sport exist in the many paintings of his horses, and one of my

[1] *Figaro in Chesterfield: A Rod for a Fool's Back.* (Chesterfield, T. Ford, 1833.)

great-grandfather himself with his huntsmen and hounds, by J. F. Herring. Sir George, indeed, had helped this artist to achieve fame. Originally the subsequently celebrated painter of horses was driving a mail coach, and one day he happened to show Sir George, who had the seat next him, his drawings. Sir George, struck by his talent, gave him a pony-cart, and sent him round the country to obtain commissions.

Sir George was among the first English sportsmen to find their paradise in the Highlands, and for some years rented, first Birkhall, and then the old house which existed at Balmoral, before Queen Victoria bought the estate and built the new castle. Both he and his wife are so fully described by their daughter, Mrs. Swinton, in *Two Generations*[1] that for their picture I will content myself with one small quotation from her. "It must, indeed, have been hard to find a prettier bride when she first came to Renishaw, with her shower of golden or light auburn curls, her peculiarly slight and graceful figure, her large happy blue eyes, her skin as fine as a baby's, and cheeks and lips like a rose. Her boy husband was just six foot high, and was also very fair in complexion. He had beautiful teeth, features which were sufficiently regular, and remarkably dark blue, kindly eyes."

It must also be explained that Sir George was finally ruined by an unfortunate combination of the expense of his style of living, a catastrophic fall in land values, the failure of the Sheffield Land Bank—which closed its doors the very day after he had deposited in it many thousand pounds realised by the sale of land—and of the action of the brother of the family solicitor, who absconded with thirty-four thousand five hundred pounds.

During the two years that followed the collapse of his finances in 1846, Renishaw was shut up and many of its treasures were sold. But it is to this period that the other curious incident in its history, to which I have referred, belongs. . . . Below the Wilderness stands a cliff, completely masked by trees—beeches with dark foliage and elephant-grey boles—and full of caves in the rock. Now the leaf-mould mounts, and silts

[1] *Op. cit.*, p. 67.

them up, so that, though still mysterious and dark, they are no longer so large as in the time of which I tell. But though many parks during the eighteenth century possessed caves containing anchorites, who had been induced to reside there by the considerable salary offered them because of their "picturesque" qualities, none, I think, ever sheltered so strange an inhabitant as was found in one of these.

A few months, then, after my great-grandfather had been obliged to shut up his home, and while he was touring the small towns of Germany (where living was so cheap) with his wife and family, and the great house stood empty, all the more desolate because of the intense activity it had so long framed, the neighbouring farmers began to complain of the inexplicable loss, now and then, of a sheep from among their flocks browsing in the quiet meadows. Sheep-stealing was still a capital offence, but though a sharp watch was kept, the thefts continued at intervals, and the offender could not be discovered. Consternation spread. Eventually, however, one spring day, a year and a half later, and just after another sheep had vanished, a party of farmers, walking along the road that borders the park, observed a spiral of blue smoke ascending over the tops of the tall trees below the Wilderness, and thought it a peculiar circumstance. They decided to investigate, penetrating up the steep, narrow paths under the budding branches along the cliff side. . . . And there, they saw that the smoke issued from the largest of the caves and, entering it, found a tall negro, naked except for a sheep-skin slung round him, roasting part of a carcass over a log fire!

The explanation of this mystery is that the poor creature was one of the last demoded victims of the craze for black servants which during the former century had been so widespread. Brought out of Africa to act as page to Lord Scarsdale at Kedleston, about forty miles away, he had begun to entertain a loathing for white people and the way of life they obliged him to follow. So he had run away, and after several days of aimless but clandestine wandering—for he did not know the country— he had found this unexpectedly secret and secluded retreat. Here he had lived for more than eighteen months, going back to something more like his own method of existence, capturing a sheep from time to time, cooking it, and preparing its fleece as a covering for his body.

To this story, the sequel is happier than might have been expected; since my great-grandfather, a very humane man, by chance returned from his travels just at the time of the blackamoor's trial and, being chairman of the Bench of Magistrates, contrived, instead of having him hanged, for him to be repatriated, sent back to a joyous, demonstrative meeting with dusky relatives in the torrid zone.

This incident, together with the tiger-hunt of fifty years before, always invested the immediate surroundings of Renishaw in the minds of those brought up in it with an air all its own, romantic and pertaining to the world of miracle. How often, as children, Sacheverell and I used to look in the deserted caves for signs of their vanished occupant, bones or the marks of fire upon the rock, or began to clear away the damp accumulation of leaves that partly blocked the entrance of some of them in order to examine the ground. Indeed, for me, it is a story that never loses its fascination. And, as I write this, and look out of window at white and endless perspectives, which, except that they are shrouded by guardian mists—though even these are in part frozen, hanging down from the white branches of the trees—seem to stretch from pole to pole, I still wonder how, accustomed to blazing equatorial suns and hot, languorous nights, that sepia-washed figure contrived to exist through the bitter winters of this part of the world, which, from its proximity to the Peak, often shows its trees encrusted with crystal, and its ground thick with snow, for months together, and how, too, his almost naked body looked, intruding with its sleek brown muscles into these Breughel-like vistas of grey and white, of icicle and iron twig.

Sir George lived on for two or three years after this kindly intervention, but never again inhabited Renishaw. His widow survived to the age of eighty-four, dying in 1880. She was the eldest sister of Archibald Campbell Tait, the subsequent Archbishop of Canterbury, and the daughter of Mr. and Mrs. Craufurd Tait of Harviestoun. Mrs. Craufurd Tait, to whom her children had been devoted, died when they were quite young, and so we do not know much of her. Indeed, her daughter, Lady Wake, tells us, in her reminiscences,[1] more of her grandmother, Lady Campbell of Succoth, wife of Sir Ilay Campbell, Lord Succoth, Lord President of the Court of Session. Of her,[2] witty, able and a well-known beauty, the granddaughter leaves us a vivid description. "Through her veins ran a fiery flood, and if she was a star in the world of fashion, to her children she was rather a portentous meteor, for their orbit was not hers; and her sudden appearances when she used to flash down upon them from her house in town to their sea-bathing quarters, where they were regularly sent both for their health and that they might be out of the way, filled their young hearts more with dismay than filial delight. Often in after years, they have described the trembling with which they used to hear the rustling of her silk dress in the passages approaching the schoolroom door."

My great-grandmother and her brothers and sisters lived much in Edinburgh and knew well Scott and those other leaders of Edinburgh intellectual life, whose very names so much intimidate the southerner of today. Sir Ilay Campbell's house was, his daughter tells us,[3] the natural resort of most of the talent of the country.

The Taits are descended from one of their name who is described on his tombstone, erected in about 1680, as a "stone-mason". This has been taken by his descendants to mean an architect. But his father, the great-great-grandfather of the Archbishop, was a gardener—though more distinguished ancestors have sometimes been found for him in pedigrees. The family quickly became prosperous, and there is in existence a fine Raeburn of Mr. John Tait of Harviestoun, a Writer to the Signet, a son of the stonemason, and the grandfather of Lady Wake, Lady Sitwell and the Archbishop. This Mr. John Tait married a Miss Murdoch, who bore the unusual Christian name, for a female, of *Charles*, for she came of an old and influential family, which had lost all its fortune for the sake of the Jacobite cause, and since its members still in their reverses remained

---

[1] *The Reminiscences of Charlotte Lady Wake*, edited by Lucy Wake. (Wm. Blackwood & Sons, 1909.)

[2] Lady Campbell's father was Archibald Murray, Lord Henderland, and her mother, a daughter of Lord William Hay.

[3] *Op. cit.*

loyal to the Young Pretender, she had been named after him.

Their son, Craufurd Tait, inherited in 1800 from his father the house and estate of Harviestoun and another estate, Cumlodden, on the banks of Loch Fyne. He was soon at work "improving" them—or, in other words, building and altering as hard as he could, without taking into account the consequences to himself or for others; a characteristic which shows a tendency to recur in his descendants.

His first attempt necessitated for its success a complete transformation of Highland habits of life, and took place at Cumlodden. In his judgement, the rough stone houses wherein his tenants dwelt, with no chimneys, and with the smoke issuing from the doors, round which, rubbing their sore eyes, the nearly nude children and women of those days grouped themselves in welcome, were unworthy of their magnificent setting. He determined to change all this, and built, so his daughter, Lady Wake, tells us, "a series of charming cottages, each having a little garden and four acres of land attached to it. Instead of the midden before the door, borders of rose and mignonette" were to enchant the senses. . . . Unfortunately the Highlanders were not interested in flowers, and entertained a more positive feeling of dislike for the continual labour which both gardens and crofts required, while financial profit meant nothing to them. They probably very actively resented the transformation. At any rate, the ideal village vanished as swiftly as a mirage, leaving, as its only traces, broken walls and fences, and, more substantial, enormous builders' accounts that had to be met. Back once more among their beloved thistles and smoky rooms, the Highlanders reverted to the ways they liked, of listless lounging through the long days of the northern summer, and of adventure with their fishing fleet during the short weeks of the herring season: while Mr. Craufurd Tait, disappointed but undaunted, proceeded to carry out "improvements" on his other estate, though even those that were now abandoned had been sufficient to impair considerably the ample family fortune.

"The old house rapidly grew," writes Lady Wake, "the improvements which succeeded each other . . . quite changed the face of the country. The highroad ran too near the house

—it was moved as though by magic half a mile lower; clusters of poor mean-looking cottages occupied ground too near the back of the house—they disappeared." In their place, Mr. Tait laid out a garden with Milton's sonorous version of the Garden of Eden from *Paradise Lost* as his model:

> Thus was this place,
> A happy rural seat of various view;
> Groves whose rich Trees wept odorous Gumms and Balme,
> Others whose fruit burnished with Golden Rinde
> Hung amiable, Hesperian Fables true,
> If true, here onely, and of delicious taste:
> Betwixt them Lawns, or level Downs, and Flocks
> Grasing the tender herb, were interposed
> Or palmy hilloc or the floury lap
> Of some irriguous Valley, spread her store,
> Flours of all hue, and without Thorn the Rose:
> Another side, Umbrageous Grots and Caves
> Of cool recess . . .

and so on.

Even Mr. Tait seems to have made no attempt to enliven this rather pedantic paradise by the introduction of "Bears, Tygers, Ounces, Pards", or by encouraging "th'unwieldy Elephant" to wreathe "his lithe proboscis" here and there for the amusement of its inhabitants. Notwithstanding, never had there been, Lady Wake testifies, a flower garden more lovely than the one thus curiously called into being. "Of great extent, it enclosed the lower part of the glen and mountain at the foot of which it lay, one of the Ochil range. A dell of lovely green turf led down from the wilder glen right through the garden, and, leaping from the rocks above, a bright and noisy burn danced merrily on through its entire length, speeding on through ferns and wild-flowers, when it suddenly disappeared. Some hundred yards below, it as suddenly emerged with a bound from a cave, falling over a little ridge of rocks into a small pool."

The attitude of "let that hill be removed!" which these extracts reveal, is well known to me; I grew up with it. (And it must be remembered that to move mountains is easier, often, than to influence those round you, and that the actual moving of them, with the illusion of power it affords—similar to that experienced by Xerxes when he ordered the sea to be flogged

—offers concrete compensation for lack of success in other, more human, directions.) The sentiments, the wish to build and lay out, are doubly familiar; for I feel them in my own heart, and have, also, heard them continually expressed, on a basis of the best excuses, round me.

Thus, when reading of Craufurd Tait's experiments, I cannot doubt that his life, which ended well over a century ago, has influenced my own, both directly and indirectly. I recall, for example, an incident that occurred in 1924, when my father, surveying with an appraising eye the comparatively small garden at Weston, a house then already in the possession of my brother, nonchalantly remarked, somewhat to the surprise of the owner, "*I* don't propose to do much here; just a sheet of water, and a line of statues. . . ." (And then, suddenly, reverting to his other principal interest—medieval times—by, as it were, catching the blue eye of a periwinkle, effected a formal introduction of us to it in the following terms: "The Periwinkle! A charming flower, and a common term of endearment in the Middle Ages.") Or I think of a sentence I found lately in a letter, written in 1939 after his retirement, by Henry Moat, my father's old servant, who was with him for nearly fifty years; (of him I shall have much to say later— and shall give many of his letters, for he was a born letter-writer). "It sounds like old times Sir G. arriving at Renishaw with a hundred disturbing plans. When I look back, he never entered any place but he commenced pulling down and building up, in short I have lived among bricks and mortar just like a builder's yard." Or I read again a letter, which I found here among the estate correspondence, written by the young sub-agent to his friend, the agent, in 1911. (In that year my father had sold to Pierpont Morgan for a large sum the magnificent Perugino he had inherited, and this explains the opening sentence.)

". . . I am wishing Pierpont Morgan to Gehenna, for now all the wild schemes which have accumulated for fifteen years are to be carried out. White, the landscape gardener was here several days last week and Lutyens one day. Already we are moving the entrance to the Chesterfield Approach a hundred yards toward Thirby Cliff. A drive to Foxton Wood is planned

which will cut up no end of good arable fields and entirely
re-arrange the fences and plantations. Three lakes are to be
made in the Eckington Woods Valley. A new drive is to be
made through Cadman Wood. A new drive and terrace are
to be made through Twelveacre Plantation and Goodness
knows what is to be done to entertain a crowd of people in the
field between the Woods when Osbert comes of age.[1] The
drive is to be continued to the Ford past Never Fear Dam. The
Ince Piece Wood is to be re-constructed. A swimming-bath is
to be made under the waterfall, and the waterfall raised to
three times its present height. A 'crowsfoot vista' is to be cut
in the Wilderness, for which plans have had to be made and
platforms erected to be able to see where they would strike.
Terraces are all to be pegged out. A pavilion is to be built in
the lake. (Lutyens' idea is a stone ship.) An extension is to
be made at the top end of the lake, ditto near the Sawmill,
and the Sawmill is to be removed, etc. etc. etc. What next, I
wonder? . . . He is talking quite seriously about this lot. Heaven
help us if he does a tithe of it. I find no time for anything
except taking levels. Estate work will be in a pretty mess
presently."

Of course, in the case of my father, this urge to build—and
especially to build gardens—was fortified by the similar strain,
equally strong, which he had inherited from Sir Sitwell Sitwell:
but though I little used to think so, now, having studied the
facts, I often wonder whether this trait, in many ways so
amiable, but which I have seen ruin other families descended
from the same blood, may not in reality have been transmitted
through many generations from the striving hearts of an obscure
Scottish stonemason and his still humbler father, the gardener,
and so have no claim to patrician origin? . . . Who knows
what schemes in stone and mortar, in trees and flowers, these
men may not have dreamt?

Alas, their grandson's dream proved to be an illusion. In
January 1814, fourteen years after Mr. Tait had inherited his
house and estates, his wife died. During that time, in the words
of his daughter, "His taste for the beautiful had been freely
indulged, he had created a paradise, and while she, his Eve,

[1] In the end, owing to various circumstances, nothing happened at all.

lived to enjoy and adorn it, he had never taken himself to account for the sums expended upon it; but the shock of her sudden removal had shattered the enchanted world in which he had lived, and he stood face to face with the appalling fact of an overwhelming debt. . . ." A few years later, Harviestoun had to be sold.

From 1814 onwards, for thirty years, the Taits, a numerous sept, frequented Renishaw. Relying on Sir George's weak, kindly and sociable disposition to make them welcome, hordes of indigent Scottish relations poured down on it from the north, making it the general headquarters for their various campaigns. Several of the younger of them found here a permanent home. But the burden of the expense thus thrust upon him was undoubtedly one of the contributory causes of my great-grandfather's ruin, and so, too, has affected the lives of my own generation, for it conditioned my father's mind to the perpetual fear of being imposed upon, and rendered him continually on the look-out for extravagance in others, and in other than the directions approved by himself. To be financially safe, he felt, one should be friendless. ("Such a mistake," he remarked to me once, without explanation, "*to have friends!*")

Again, for the play of action and reaction upon lives much later in time, it should be remarked that Archibald, my great-grandmother's youngest brother, was brought up at Renishaw, and this also was not without its consequences. His lameness was cured through Sir George sending him to a bone-setter of the period: without which treatment it is doubtful whether he could have filled the office of Archbishop. Subsequently he became my father's guardian—for my grandfather died when my father was two—and no doubt his ultra-religious zeal was, in its turn, largely responsible for my father's unbending atheism, the certainty of his conviction. Admittedly his childhood and boyhood were martyred by religion, and Renishaw is still full of holy books, given by the Archbishop, and containing, in his handwriting, exhortations to his ward to attend church constantly. I once asked my father, I remember, how he had escaped the contagion of the prevalent church fever.

"Well," he replied, "when I was three or four, I came to the conclusion that I was too young to understand such things properly, and so had better reserve my judgement until I was old enough to form an opinion of my own." And when he grew up, his lack of belief assumed a very positive form. He could not be said to "cleave ever to the sunnier side of doubt". He was no mere agnostic.

In addition, however, to the suffocating religious atmosphere of his home, an incident, or an adventure, when he was a boy of nineteen, had helped to crystallise his disbelief; he had, during a vacation from Oxford, been one of the two chief protagonists in the first direct exposure of a fraudulent medium. This lady had long been the most famous of her kind, possessed the trust of Sir William Crookes, and was the regular vessel of his psychic experiments; moreover, the *séance*, in which her body had been found masquerading as a spirit, had taken place at the headquarters of the British National Association of Spiritualists itself. . . . Previous to this, it had been given out by the members of the faith that anyone touching a manifestation would die, so that my father's action in holding the "spirit" and preventing her from escaping had required courage and enterprise.[1] But, henceforth, until he became an old man, and his attitude softened, indeed completely altered, there were no spirits, no ghosts, neither angels nor devils, no God, nothing behind the scenes, as it were, but the Law of the Survival of the Fittest—and the fittest were those at present in possession.

Nevertheless my father, in spite of his convictions, remained attached to the Archbishop, who was very kind to him. As a boy, when in London, he always stayed at Lambeth, and later, when he first went to Oxford, he was touched by the fact that the Archbishop had written, with his own hand, seventy letters of introduction for him. The Archbishop died before I was born, but I bear him a slight grudge—it would be stronger, if I liked port better—because during the long visits of those days, which he paid to Renishaw, he often suffered from episcopal sore throat (an occupational disease, one imagines). Port was then held to be the best disinfectant, and, as only the best appeared in the butler's eyes good enough for the Archbishop, a bottle of 1815 port, the finest vintage ever known, was

---

[1] I have reprinted an account of my father's capture of a spirit, for those interested, in Appendix A on p. 255.

always taken up to his room, and he gargled away bottle after bottle, year after year, until the large stock became exhausted.

My father could not recollect his father, Sir Reresby, and though I lived so much with my grandmother, Lady Sitwell, who will often appear in these pages, I know little of him, except that he was a man of strong temper and deep affections, who suffered greatly by the ruin of the estate. To him, the shutting-up of his old home, and the forced dispersal of much of its contents, came as a shattering blow. In an effort to be helpful, he found that he had made himself responsible for his father's enormous debts, and that there was no prospect of the property recovering within his own lifetime. He had married when his affairs had appeared to be in a less lamentable condition, and the feeling that he could not support his wife and children in the style to which he was accustomed, preyed on his spirits. Singularly enough, his early death helped to rectify the position, and during my father's long minority, the estate, owing to my grandmother's management of it, recovered.

When he was a cornet in the First Life Guards, my grandfather devoted himself chiefly to sport, but he had other sides to him, for he was a friend both of Ruskin and of the philanthropist, Lord Shaftesbury, and was an accomplished watercolour artist. For a few years before his marriage, he had lived alone at Renishaw, only part of it being then furnished. My grandmother did not see the house, until she was on her honeymoon. She describes in her diary her first visit, in October 1857: "I peeped out very anxiously between the trees, as we came near Eckington, but instead of seeing the *house*, to my surprise we saw about thirty men on horseback with white favors, and flowers in their horses' heads, they rode in front and on both sides of the Dog-cart, which felt like an odd sort of triumphal car, and drew up in line at the gates and again at the great door to cheer us, and to welcome me. 'Another cheer for Lady Sitwell, another.' I thanked them as best as I could, but was glad to escape to the solemn house. . . . Reresby's Batchelor rooms are so pretty and so droll, and we had a pleasant evening in them, with Eckington Church bells ringing as if we had *all* been married that morning, and the wind howling through the empty passages of this huge house. The next morning Reresby tried to show me over it, thereby making me sadly confused in my head, and afterwards I tried to explore alone but could not get it done, some distant door slammed, or the wind howled like a human voice, and back I ran, never stopping till the *two* boudoir doors were shut behind me." After a week, they left, to go to Rome. ". . . Frank the gardener made me a parting bouquet of lovely ferns and orange blossom, and I gave my last look at the little boudoir with real regret, and again from the train at the grand old house standing in full sunshine, looking as if it wondered how it *could* be left, dismantled and deserted."

When they returned from Italy, they made their home at Renishaw, living in a quiet way there, with much sport and wood-carving—his hobby—and a great deal of religious and charitable activity. But four years later, my grandfather died at the age of forty-two. His widow, sad and lonely, with the responsibility of two young children to care for and the wreck of the Sitwell fortune to nurse back to health, lived thenceforth mostly at Scarborough, only paying visits to Renishaw.[1] And during the years of my father's minority, by her constant attention and cleverness, she pulled the estate round. She was, indeed, a woman of remarkable ability and charm, with latent fires in her, a great personal dignity and an inflexible but softly masked will. And with her, we approach a family of whom I believe many members to have been of outstanding character —not necessarily always pleasant.

My grandmother was the daughter of Colonel Hely-Hutchinson, a brother of the 3rd Earl of Donoughmore. His grandfather, the founder of the family, was John Hely, son of Francis Hely of Gertrough, and he married the niece and heiress of Richard Hutchinson of Knocklofty, whose name he soon added to his own. An eminent lawyer and statesman, and a magnificent orator—as a young man he had been an intimate friend of Quin, and it was said that the great actor had helped him with the preparation of his oratorical effects —he was known as "Silver-Tongued Hely-Hutchinson", and his portrait by Sir Joshua shows us a man with a certain appearance of fervour and animation. A friend of Edmund

---

[1] I have treated fully of this period in the preface to *Two Generations*.

Burke and many other celebrated politicians, he possessed as many, and almost as distinguished, enemies. Nobody, I believe, ever attempted to disparage his ability or to deny that he was a most extraordinary character, but he was accused of venality, and his opponents described him as a "harlequin genius" and declared that he had "received more for ruining one country than Admiral Hawke had been given for saving three", and that he was "so avaricious, that if King George III gave him Ireland one day, he would ask for the Isle of Man the next", while the *Dictionary of National Biography* sums up by saying that, in spite of "many public and private virtues", his political career "was throughout vitiated by an intense and inordinate desire to aggrandise his family".

In fact, he was a master of the bland art of nepotism, at which many of his nation excelled. As Secretary of State for Ireland before the Union, he enjoyed, therefore, the most interesting and fruitful field for its exercise, and some of the coups he achieved were so remarkable, even in that day, as to seem worth recording. For example, a son of his, Lorenzo, continued to draw army half-pay—£133: 5: 8 a year—long after he had become a clergyman of the Established Church of Ireland, and also long after the Act of Union had been passed. But even this arrangement must have appeared simple in comparison with the other which follows. . . . The Chief Secretary contrived to obtain a commission as Colonel-in-Chief for one of his nieces or favourite cousins. This young lady never, of course, commanded—or even joined—her regiment, nor, though a Colonelcy was a valuable thing to own in days when commissions were articles of commerce, varying in value like stocks and shares owing to the state of the market, did she dispose of it. On the contrary, being evidently no believer in small profits and quick returns, she held on to her investment until her death at an advanced age—though as an old woman she used energetically to denounce the authorities for having, a little while before, removed her from the full pay list and placed her on half pay.[1]

[1] See *Secret and Confidential*, by Brigadier W. H-H. Waters, C.M.G., C.V.O. (John Murray, London, 1926.) General Waters is a great-nephew of Lord Hutchinson of Alexandria.

In 1785 Hely-Hutchinson accepted a peerage for his wife, who was created Baroness Donoughmore. He had six sons, nearly all of whom were remarkable men.[1] The eldest, who had commanded the Cork Legion in 1797, was made an earl in 1800, and was an enlightened statesman and a great friend to Catholic emancipation. After his death, the Catholic Association described him with enthusiasm as "the hereditary patron of the Catholics". . . . The second son, John, was the real founder of the English power in Egypt. He possessed abilities of the highest order. When Sir Ralph Abercromby went there to take charge of the Army of the Nile, he insisted on Hely-Hutchinson being appointed as his Second-in-Command—perhaps because he so well understood the French Army and French mentality, having been educated partly at the Military Academy of Strasbourg, and later, during the French Revolution, having held an appointment for a time on the Staff of Lafayette. After Sir Ralph's death he took command, and in 1801 turned the French out of Egypt. Bunbury[2] describes him at the time of his great campaign in these rather unflattering terms: "He was forty-four years of age, but looked much older, with harsh features, jaundiced by disease, extreme short-sightedness, a stooping body and a slouching gait, and an utter neglect of his dress". He shunned "general society, was indolent, with an ungracious manner and a violent temper". A portrait of him by Thomas Phillips, now in the possession of my brother, depicts him on the other hand in his scarlet coat and white buckskin breeches as a good-looking and elegant man, with a somewhat cynical aplomb; a real eye-glass face; and it seems odd that, if Bunbury accurately describes his characteristics, he should have been so intimate a personal friend of

[1] Another brother, Christopher, was instrumental in capturing the French generals, Lafontaine and Sarrazin, at Ballinamuck, at the time of the attempted invasion of Ireland. After the passing of the Act of Union, he left Ireland in disgust, became aide-de-camp to his brother John, accompanied him as a volunteer to Egypt, was member for Cork, again attended his brother—now Lord Hutchinson of Alexandria—this time on a diplomatic mission to Berlin and St. Petersburg in 1806, and then enlisted in the Russian ranks the following year, and took part in the Polish campaign. He voted for parliamentary reform, and was turned out of France—where he always went for a holiday between sessions—with his family after 1815, because of his liberal opinions and friendships.

[2] *Narratives of Passages in the War with France*, 1799-1810. (1854.)

the Prince Regent, that model of worldly elegance. Moreover, all the other members of his family were unquestionably handsome, of a fine, intellectual appearance and with a look of distinction.

Of his famous campaign, the *Dictionary of National Biography* remarks that his "movements were at first slow and cautious, but when his plans were formed, he carried them out with great sagacity and success". On his return to England, the General was granted the resounding title of Lord Hutchinson of Alexandria and Knocklofty, with a pension of £2000 a year attached to it, and, in 1807, was made Military Plenipotentiary in Russia at the time of the Treaty of Tilsit. After his retirement, he lived for many years in a cottage in the garden of the Royal Pavilion at Brighton, and acted on several occasions as intermediary between the Prince and Princess of Wales. When the Prince succeeded to the throne, he chose to send Lord Hutchinson on a private mission to Caroline, with an offer to her of £50,000 a year on condition that she surrendered all English royal titles and would undertake not to set foot in England again; but she refused to listen to these proposals and started for England the next day. In 1825 the General succeeded his brother as 2nd Earl of Donoughmore. My great-grandfather, Colonel Hely-Hutchinson, his favourite nephew, lived much with him at Knocklofty. In 1832 Lord Donoughmore died and his nephew, my great-grandfather's elder brother, inherited the earldom. . . . From this family, I am sure, my father took much in his make-up, his voice and power of speaking in public—he was an unusually good public speaker, though he required, to be at his best, a large audience—, his financial outlook and grasp of practical detail, and also his essentially forensic point of view, which enabled him to champion, clad in the shining white armour of unquestionable justice, any cause which happened to appeal to his way of thinking or feeling.

Of Lord Hutchinson of Alexandria's brother, Francis, and of his wife I know little, except that he, too, like so many of his family, was for some time a member of Parliament, and that she was a cousin of his. Of their son, my great-grandfather, I have given an account in another book,[1] but this time I will

[1] *Escape With Me!*

repeat myself. From his portraits, he was a startlingly handsome and agreeable-looking young man, and his career displays
all the adventurous qualities of his family and his race. He ran
away from Eton at the age of twelve, and joined a Portuguese
regiment, since the English army would not have him at that
age, in order to fight in the Peninsular War. (The Duke of
Wellington, his godfather, subsequently obtained for him as
soon as he was old enough a commission in an English regiment.) He fought or travelled or lived in Spain, Portugal,
Germany, France, Holland, Belgium, Switzerland, Austria,
Denmark, Norway, Sweden, Russia, Poland, Italy and South
Africa.

When stationed in Paris in 1814, he formed an attachment
for a Polish Countess, a daughter of the Prince de Ligne, who
had been married against her will to a man thrice her age,
and for a long time they were lovers. Thirty years or more
after this liaison had been broken off, when he had become a
most respectable married man, revelling in the conventions of
the mid-Victorian age, she died, a widow, and left him all the
immense Polish estates and possessions of her late husband.
At the request of his wife, however, he relinquished these
legacies. . . . But when my brother inherited his house, Weston,
about twenty years ago, we found in the library, discreetly
framed on the inside of a blotting-pad, a miniature of Sidonie,
portraying her as a radiant young creature, with masses of fair
curls and muslins, in the style of the Empire; all that was left
of this romance.

During his travels, the Colonel[1] kept a diary. Some of it
is in Spanish, which lends it variety, and there are certain
erasures made by his wife, and later by his daughters, who
acted as self-imposed censors, cutting out any remarks that
offended their epochal sense of morality. Even their efforts
could not altogether banish from every entry the signs of his
susceptible disposition as a young man, but, in spite of them and
his extensive travels, the few dull patches that went to the
composition of his character—for in life he was apparently

[1] I call him "the Colonel", for as such I have always heard him referred to
by his grandchildren. But the Army List for 1816 gives him as being a Captain, with rank dating from 22nd July 1813, in the "78th (Highland) Regt.
of Foot (or the Ross-shire Buffs)".

anything but dull—all contrive to make, together, a powerful impression in the pages of his journal. Devoted to details of agriculture and commerce, one is irresistibly reminded, when reading it, of Arthur Young, author of the *Travels in France*, of whom Miss Maxwell has written in a recent book,[1] "When attempting to describe a house, he will give merely the measurements of the rooms, and only the baldest account of the scenery". The Colonel had a similar passion for seeing countries, and he is for ever measuring statues and basilicas, gardens and waterfalls, battlefields and armies: he even measures the month, beginning the new one with, let us say, "1st November. November has 30 days." He tots up leagues indefatigably, but the patience of at least one reader is stretched almost beyond the point of endurance, when, having gone to Russia and Poland, he begins to measure in *versts*! Nevertheless, if the book were pruned, rigidly pruned, a good deal would emerge of interest.

In most of the entries, a curious, very British, censoriousness is evident, and I shall now make one or two brief quotations to prove their quality.

"*Lisbon, 27th February (1814)*. . . . The people are wonderfully altered since I was here the first time. They have entirely left aside the *Capote*, wear round hats and dress to a degree smart and clean, without anything tawdry, which formerly they valued themselves upon. They ride on saddles made after the English fashion and cut short their poor horses' tails to make them look English—they ape and endeavour to copy us, and do everything, but to think and act like Englishmen.

"*Sunday 6th March*. I went to General Neronha's funeral. He was buried at 9 o'clock last night with all the honours due to an eminent General, and with the pomp and swaggering of his Nation. Before the body arrived at the Church, the conduct of the spectators was shameful, and shewed a great lack of Religion, and certainly of feeling. The principal people of Lisbon assembled in the Church, and it was more like a Levée than a solemn meeting, everyone talking upon trivial subjects and laughing. During the Service, three gentlemen behind

[1] Constantia Maxwell, *Country and Town in Ireland under the Georges.* (George G. Harrap & Co., 1940.)

me were engaged in dispute; whether Admiral Martin (by whom I was standing) was a Christian or a Heretic. The firing of the guns from the Castle was fine and awful. . . ."

These entries have a little of the atmosphere of Beckford's *Letters from Spain and Portugal*, though they are written twenty years after, and have not been touched up, as were Beckford's. A year later, a laconic entry possesses a certain family interest:

"*Paris, 1816*. The month of March passed in a most particularly dull manner. No society, bad weather, no hunting, and my brother in a rascally prison for having helped in saving the life of a Frenchman."

This last grumble relates to the sentence passed upon his elder brother, John—afterwards 3rd Earl of Donoughmore— for having helped General Count de Lavalette to flee from France. The general had incurred the death penalty by his Bonapartist activities, but on the day upon which he was to be guillotined, his wife dressed him in her own garments and smuggled him out of the Conciergerie in a sedan-chair. But Paris was so well guarded by English, Austrians, Russians and Prussians that he could not succeed in leaving the city. For a long time he hid in holes and corners. At last his friends appealed to General Sir Robert Wilson, who was noted for his chivalrous generosity, and he, aided by the two officers Bruce and Hely-Hutchinson, dressed Lavalette as an English officer and smuggled him in a cabriolet through the barriers and over the frontier into Belgium. "The English gentlemen", says a writer in the *Daily Telegraph*, who refers to the incident many years later,[1] "were arrested in Paris and tried before the Court of Assizes of the Seine. . . . They were sentenced to a brief term of imprisonment; but they found their reward in the cheers and embraces of the spectators in court, and in the applause of all liberal France." . . . John Hely-Hutchinson was sentenced to three months' imprisonment and was deprived by the King of his commission; but he was soon pardoned and returned to his regiment. His brother, however, continued to regard him as very ill-used.

In the winter of 1817-1818, when he was twenty-seven years of age, my great-grandfather went to Italy, for pleasure and

[1] 17th August 1874.

the improvement of his mind. At Weston there is a walnut, each half of which contains a kid glove of Princess Pauline Borghese's, Napoleon's lovely sister, famous for her small hands, though her whole body was celebrated so exquisitely by Canova. Of her he gives a lively account on 30th December 1817:

"I dined with a beautiful and famous personage, who thinks of nothing but her little handsome person and of her dress. She is illiterate, and amusing when she does not attempt to read Tasso. Her court is made up of Singers, *some* Sycophants, and of young handsome officers. It is astonishing how people are breaking their heads to get even a sight of her."

His account of the Roman Carnival, too, is not without charm:

"*7th January 1818.* The sight of one Carnival at Rome will, I think, content me for all the rest of my life. Pelting *confite* is amusing to those who like such fun. The masks are good, but little to say for themselves. The most curious part is to see about twenty thousand—they say forty thousand—people ranged by an impudent soldiery on either side the Corso, a charge of cavalry ensues in the space of a few minutes, and then the Horses, who run from one extreme of the Corso to the other without riders. The last day finished with an exhibition of rather a singular nature, which is called *moccoletti*. After the Horse-race, the Corso is one sheet of fire—everyone carries lighted candles and the carriages are filled with them. A great noise is heard, crying out '*Morte a chi non porta moccoletti!*' . . . From the Principessa Borghese's balcony we saw the sight remarkably well, and covered the people underneath with wax —they try to put out each other's candles, and you will see a Clown blow out the *moccolette* of a Princess, and push his way into the carriage to light it again, and perhaps then blow it out a second time. . . . These people are the most good-natured and illiterate fools I ever met; they are just fit to live under their present government."

At the monumental and magnificent Royal Palace of Caserta, near Naples, two months later, the young officer mingled with the disapproval he meted out, some enjoyable measuring:

"The palace has 746 feet in length by 576 in breadth, and

is rectangular. It is 113 feet in height with 2 *grands étages* and 3 smaller. Vanvitelli was the architect. The rascal ought to have been hanged five times over for laying out, or rather throwing away, so much of his country's money. And it is yet unfinished. The Staircase is fine—the gardens and waterfall, of both of which they so much brag, are quite horrible. As to the Aqueduct, it is nothing to those who have seen Lisbon, Pont du Gard or Llangothlen. . . . I hate kings more than ever."

It is of a certain interest, besides that which attaches to the difference in feeling manifested between two periods a hundred years apart, to compare Colonel Hely-Hutchinson's account of the palace with that of his great-grandson, Sacheverell Sitwell. In the century that had elapsed, Caserta had been forgotten, buried under the dusty accumulation of Ruskin's crockets, pinnacles and gothic lace and lavender, and it was my brother's book—his first prose work, written at the age of twenty-two—, fresh, strange and lovely as the music of *Petrouchka—Southern Baroque Art*, and especially the essay in it entitled "The Serenade at Caserta", which again brought sightseers to this shrine of the eighteenth century, when it was said by English travellers "to be the greatest building since Roman times". Alas, discursive and disquisitional as I want this book to be, I must nevertheless refrain from a very lengthy quotation, and content myself with the passage which follows.[1]

"Those who object to the conscription of labour in Russia can take pride in Caserta, built in the last days of despotism. It is the work of slaves, some of them negro, but in great proportion European. This last great work of slave labour is heartless as you would expect. The staircase, with its ceremonial landing, the chapel and theatre are famed for their marbles. . . . The porticoes leading through the house recall drawings by Bibbiena. Beyond them lie the gardens, rising for two miles up a hill, and of such length as to necessitate a carriage. The innumerable groups of statuary on successive landings along the cascade become monotonous. The water drips down slowly past you, passing from basin to basin, between the two straight roads that border it. Arriving at last at the height of the

[1] *Op. cit.* (Grant Richards, 1924), pp. 58-9.

hill, where a mere fall of water into the topmost basin precipitates this small avalanche, there awaits you the biggest and most imposing of the statue groups. But it is the view when you turn round on your ascent, which is the culmination of this immense work. Very far down the avenue, just filling the space between its two arms, lies the palace, absolutely still and uninhabited. On the left there is Vesuvius, like an inkpot with a cut-down quill pen in it. Then the eyes naturally travel again down the groove laid for them. The trees of the avenue, as they fade and grow smaller in the distance, have the air of gently spinning like tops in a slight mist. But the dropping water and the hot afternoon turn them to hundreds of bells, smaller almost than any leaf. These millions of little tongues are lolling, or beginning to chatter, and the whole volume of their song, swinging as it goes along all the bells it touches, eventually jumps right off the trees over the palace. And there, in the heart of the mist, over the middle of the palace roof, far enough at sea for this music to be heard, lies Capri, looming out of the mysterious sea like a huge whale's back. . . ."

Of the landscape so imaginatively described above, all that Colonel Hely-Hutchinson notes is, "The hills around are bleak and naked, with few even of those miserable olive trees upon them."

In April our traveller had reached Venice, where he indulged in an orgy of measurements and statistics. At the Armoury, "the ropewalk has 995 feet in length. The whole is three miles in circumference." Then, swelling to a mood of Jeremiah-like prophecy, his culminating paragraph runs: "Since the revolution there are eighty palaces in Venice utterly destroyed and two hundred houses, the population amounts to only a hundred thousand. . . . There is no commerce of any sort, not a single English flag in the harbour. All foreign productions are prohibited. From January to June the entry made in English vessels was of 4000 tons. From June to November of the same year it had diminished to 300. . . . Before the Revolution there were 15,000 gondolas here, now there are not 4000. In fifty years, Venice will be no more."

Colonel Hely-Hutchinson's entries in his diaries of travel become more dry as he grows older, until finally he no longer went so far afield. In the spring of 1825 he married Harriot, the daughter of Mr. William Wrightson of Cusworth, and the widow of Frederick North Douglas, the only son of Lord[1] and Lady Glenbervie, and thenceforward, apart from long visits to Ireland, divided most of his time between London, where he had a house in Brook Street, and Weston in Northamptonshire. After his wife's death, he went abroad for a change: he was by that time an old man, and took with him two of his grandchildren—my father and my aunt, then very young. My father told me that, when they reached Brussels, the veteran offered them the choice of a treat; they could visit with him the field of Waterloo, upon which he had fought, or he would take them to a circus. . . . Unhesitatingly, they both plumped for the circus. But the old gentleman seemed in no way put out.

Another anecdote which my father told me of him, suggests that his mind, in spite of its prosaic aspects, possessed a more sensitive and romantic side. Shortly before he died, at the age of eighty-four, he looked earnestly at my father and his sister Florence, then aged fourteen and fifteen, and said, pointing to my aunt, "You are to be a painter!" and to my father, "You are to be a poet!"

But, indeed, he had always shown a respect for art and artists; in Rome in 1817, he visited Canova's studio, and was

[1] Sylvester Douglas, born in 1743, was an able Scot with a precise mind. He first studied medicine, but then changed over to the law and was called to the bar in 1776. He married Katherine, daughter of Lord North, and it was owing to his thus being son-in-law of the Prime Minister, no less than to his natural perseverance, that he owed his quick preferment in politics. He filled many posts, and was created an Irish peer in 1801. He left at Weston a diary computed at two million words, and my brother and I were responsible for the publication of selections from it, *The Journals of Sylvester Douglas* (Lord Glenbervie), which were edited by Mr. Francis Bickley and published by Constable in 1928. Since Lord Glenbervie liked a life full of news, and to be "behind the scenes" on every possible occasion, the book sheds new light on many characters and events of the time, notably on the conduct of Queen Caroline, to whom Lady Glenbervie had been lady-in-waiting.

Lord Glenbervie died in 1833, a lonely and sad old man, who had outlived his wife by thirteen years, and his only son by fourteen. He had been particularly devoted to them, and his later diaries are full of his unhappiness.

He had been examined as a witness for the defence in the trial of Queen Caroline; and Sheridan, shortly afterwards, wrote a pasquinade beginning

> "Glenbervie, Glenbervie,
> What's good for the scurvy?
> For ne'er be your old trade forgot."

plainly a great admirer of his work. And when in Paris in 1818, he records:

"*July*. Accompany Sidonie Potocki to see the atelier of Monsieur Garneray. He is remarkable for his manner of painting Gothic architecture and flowers. . . . Nothing has given me more pleasure than the studio of Monsieur Redouté,[1] No. 6 Rue de Seine. He is the first flower painter in Europe. His collection of roses which he is just finishing is superb. Redouté took us to see the atelier of Monsieur Gérard (élève de David), the first historical and portrait painter in France. What a work is his entrée d'Henri IV à Paris, for which he is only paid forty thousand francs!"

Unlike so many other members of the family, however, Colonel Hely-Hutchinson entertained—as the reader will have deduced from the entry concerning Caserta in his diary—a horror of over-building. No doubt Weston, a compact and pretty manor-house, appealed to him for this reason. And after his first visit to his daughter at Renishaw—this, it must be remembered, was subsequent to the sale of much of its contents, so that no doubt many of the rooms looked bigger for being so bare—he remarks in a letter, "By whom, or by how many, Renishaw was built, it is a folly."

His wife, Harriot, had been brought up in her father's enchanting house, Cusworth, near Doncaster; one of the most beautiful William and Mary houses in the north of England. Later she had inherited from her maternal aunt, Miss Heber, Weston in Northamptonshire. It is a place full of the past, and I have never known rooms in which you could hear more clearly the heart-beat of other centuries than our own. Five years ago, Mr. Francis Bamford edited a book of some of the letters my brother found there;[2] a correspondence of great interest to all students of social life in England in the latter half of the eighteenth century. All the letters were written *to* the lady whose name gives the title to the volume[2]—with one

[1] Pierre Joseph Redouté, the great painter of roses and lilies, was born in Belgium in 1759. He was the son of another celebrated artist, Charles Joseph Redouté (1715-1766), and brother of two others. Among his pupils were Marie-Antoinette, Josephine and Hortense. He died in Paris in 1840.

[2] "*Dear Miss Heber* . . ." Edited by Francis Bamford, with prefaces by Georgia and Sacheverell Sitwell. (Constable & Co., 1937.)

exception, the first letter in it, written by herself at the age of seven or eight years, and addressed to her father at Bath. Surely among the most charming and evocative letters ever written by childish hands, it takes you for the moment, while you read it, straight into the vanished world from which it comes: you can see the very colours of the room in which the little girl writes, the stripes of the curtains, the formidable erection of powdered hair worn by her grandmother, who sits with her; you can smell the fumes from the kitchen, mingling with the heavy scents of the drawing-room on that winter's afternoon now so far away.

HAYES, December the 3rd [1765?]

I am in great hast to thank my dear Papa for his charming long Letter old John brought me this morning, which gave me so much pleasure that Sister Harriot and I jumped for joy, and was in such a hurry that we had scarce patience to let my Grany put on her Cloaths before she read it. And truely I believe she was as ready as we was to know how our dear friends at Bath did.

As you was so good to give me an acco't how you spent your time, I must in return tell you how we go on. At our first coming home from the "Magpye", our little Parlour seemed dull for want of the good Company that was gone to Bath.

But in a day or two came Mrs. Lethieullier and two Miss Ire-mongers and Mrs. Otty, who taught us to sing *A Little flurtation*. I asked her the meaning of the word (as I love to know all I can); she flaped her fan and told me that was flurtation; then I was satisfied. They invited us to dinner, and my Grany wish'd papa and mama co'd have seen their two little girls sitting amongst all the fine Silver dishes, as grave as two Judges with their man Richard behind them, for we went without a maid. My Grany said we was good, but we must not praise ourselves.

Last Sunday afternoon I went to church, and when we came home and was reading our Books and saying our Catechism, in came my aunt and cousin Blencowes, and soon after Mr. Lane with his Black man Toby, who we see in the kitchen. He asked my sister Harriot to kiss him, but she said, "Sir, I've got a sore Nose and desire you'l excuse me."

We shall be very glad of the little Book, for I think King Baldad[1] was a clever old man to find out so nice a Spring, and if it does you good, shall love his memory.

We often look in the map and particularly at Bath, which my sister Harriot put her finger upon today, and said "There is Bath, but I wish you wo'd show me my dear mama there, for I cannot see

[1] King Bladud, the legendary founder of Bath.

her." I hope it will not be long before you come home and say you love your Harriot, Eliza and your and mama's dutyfull daughter, M. HEBER.

Pray tell Miss Filmer we never forget to drink her health every day when we have drunk yours and mama's. Richard has mended the pen, so I must tell you that Grany and her two girls sit close together at the same table, which often moves so sudingly that you are not to wonder at the fine black spots in this.

Bath, however, could do nothing for her father, for whom, in this letter, the young writer shows so much affection, and he died, the following summer, at the age of thirty-nine.

And now I will finish this account with an extract from a letter to Miss Heber from her sister, Harriot, my great-great-grandmother, describing her arrival at Cusworth after her marriage:

26th July 1788

MY DEAREST MARY,

. . . This will inform you and my mother that we arrived here very well by Tea time yesterday—the place is indeed beautiful, much more so than I cd. have imagined. With the first sight of it I cd. but be highly pleased. But nothing cd. equal the impression I recd. from the affectionate wellcome my Dearest Wrightson gave me the moment after I entered his House. . . .

I must now . . . endeavor to make you smile by giving you an account of our cheerful reception at Doncaster, thro' wch place our carriage was the whole way surround'd by people paying their compts: the Bells had been ringing the whole Day. I really cd. not help laughing to see how much I was the object of curiosity; every window was crowded with people, to whom Wrightson had nothing to do but Bow and say "Howdy" and laughing too all the way. I am sure they must have thought us a very merry couple.

I have been writing the above while my Hair was Dressing; fear you can hardly read it. Yesterday even. my time was fully imploy'd. Mr. Wrightson was shewing me my room in the House and taking me the Shrubery, etc., till it was late and we were tired; this morng. I had notes to answer, the Housekeeper to talk to, Old Nancy to interrogate, etc., etc. And walk'd in the Park a great while, so you may think I had not much time to spare, allowing too for Dressing. I have left many things and want many things, but have not time to tell you of them now as the Phaeton is just coming to the Door and a servant is waiting for this.

Thomas, the Huntsman, a *Drole creature*, a great friend, *you know*, to early hours—I had not been arrived 5 minutes before he went up to Mr W. and said indeed he liked my *looks mightily*. Burn this scrawl when read.—Yours affte., HARRIOT WRIGHTSON.

Both these letters show the aptitude for self-expression which seems to come naturally to those of Heber blood.

The chief house of the Hebers was at Hodnet, in Shropshire, an estate they had inherited from the Vernons. One of the Hebers had fought in the Duke of York's army at the battle of Wakefield in the Wars of the Roses; but the family produced its two most distinguished members toward the end of the eighteenth century, in Richard Heber, the greatest of bibliophiles, and his half-brother, Reginald, Bishop of Calcutta, and author of the hymn "From Greenland's Icy Mountains".[1] Born in 1773 and 1783 respectively, they were first cousins of my great-grandmother's. Richard Heber, to whom Walter Scott referred as "Heber the magnificent, whose library and cellar are so superior to all others in the world", was certainly a most extraordinary character. For some years he represented Oxford University in Parliament, but, finding that to him the claims of book-collecting dominated and superseded all others, eventually resigned. Campbell called him "the first and strongest of all bibliomaniacs", and his best-known dictum was "No gentleman can be without three copies of a book, one for show, one for use, and one for borrowers". When he died at the age of sixty in 1833, he possessed eight houses, crammed with books, "overflowing all the rooms, chairs, tables and passages—two in London, one at Hodnet, one in the High Street of Oxford, others at Paris, Brussels, Antwerp and Ghent, besides numerous smaller hoards in other parts of the continent".[2] After his death, the series of sales of the volumes belonging to him—which Dibdin estimated at 127,500 and Allibone, more precisely, at 146,827—lasted for over three years. And from these sales was formed the Britwell Court Library, the disposal of which constituted the greatest and most sensational bibliographic event of the present century.

[1] Bishop Heber's best known poem, apart from hymns, was his Oxford prize poem, "Palestine" (1803). Sir Walter Scott was having breakfast at Brasenose with Heber just before the poem was sent in, and remarked that there was no allusion in the poem, which otherwise he praised, to the fact that no tools were used in the construction of the Temple. Heber at once invented the subsequently celebrated lines—
> ". . . No hammers fell, no ponderous axes rung;
> Like some tall palm the mystic fabric sprung."

[2] *Dictionary of National Biography.*

Reginald Heber wrote a few poems which are remembered, and some interesting books of travel. And from him were descended two writers, Mary Cholmondeley, thirty or fifty years ago a well-known novelist, and Stella Benson. So it will be seen that several authors have the blood of this family in their veins, and sometimes I wonder, too, whether another gift —if it can be described as a gift—which both my sister and I possess to some degree may not come to us through the Hebers. . . . A walnut cabinet which stands in the Justice Room at Weston has, pasted inside one of its panels, a piece of discoloured paper, on which is recorded in faded ink this curious story. "Mrs. Jennens" (the great-grandmother of Mrs. Wrightson) "dreamt that an express came with an account of the death of her sister, Lady Probyn; that the latter had appointed her sole Executrix, and had left a cabinet to Mrs. Betty Blencowe, in which were secret drawers containing several valuables. She told her dream to Mrs. Welch, then staying with her. A year afterwards, an express came, Mrs. Welch reminded her of her dream, and upon opening the Will it was found that the cabinet was left to Mrs. Blencowe, and Mrs. Jennens was directed by her dream to the secret drawers, where she found diamonds and other valuables, which were afterwards given to her daughter, Mrs. Peareth." . . . Is this an instance of the same faculty—possibly hereditary, and certainly more common than is allowed—which, for example, enabled me to dream correctly beforehand of a winning number at the roulette table? . . . In my sleep a voice said to me, "Back the number fifteen when the casino clock is at the hour". The following afternoon I went into the rooms, and a little later, seeing that the minute hand of the clock marked the hour—six o'clock— precisely as the ball was thrown, I hurriedly did as I had been bidden, and put on all the money I had brought with me. . . . And, I won! On other occasions, too, I have dreamed of events that were subsequently to occur, though these were not so pleasant, and these dreams I will narrate fully in their place.

CHAPTER THREE

My Mother's Side

Now I must turn to my mother's side of the family, and first to her father's grandfather and grandmother, Lord and Lady Conyngham. . . . The Conynghams derived from an Anglo-Norman family, long settled in Ireland. The 3rd Lord Conyngham was created a marquess in 1816, and he served as Constable of Windsor Castle and Lord Steward of the Household for nine years. These posts and dignities he owed, it is presumed, to the influence of his wife with the Prince Regent, later George IV.

For the whole florid decade of King George's reign, the three most caricatured and ridiculed persons in England were the Monarch himself, his friend, Lady Conyngham, and the Duke of Wellington; the lengths to which the cartoonists and pamphleteers pushed their libels, even though one of the trio was the King, and another the hero of England, and, more than that, of the whole of Europe, was startling indeed. And towards the end of King George's life, the coarse and brutal attacks upon his physical infirmity—he suffered from dropsy—are, even in this ruthless age in which we now find ourselves, almost unbelievable; though they are paralleled by the description Fielding, a sufferer from the same disease, gives in his *Journal of a Voyage to Lisbon*, of the crowds at the docks in London laughing at his swollen form as he was carried on board ship.[1]

Sometimes, then, looking at these caricatures, you will find yourself wondering whether, if the Duke of Wellington were so plainly and vindictively misrepresented, the same may not be

---

[1] ". . . I think upon my entrance into the boat, I presented a spectacle of the highest horror. The total loss of limbs was apparent to all who saw me, and my face contained marks of a most diseased state, if not of death itself. . . . In this condition I ran the gauntlope (so I think I may justly call it) through rows of sailors and watermen, few of whom failed of paying their compliments to me by all manner of insults and jests on my misery. No man who knew me will think I conceived any personal resentment at this behaviour; but it was a lively picture of that cruelty and inhumanity in the nature of men which I have often contemplated with concern. . . . It may be said that this barbarous custom is peculiar to the English, and of them only to the lowest degree. . . ."
Fielding died during the visit to Lisbon that ensued.

true, in at any rate a lesser degree, of the two other victims. The verdict which, in conversation with Raikes, the Duke of Wellington passed on George IV, many years after his death, is well known: "He was, indeed, the most extraordinary compound of talent, wit, buffoonery, obstinacy and good feeling—in short, a medley of the most opposite qualities with a great preponderance of good that I ever saw in any character in my life". His judgement on Lady Conyngham is less familiar; he remarked that during the King's reign, no great decision·in English policy or matters of State had been taken without her counsel and consent.

It is singular that when so much labour has been spent in rehabilitating people of far less historical and personal interest, this woman, so powerful in her own day, should have found no writer to undertake her defence. No champion comes forward to refute with incontrovertible evidence the vague but general accusation of greed, stupidity and want of feeling levelled at her by her contemporaries. My own purpose, however, in trying to summon her for a moment from oblivion, is in no way to whitewash her, but merely to recall to memory a few points in her favour to set against those to which, if the public at all remembers her, it yet clings in her despite, and to examine the curious circumstances wherefrom she sprung. Apart from this, she is too far away now for me to feel much of the piety of a descendant rushing to the rescue of an ancestress.

The beginning of Lady Conyngham's real ascendancy over the King coincided with the beginning of his reign—and it may be noted that he had succeeded to the throne on the 29th of January 1820 at the age of fifty-eight, and that Lady Conyngham herself was already over fifty—and only ended, after ten years, with his death. During this entire decade the public attention was fixed upon her every action and word. And if, as I have said, the Duke of Wellington, most unbiassed of observers, did not join in the chorus of her dispraise, the rest of her contemporaries were not so lenient.

Princess Lieven,[1] that rattling bag of bones animated by so

[1] Dorothea, Princess Lieven, the wife of Prince Lieven, who was sent to England as Russian Minister in 1812. Shortly after, he was made Ambassador, which post he filled until his recall in 1834.

Plate IV

SIR GEORGE SITWELL
THE AUTHOR'S GREAT-GRANDFATHER
From the water-colour by Octavius Oakley at Renishaw

Plate V

THE WARNEFORD AND SITWELL FAMILIES

From the silhouette by Francis Torond

In the group on the right are Francis Hurt Sitwell and his Wife with their children Mary, afterwards Lady Wake, and Sitwell Sitwell

Plate VI

COL. THE HON. HENRY HELY-HUTCHINSON, THE AUTHOR'S
GREAT-GRANDFATHER, WITH HIS DAUGHTER, LOUISA LUCY,
AFTERWARDS LADY SITWELL
From the painting by John Phillip, by kind permission of Sacheverell Sitwell, Esq.

Plate VII

THE SITWELL CHILDREN
By J. S. Copley
Frank, Mary, Hurt and Sitwell Sitwell

Plate VIII

ANNE, COUNTESS OF MORNINGTON
READING THE NEWS OF WATERLOO AND SURROUNDED BY
THE BUSTS OF HER ILLUSTRIOUS SONS
After the painting by her grand-daughter, Lady Burghersh

Plate IX

LORD ALBERT CONYNGHAM, AFTERWARDS ALBERT DENISON,
1st LORD LONDESBOROUGH, THE AUTHOR'S GREAT-
GRANDFATHER
After the painting by Sir Francis Grant

Plate X

HENRY, 7TH DUKE OF BEAUFORT, K.G.
THE AUTHOR'S GREAT-GRANDFATHER
From the painting by Winterhalter, by kind permission of the Duke of Beaufort

Plate XI

THE PRINCE AND PRINCESS OF WALES ON THE SPA AT SCARBOROUGH, 1871

From the painting by J. J. Barker

From left to right in the group before the lamp standard : The Duchess of Beaufort, The Duke of Beaufort, H.R.H. the Prince of Wales, H.R.H. the Princess of Wales, H.R.H. Princess Christian, Lord Londesborough, Lady Londesborough, H.H. the Duke of Teck and H.R.H. Princess Mary, Duchess of Teck

Plate XII

HENRY, FIRST EARL OF LONDESBOROUGH,
THE AUTHOR'S GRANDFATHER

Plate XIII

THE AUTHOR'S MOTHER
From the painting by Sir William Richmond

Plate XIV

THE SITWELL FAMILY
by J. S. Sargent

Plate XV

Elliott & Fry Ltd.

AUGUSTIN RUBIO WITH VIOLET GORDON WOODHOUSE

lively an ill-will, and a person as much feared by the stupid and uncritical as Lady Oxford in our day—but with more reason, since Lady Oxford's kindness in act as opposed to word never fails—opens the attack. On 26th April 1820 she ends a letter to Metternich:[1] ". . . can one imagine anything more absurd than an amorous and inconstant sexagenarian who, at the beginning of his reign, gives up all his time to a love affair? It is pitiable." Then, on 24th May of the same year, Charles Greville[2] proceeds to the assault with a triple-barrelled firing of anecdotes of an uncomplimentary nature. The first is that delightful story of Lady Hertford, the discarded and supplanted favourite of the new King. "Somebody asked Lady Hertford 'if she had been aware of the King's admiration for Lady Conyngham' and 'whether he had ever talked to her about Lady C.' She replied that 'intimately as she had known the King, and openly as he had always talked to her upon every subject, he had never ventured to speak to her upon that of his mistresses'!" Then he tells us that when the King was riding in the Park with Lady Conyngham, Lord Beauchamp,[3] Lady Hertford's grandson, exclaimed, "By God, our grandmother must learn to ride, or it is all over with us". And finally he repeats that when members of White's were discussing Lady Conyngham's looks, someone said "she had a leg like a post", and Copley[4] added "A poste Royale". In June of the following year, he notes: "The King dined at Devonshire House. . . . Lady C. had on her head a sapphire which belonged to the Stuarts, and was given by the Cardinal of York to the King. He gave it to the Princess Charlotte, and when she died he desired to have it back, Leopold being informed it was a crown jewel. This crown jewel sparkled in the headdress of the Marchioness at the ball." And, at the end of 1821, Princess Lieven obliges Metternich with a characteristic vignette of the favourite, "Not an idea in her head; not a word to say for

[1] *Private Letters of Princess Lieven to Prince Metternich (1820–1826)*, edited by Peter Quennell. (London, John Murray, 1937.)

[2] *The Greville Memoirs (1814–1860)*, edited by Lytton Strachey and Roger Fulford. (Macmillan, 1932.)

[3] Richard Seymour Conway (1800-1870), afterwards 4th Marquess of Hertford, and the great connoisseur.

[4] John Singleton Copley, the son of the portrait painter, and afterwards the Lord Chancellor, Lord Lyndhurst.

C

herself; nothing but a hand to accept pearls and diamonds with, and an enormous balcony to wear them on". After a visit to Windsor in June 1822, she treats us to a remarkable conversation piece, etched with the purest and most corrosive acid: ". . . here is one of the scenes between the trio—King, Favorite and Myself:

"The King, pointing to Lady Conyngham: 'Ah, heavens, if she were what I am!' I was at a loss to understand what this meant. Ought Lady Conyngham to be a man? The King stopped, sighed, and then went on: 'If she were a widow, as I am a widower, she would not be one for long.'

"Lady Conyngham: 'Ah, my dear King, how good you are.' . . . The King: 'Yes, I have taken an oath'; then turning to me, he added in a low voice, 'Patience; everything in good time.'

"I could not help thinking of the mysterious nocturnal visits of the man midwife,[1] and a whole chemist's shop flashed through my mind. I am not sure I did not shiver as if I were cold."

All through the reign, the volume of ridicule and denunciation continues, until it culminates in two passages from Greville. On 14th May 1829 he writes in his diary: ". . . the influence of Knighton and that of Lady Conyngham continue as great as ever; nothing can be done but by their permission, and they understand one another and play into each other's hands. Knighton opposes every kind of expense, except that which is lavished on her. The wealth she has accumulated by savings and presents must be enormous. The King continues to heap all kinds of presents upon her, and she lives at his expense; they do not possess a servant; even Lord C.'s *Valet de Chambre* is not properly their servant. They all have situations in the King's Household from which they receive their pay, while they continue in the service of the Conynghams. They dine every day while in London at St. James's, and when they give a dinner it is cooked at St. James's and brought up to Hamilton Place in Hackney Coaches and in machines made expressly for the purpose; there is merely a fire lit in their kitchen for such things as must be heated on the spot. . . ." After the King's death, again, Greville had an enjoyable gossip with one of the

[1] Princess Lieven's name for Sir William Knighton.

Valets de Chambre or Pages of the Backstairs, as they were known, and makes the following entry of what he had learned in that direction. "It was true that last year, when she [Lady Conyngham] was so ill, she was very anxious to leave the Castle, and that it was Sir William Knighton who with great difficulty induced her to stay there. At that time She was in wretched spirits, and did nothing but pray from morning to night. However, her conscience does not ever seem to have interfered with her ruling passion, avarice, and She went on accumulating. During the last illness wagons were loaded every night and sent away from the Castle, but what their contents were was not known, at least he did not say. All Windsor knew this." In the copy of the *Greville Memoirs* in the Library of Windsor Castle there are a few marginal comments, some thought to be by Queen Victoria, others by Lord Sydney, who had been page to George IV. One such note, probably by Lord Sydney, relates to the statement I have just quoted and runs, "Believed not to be true". This is almost the only favourable contemporary reference to her—and it is a later aside.

Feeling against the favourite was so strong that, in their violence, the writers contradict themselves. Thus some refuse to believe she was ever the King's mistress, and at the same time assign her children to him, while others maintain that she *was* his mistress and that the children are Lord Conyngham's. Greville,[1] in referring to the King and Lord Francis Conyngham,[2] alleges, "Now Bloomfield sits among the guests at dinner at the Pavilion; the honours are done by the Father on one side and the Son on the other". And Creevey,[3] in a letter to his step-daughter headed from Croxteth, 23rd December 1822, writes: ". . . Brougham says *many of the best informed* people in London, such as Dog Dent and others, are perfectly convinced of the truth of the report that dear Prinney is really to marry Ly. Elizabeth Coyngham; on which event the Earl[4]

---

[1] *The Greville Memoirs (1814–1860)*, vol. i, p. 123.
[2] Afterward 2nd Marquess of Conyngham. Lord Chamberlain, 1835–1839.
[3] *The Creevey Papers. A Selection from the Correspondence & Diaries of the late Thomas Creevey, M.P.*, edited by the Rt. Hon. Sir Herbert Maxwell, Bart., M.P., LL.D., F.R.S. (John Murray, 1905.)
[4] William Philip Molyneux, 2nd Earl of Sefton.

here humorously observes that the least the King can do for the Queen's family is to make Denison 'Great Infant of England' ". To this statement a footnote is appended—though we are not told whether Creevey or Sir Herbert Maxwell is responsible for it—which informs the reader that the Infant in question was "Lord Albert Denison Conyngham,[1] third son of Elizabeth Denison, 1st Marchioness of Conyngham. He was born in 1805, and was supposed to be the son of the Prince of Wales (George IV)."

In the middle of all the accusations that fly through the over-heated air of that short reign, we remember suddenly that Lady Hertford was a deeply wounded and resentful woman whose vindictiveness age could not stale, and that Charles Greville was always jealous of success of every kind, and on every occasion manifested a total lack of feeling, fed by the prying mind of a born sycophant and lackey. Surreptitiously his fingers turn the pages of his master's letters, he says nothing at the time, takes his orders, and then returns home and jots down in his diary what he has read, and his disgust at it. Certainly we are the richer for the scavenging of this golden dustman, for his little talks with the Pages of the Backstairs: but we need not think him a nice character or believe all that he says. We recollect, too, that Princess Lieven, with her moral strictures and her very witty descriptions, was, at the very moment of writing them, the scraggy, undecorative mistress of Prince Metternich.

The pictures they give us of Lady Conyngham are too vehement, too emphatic, for all their vividness. Resentment at the influence of the favourite enters into each mention of her and, though certain features in the delineations of her tally, in the main they are contradictory. A famous beauty—though admittedly past her prime—, they show her to us as a fat, middle-aged woman totally lacking in charm; at one moment we are told that she was stupid, ugly and grasping, at the next we are asked to believe—which is true—that she was able to capture and, until his death, retain the affection of the most capricious, cultivated, elegant and original, if eccentric, prince that England had seen for two centuries: we are told that she

[1] Afterwards the 1st Lord Londesborough.

was avaricious in the extreme, but we are not informed that she was herself a rich woman, the daughter of an immensely rich man, and the sister of a multimillionaire. Similarly the gossips maintain that she was the mistress of the King, and that certainly one, and probably two, of her children were his, and then we find out that, unless during the period that Lady Conyngham was living chiefly in Ireland, some previous connection had existed between them—and of this, though a few curious hints exist, there is no evidence—Lord Francis was born some seventeen years, and Lord Albert fourteen, before their mother's acknowledged ascendancy began. Lord Conyngham's marquessate is said, again, to have been due to her influence with the Regent, but he was created a marquess four years before the friendship is supposed to have started! . . . But everything she does is wrong; the diarists and letter-writers attack her for her influence in politics, and at the same time accuse her of taking no interest in public affairs; she is pilloried for inducing the King to abandon the Whigs and support the Tories, and then, when she becomes the powerful advocate in royal circles of Catholic emancipation, the fury of the same Whig diarists knows no bounds.

As to whether she was, or ever had been, in fact, the King's mistress, it is impossible now for us to judge. Nobody even tells us definitely when they met. But, quite apart from such speculations, it is plain, I think, that in his mature years the King, that extraordinary man, so unanchored to reality for all his talents and kindnesses and social graces, valued her friendship especially for the atmosphere which she provided in his home. He admired no doubt the particular type of beauty which she possessed—since, with her massive frame, fair hair and fine complexion, she a little resembled Mrs. Fitzherbert, his wife, and the woman who, in spite of his frequent anger—and with how little reason!—against her, remained his ideal. But, above all, he enjoyed her company and that of her sons and daughters, because he loved family life—so long as it was not that of his own family—, he loved young people—so long as they were not his own young people. This, of course, is the meaning of the scene witnessed by Princess Lieven, who told Lady Harrowby, who, in her turn, made it grist for Greville's mill; a scene which, since he misunderstood it, so deeply shocked, and therefore enchanted, him. Lady Conyngham had given the order for the hundreds of wax candles in the chandeliers of the Saloon of the Pavilion to be lit. "When the King came in, she said to him, 'Sir, I told them to light the candles as Lady Bath is coming this evening.' The King seized her arm and said with the greatest tenderness, 'Thank you, thank you, My Dear; you always do what is right; you cannot please me so much as by doing everything you please, everything to show you are Mistress here.' "[1]

Another cause of her power over him, and its long duration, is to be found in the King's laziness. As he grew older a kind of torpor enveloped him, until, at the end of his reign, he was called at six or seven in the morning, breakfasted in bed, transacted what business his Ministers could induce him to transact, still in bed, read every newspaper all through, got up in time for dinner at six, and retired to bed again between ten and eleven. In the night he would often ring his bell forty times, and, though a watch hung by his side, he would not make the effort of turning his head to look at it, but would ring for a Page to tell him the time: similarly, he would not even stretch out his hand for a glass of water. This was at Windsor, when he was in failing health: but even at the Pavilion, in the early 'twenties of the century, though he liked feminine society, he did not wish to be bothered and fussed. Lady Conyngham never offered her advice unless the King sought it—and her triumph was that, in consequence, he always *did* seek it. Otherwise, she did not interfere, except to make life more pleasant for him. She left him in peace, in his stifling rooms, of which others—but not she—complained that they were like a furnace, to concentrate upon the Things That Mattered; to consult with his cook upon the acquisition of an old master or the invention of a new dish, to design a piece of jewellery— composed, no doubt, of a Crown jewel or two—for Lady Conyngham, a new wig or waistcoat for himself, a new slin jacket for the Hanoverian Hussars. There were tailors to be seen, and the makers of chandeliers and curtains. He had thought out a new carved dragon, with golden and silver scales,

[1] *Memoirs*, vol. i, p. 118.

for the Music Room, and a new draping for the curtains.[1]
He must order a new kind of shoe that, though elegant, gave
room for gout. He must see the architects about new ideas for
the Royal Pavilion itself, for the Cottages and the Fishing
Temple on Virginia Water, as well as for the great schemes he
had just begun to prepare for Windsor, and he must talk to
Nash about the new Buckingham Palace and about plans for
London in general. He might, too, if he had time for it after
he had read the papers, think of a new battle in which he had
taken part—he was tired of Salamanca and Waterloo, and
that fisticuff battle with the butcher that he had been relating
lately—to tell to that old stick-in-the-mud, Wellington. (He,
the King, might be only a constitutional monarch, but he still
retained some prerogatives: the King's truth was different
from other men's truth, and even Wellington, the most truthful
man alive, could not question it.) So there was plenty to do,
really important things; and if the Ministers wanted to see him,
well, they could wait. Let them wait! He had already saved
Europe once, with his plan for the league of Continental
Powers which culminated in 1814; it had been his idea. And
no acknowledgement for it, no gratitude had he received! . . .
So now they could kick their heels in the anteroom. . . . Sometimes he kept them there for four or five hours.

Caroline was dead, the old King was dead, so he could do
what he liked. He most emphatically did not wish for the
influence, which he knew he *must* have in his *entourage*, to be
wielded by someone who would attempt to interfere with his
genuine passion for the arts and for music, who would try to
frustrate his continual and immense plans for rebuilding
palaces and cities, or would want to help him by urging economies
and by endeavouring to curb his extravagances—after all
he was King now, and the money was his, and bore on it his
likeness (not a very good one, by the way, he reflected). And,
in other directions, the woman presiding over his house must
be one who would never protest at his suddenly, without a
word, summoning the choir from St. George's Chapel to sing

[1] The drawings of these for the great reception rooms in the Royal
Pavilion, now in the possession of the Brighton municipal authorities, have
scrawled on them "Passed by H.M."

to him after dinner in the Dome, who would not deprecate his action if, when his private orchestra was playing a favourite piece, he decided to join in its rendering with a dinner gong, or tell him that it was unwise to mimic his Ministers or a foreign Monarch in front of a large gathering (and his new imitations, he was aware, were better than ever!), or declare that it was undignified of him to receive that young Italian composer, Rossini, whose work he so much admired, but whom many of his friends regarded as rude, conceited and flashy, not a fitting guest for their King. . . . Lady Conyngham filled this rôle; if she liked jewels, and spending money on them, so did he. He would design them for her. And it was a pleasure, too, to have Francis and Albert and Lady Elizabeth about him. . . . In these ways that we have mentioned, and in the company he liked, he was able, if only for a time, to banish the spectre of boredom which he so much dreaded. Ever since he could remember, he had sought, by means of diversions and pleasures, often deliberately unworthy, and with the aid of his charming manners and lively company, to avoid the form, the ceremony, the constraint, that his presence had, all along, inevitably imposed, and now, since he had succeeded to the throne, more than ever entailed. Looking back, it seemed as though his whole life had been spent in this vain attempt to escape from his own gilded and unwieldy shadow, the splendid, pompous shadow that passed like a wind over every room he entered, as the men bowed their heads and the women swept down in a curtsey. . . . Only in this circle, and with these individuals, could he relax.

Lady Conyngham, for her part, loved power, no doubt, and in her composition had some of a pirate's qualities. Perhaps the jewels and the compliments reminded her, too, how far she had travelled, for she, also, may have been trying to escape a shadow, though a shadow of different sort, of early poverty and disregard. . . . Certainly she was not merely the middle-aged woman of coarse appearance with whom the caricaturists of the period make us familiar. The portrait of her by Sir Thomas Lawrence, in the possession of the Countess of Londesborough, shows her as a very beautiful and dignified woman. And it is to be observed, in respect of this, how many of her descendants,

Conyngham as well as Denison, have been noted for their beauty. As her granddaughter and my great-aunt, Lady Treowen, when an old lady, remarked to me of herself and her several sisters, "We gals were a damned good-looking lot!" ... But the most curious and unexpected tribute to Lady Conyngham that reaches over the years, is that Greville, writing a quarter of a century later, admits that Queen Victoria entertained a regard for her, and was grateful to the favourite for her treatment of the Duchess of Kent and herself in the time of her domination.

There seems at this distance to be no means of deciding whether Lady Conyngham enriched herself at the expense of the Crown or not. If many Crown jewels had passed into her hands, Queen Victoria, I imagine, would not have pronounced so favourable a judgement upon her. Doubtless she received presents of jewels, but, where money was concerned, the Conynghams were at that time a very rich family, the income of Lord Conyngham's inherited estates being estimated at £70,000 a year; while, though it is true that Lady Conyngham at her death left £200,000, it must be remembered that this was probably her portion, for her father died a millionaire, and her brother became even wealthier, bequeathing to his younger nephew, Lord Albert, in 1849 a fortune of over £2,300,000; then an even greater sum than it would be today.

The history of Lady Conyngham's family, the Denisons[1]— of whom she became sole heir—is, though obscure, remarkable for the contrasts it affords. The name *Denison*, we are told by a local writer in 1865, is "even to the present day nearly as common about Leeds, as Smith in London, or Jones in Wales, or Campbell in Scotland, though it is rarely met with in other parts of Her Majesty's dominions". Joseph Denison, described at the time of his decease as "merchant of St. Mary-Axe", the father of Lady Conyngham—not, as sometimes stated, the

[1] This short account of the Denisons is derived from family tradition, from the *Complete Peerage*, from an article in the *Gentleman's Magazine* (vol. lxxvi), July-December 1806; on Joseph Denison, from an article by "Sylvanus Urban, Gent" in the *Gentleman's Magazine* (vol. xxxii, New Series) for 1849 (July to December), from information contained in *Biographical Sketches of Leeds and Neighbourhood*, by the Rev. R. V. Taylor, B.A. (London, 1865), and the entries in the *D.N.B.* under the heading "William Joseph Denison" and "Lord Albert Denison".

grandfather—was born about 1723, the son of very poor parents in or near Leeds. It is said that when he travelled up to London, as a boy of seventeen, he remained ignorant of reading and writing. The journey he accomplished in one of the ten-horse carrier wagons of the time, sometimes riding in it, and at others trudging along by the side of the horses. A later Dick Whittington, he was buoyed up by the hope—in which he was not to be disappointed—that he would find the streets of London paved with gold. He must have educated himself, if the stories of his illiteracy are true, with considerable speed, for, before long, he had become clerk in the counting-house of Mr. Dillon, an Irish Catholic, then the head of a considerable business, though in after years he was glad to act as clerk for his own former employee, Joseph Denison. Denison constituted, we read, "an extraordinary instance of success and prosperity in all his undertakings", and by, as one writer phrases it, "unabated industry and rigid frugality", or, in the words of another, "continuous working and scraping", the young man amassed a vast fortune. In his early struggles, he was very much helped by his wife, who came from the same locality as himself, and was named Sykes. She kept his books and looked after his affairs while he was away on business. She died without issue, some time at the beginning of the 1760s, and subsequently in 1768 he married Elizabeth, only child of Mr. Butler, variously described as "formerly a hatmaker in or near Tooley Street, Southwark", or, more grandiloquently, as "the daughter of a Lisbon merchant". (Perhaps this description should have run "*Leghorn* merchant": for it was from that part of the world that all the straw for hats was then imported.) This lady, who, all accounts agree, was "a well-educated and very amiable woman", bore him three children.

According to another writer of the nineteenth century, "the good fortune which attended on the Denisons in their 'rise and progress' to opulence and title has seldom or never been surpassed". For Mr. Joseph Denison was "the father of Mr. William Joseph Denison, M.P., of Denbies, the wealthy banker", while one of his daughters, Maria, married Sir Robert Lawley, created Lord Wenlock, the other married "the late Marquess of Conyngham" and "became the especial favourite of George IV", and his grandson and eventual heir "wore the coronet of Lord Londesborough".

William Joseph Denison, Lady Conyngham's brother, is presented to us as "a man of sound principles and excellent character, who, though less penurious than his father, pursued the like process of accumulation". He now owned the estate of Denbies in Surrey, his father having bought it from Jonathan Tyers, the former proprietor of Vauxhall Gardens, and he had become the chief landowner in Yorkshire, owning above 60,000 acres of that county, which his father had left some fifty or sixty years before as a penniless youth. He sat as Whig member for Camelford from 1796 to 1802, and for Kingston-upon-Hull from 1806 until his death forty-three years later.

In the gap which intervened between these two portions of his parliamentary career, he wedded his patriotism to the Muses, and produced a very long, rolling and resonant poem, kindly described by the writer on him in the *Dictionary of National Biography* as being "of some merit". It was of a sort always admired in England during a crisis. Its theme was Napoleon's threatened invasion of 1803, and I give two samples for their appositeness: First—

> Come when he will—elate in frantic pride,
> With vassal kingdoms crouching by his side—
> Deck'd with the pageantry of Eastern State,
> Tortur'd with restless and malignant hate,
> Drunk with success, array'd in hostile form,
> Old England's Genius fearless meets the storm.

And now, the great patriotic finale—

> But if decreed by Heav'n that fall we must;
> And what she wills, is ever right and just;
> If doom'd to swell (ordain'd by angry fate),
> This modern Attila's revengeful hate;
> Then Europe's sun is set in endless night—
> Then Faith, then Honour, wing their hasty flight—
> Then all the Ties of social life are o'er,
> From Moscow's snows, to fair Ausonia's shore—
> Then Gothic Darkness spreads its baleful shade—
> Then Art, then Learning, Laws and Freedom fade!
> For happier climes they hoist th' indignant sail,
> While savage Force and Anarchy prevail—

While all the Science polish'd Greece bestow'd,
Of every Muse the once admir'd abode—
With all that Genius, all that Taste inspire,
Sink in the flames to please a Despot's ire.
Long ere that moment let me meet my doom;
Grant me, great God, the refuge of the tomb.[1]

The writer of a short account of W. J. Denison after his
death states: "It has always been understood that a peerage
was offered to the late banker, through the intervention of his
sister (Elizabeth), who obtained a marquisate for her lord . . .
and a barony for her brother-in-law, Sir Robert Lawley (Baron
Wenlock in 1831[2]) . . . ; but the honour was respectfully
declined by the staunch old Whig, who considered that his
patronymic was more in its place at the head of his own ledger,
than in the pages of the peerage". . . . Certainly, all the diarists
agree that he disapproved most strongly of the relationship
between Lady Conyngham and the King. In a letter[3] to Miss
Ord, his stepdaughter, headed "Whitehall, Feby. 5, 1828",
Creevey tells how he had been left alone at about one in the
morning with Mrs. Michael Angelo Taylor, the friend of the
Whigs; who began a conversation with him—as one might
think, rather unwisely—with the words, " 'As I know, Mr.
Creevey, I may trust you with anything' ", and had then proceeded to tell him that her friend "poor Mr. Denison" was
" 'broken-hearted about his sister, Lady Conyngham' ". He
had told Mr. Taylor that from the first he had protested against
her living under the King's roof. "Not that even now he can
suppose there is anything criminal between persons of their
age", but because it created so much scandalous talk, which
he could go nowhere without hearing. Finally, together with
Lord Mountcharles,[4] he had "called formally" upon his sister
to leave the King, and had assured her that he would
alter his will if she refused, but she treated all such suppli-

[1] *Address to the People of Great Britain*, by W. J. Denison, Esq. Printed for
James Asperne (successor to Mr. Sewell) at the Bible, Crown, and Constitution, No 32 Cornhill; by W. Lane, Leadenhall Street. Price one penny
each, or 6s. the 100.
[2] It is to be noted that this barony was conferred by King William IV.
[3] *The Creevey Papers*.
[4] Formerly Lord Francis Conyngham, subsequently 2nd Marquess
Conyngham.

cations and threats only "with bursts of passion and defiance".

Perhaps his unhappiness in the past concerning his sister may have influenced Mr. Denison, for some reason we cannot fathom, against his other nephew, Lord Albert, and may have been responsible for an act of his which, in a man otherwise of amiability and principle, seems quite unaccountable. One of the writers I have quoted upon the Denisons tells us that, about three years before his uncle's death, my great-grandfather fell into difficulties over his speculations in railways, a transaction upon which he had entered with Mr. Denison's full knowledge and approval. Yet the old man allowed his nephew, with his young family, "to fly from the writs out against him to the semi-penal settlement of Boulogne-sur-mer, and reside there a twelvemonth . . . rather than come down with the tune of £2000; yet to this very gentleman—a man of the nicest honour —he had at that very period bequeathed more than two millions". Lord Albert—pronounced "Orbert", by the way— inherited this great fortune in 1849 and assumed, under his uncle's will, the name of Denison.

As I have said, there were those who alleged that he was the son of George IV. Certainly in appearance he in no way resembled that monarch, for he was tall and thin and dark, being described by a contemporary as "like a comb, all teeth and backbone". But he was, as his picture by Grant that hangs at Blankney shows us, an extremely imposing and romantic figure, with his great height—he was six feet four or five inches —, his dark, curling hair and side-whiskers, his features of a rather Latin regularity, and his eyes of a Spanish pride and melancholy. He had also the reputation of being a wit, and things he said I have heard repeated in my own lifetime. Age, however, seemed to have dulled them.

For a time Lord Albert was a cornet in "The Blues", then he served in the Diplomatic Service, and translated a fashionable novel by Carl Spindler, a German author who wrote dozens of romantic stories. This book, *The Natural Son . . . a German tale descriptive of the age of the Emperor Rudolph II (1552-1612) by Lord A. C. in 3 volumes*, appeared in 1835. Later he entered the House of Commons, sitting as Whig member for Canterbury. But the real business of his life was the collecting of beautiful and rare objects, and in this connoisseurship resides the single resemblance that can be found to his reputed father. In addition to his London house, he purchased Londesborough Lodge at Scarborough—a house which played so great a part in our own young lives—, Londesborough itself, and in 1850 the magnificent classical house of Grimston in Yorkshire. This mansion, probably the last fine Italianate villa to be built in England, had been designed, for the second Lord Howden[1] and his Russian wife, ten years previously by Decimus Burton, and Lord Albert filled it and his London house with precious and lovely objects, old masters, French furniture, Greek statuary and armour. (In his portrait by Grant, one elegant hand rests by the side of a vast vizor.) Smaller objects included Celtic and medieval jewellery, ivory caskets, drinking-cups, Limoges enamels, and several articles connected with magic, especially Dr. Dee's famous mirror.[2]

[1] He was the grandson of John Cradock, Archbishop of Dublin. His father, a well-known soldier, after being made Lord Howden at the age of seventy, suddenly discovered that he was descended from Caractacus, King of the Britons, and accordingly changed his name to Caradoc. The son, Sir John Hobart Caradoc, 2nd and last Lord Howden (1799-1873), was an interesting character, good-looking and somewhat eccentric. In Paris, where he was military attaché, he was known as Le Beau Cradock, and there he met Katherine Shavronski, Princess Bagration. She was a widow, and a great heiress in her own right, being the great-niece of Potemkin. Cradock—as he then was—eloped with her; but to the consternation of both of them, the Czar, since he had not been consulted, refused to recognise the marriage. He ordered Katherine's estates to be seized and a decree of banishment to be issued against her. Cradock himself inherited little money, but he at once set himself to the rebuilding of Grimston, an enormous house, and the laying-out of its gardens by Nesfield, the very talented landscape gardener. The place was planned to be of a scale and grandeur to which his wife was used and included "a riding school for this exotic pair . . . to take their exercise, even in the Yorkshire winter"; though they still lived in Paris. Later, Lady Howden received a large annuity in compensation for her Russian estates, but the marriage was a failure and they were legally separated in 1847, when Lord Howden was appointed Ambassador to Brazil, and later to Spain. He died in Paris in 1873, and was buried in the grounds of the Casa Caradoc, his villa near Bayonne, where, we are told, he had made a home for himself and "for other connections that he had formed " since the breakdown of his marriage.

(See *D.N.B.* and two articles on Grimston by Mr. Christopher Hussey in *Country Life* for 9th March and 16th March 1940.)

[2] Dr. John Dee, mathematician and astrologer (1527-1608). ". . . the magician did not himself see the vision in the glass, but he had to depend upon an intermediate agent, a sort of familiar, who in England was known by the name of a *skryer*, and whose business it was to look into the glass, and

He had bought much of the furniture from the Petit Trianon and in the simplicity of this, and in his passion for Greek antiquities, can perhaps be traced an artistic reaction from the rococo and gothic fantasies among which his youth had been spent, from the writhing dragons and clustered domes and bamboo staircases in wrought iron of the Royal Pavilion, the chinoiseries of the Fishing Temple and the gilded, blazoned halls of Windsor Castle. Nor was he interested alone in archaeology, the furniture and objects I have described, and in the pictures of the old masters: he appears also to have been a patron of the modern school of his epoch; what Augustus John has been to my generation, Landseer was to his (Ruskin had praised him, and, further, had formulated and explained his esthetic theories for him), and Lord Albert had bought the most celebrated of all Landseer's works, "The Monarch of the Glen".

Lord Albert was responsible for the publication of two sumptuous illustrated catalogues of the pieces of art and antiquity in his possession,[1] and was an author, as well as a translator—though of only one book. In 1849 he caused to be printed a small volume of travel sketches for private circulation.[2] In 1848 he had been very ill, and towards the end of that great revolutionary year he set out to find a warmer climate, accompanied, as he tells us, by "a wife, a plump and rather pretty English maid, and an English valet . . . an exception to the latter part of the rule 'that a servant may be a good servant for the first five years, a good master for the second five

describe what he saw. It is thus quite evident that the wise man who believed that he could command the spirits of the unknown world, lay at the mercy of a very inferior agent, of whom he was easily the dupe. Such was no doubt the case with Dr. Dee, who seems to have tried several '*skryers*' with little success until he became acquainted, soon after the year 1580, with Edward Kelly, a clever unprincipled man, who led Dee into a number of romantic adventures. . . ." Thomas Wright in *Miscellania Graphica*.

[1] One is entitled *Miscellania Graphica, Representations of Ancient, Medieval and Renaissance Remains in the possession of Lord Londesborough, engraved and described by F. W. Fairholt, F.S.A. The historical introduction by T. Wright, M.A., F.S.A., London, 1857;* and the other, *An Illustrated Descriptive Catalogue of Antique Silver Plate formed by Albert, Lord Londesborough. The Engravings and Letterpress by F. W. Fairholt, F.S.A., 1860.*

[2] A rare book, of which I have only seen one copy: *Wanderings in Search of Health,* by Lord Albert Denison, K.C.H., F.S.A. (London, printed for private circulation, 1849.)

years, but is a hard master for the third five years of his service' ".

The book that my great-grandfather wrote as a result of the voyage that he thus undertook, opens a window upon the eastern end of the Mediterranean as it existed in those days, and his accounts of it—and of Malta, Sicily and Italy—are authentic and lively, albeit his mind appears to have been somewhat formal despite its Whiggish mould. At the same time, a certain unintentional air of originality has been imparted to the chapters concerned with Greece, by the insistence of the printers on rendering "Armenian" as "American"; thus, "I met a group of American peasants, and asked to buy a terracotta they had recently excavated" is a common adventure. . . . I am, as I have said, fortunate in having so many written records by members of the family, and I propose for a moment to pause and contemplate the vista which this particular window affords, so that we may learn indirectly, through the people and places he describes, a little of the author.

After a stay in Malta, the party proceeded to the Piraeus. Accounts of Greece between 1830 and 1850 are rare; English tourists were then as few as fifty years later they were numerous. Even schoolmasters, inured for a lifetime to English schools, feared the discomfort of staying in this country, rescued so recently from the Turks. The windows of the houses lacked glass, and there was scarcely any furniture in the living-rooms, for, only two decades back, it had been the custom of even the wealthiest citizens of this impoverished and enslaved land to sit cross-legged upon the floor and sleep on a divan. Chairs and beds were therefore still somewhat new-fangled, while to travel through the country was both difficult and dangerous. Though there was as yet little revolutionary ferment here, brigands were common, and even more ferocious—and certainly less picturesque—than in Southern Italy across the water, where it was still their habit at this period to appear disguised as Punchinellos, in loose, glittering white clothes, tall, pointed caps of white felt and black masks with enormous black beaks.

The sybaritic Lord Albert, however, seems to have been willing to face considerable discomfort in order to acquaint himself with places of interest and beauty, as we can see, for example, by his description of the quarters that he and his wife were obliged to share at Macropoulos. "I found Lady Albert in melancholy mood, established . . .; our two truckle beds and a little table for our dinner, with two chairs, were the furniture of a large loft and granary, open by many cracks in the tiles to the sky,—receiving light from the door alone, and warmth from an earthen pan of coals, which, by the way, gave me a dreadful headache all night. A lighted lamp swung in the draughts of wind before a Byzantine Virgin and Child, and holes pierced in the floor gave us the advantage of all the noises from below, which were manifold,—our place of shelter being the village coffee-house. . . ."

Lord Albert first settled in Athens, spending three months there, and visiting, as well, during that time the famous places in its immediate neighbourhood, such as Eleusis and Daphnae. His book enables us to see the city as it then existed, a small collection of huddled, wooden shacks appearing to have drifted on a sea of impenetrable dust against the bottom of that august and glorious rock, the Acropolis. In spite of the long history attached to it, it was thinly-built, squalid and unpainted, a sham capital of a few streets, set in surroundings of unparalleled loveliness; a bare, high, rocky country, more beautiful in its bareness, in its supreme elegance and rhythm of line, than all others in their richness. At every point, probable and improbable, this landscape encountered the sea. Formerly peopled by nymphs and fauns and by marble statues of the gods, it was now inhabited by a handsome race of brigands dressed in the clothes of the mountaineers of Albania, from whom they were descended. The men, for instance, in the neighbourhood of Athens wore red caps with tassels, white shirts and white kilts, the women "white robes, embroidered with some dark colour, and very picturesque. The head-dress of the young women, worn on festivals, proves the inhabitants to be cautious in investing . . . : it is a sort of cloth helmet, or rather skull-cap, covered with coins of the present day."

Over this strange, lovely, poverty-stricken land, the centre of a Court that must have been most difficult to collect in a nation composed of peasants who had only just ceased being slaves, reigned the Bavarian Otho,[1] the only ruler of his abortive dynasty. Lord Albert writes of this King, "In no single instance have I heard him well spoken of. . . . Those that do not like to speak ill of him are silent." His unpopularity had been in part due to a tactless wish he had expressed to introduce small colonies of industrious Bavarians into the idyllic prospects of which he was monarch.

This sovereign and his pretty and amiable consort lived in a newly erected echoing palace in the German neo-Greek style of the 'thirties. It looked enormous set in the middle of their unbuilt yet tumble-down capital. Lord Albert thus describes his first visit to it, no doubt comparing it in his mind with the luxurious state that had been kept in the Royal Pavilion, and with the grandeur of Windsor. "One solitary servant was in attendance, in a vast, dimly-lighted hall. We had to find our own way up a large gloomy stair-case, into a long, lofty corridor. This was also scantily lighted. Doors opened into it on either side. Two servants were stationed there. We were shown into a room where the grand maître de la cour was waiting to receive us. . . . In about five minutes a side-door was opened, and we were ushered into the presence of the king and queen, the only persons in waiting being the grand maître and the grande maîtresse de la cour. . . . The king is plain, with a slim figure." After the fashion of his subjects, he often sported a white kilt, and in his portraits was nearly always so represented, but tonight he was wearing, instead, "an elaborately embroidered Greek dress of blue and silver. He charmed me", the author adds, "by talking to me of the British Archaeological Association, having, of course, been primed for this by . . . the Austrian Minister. . . ."

The Queen unfortunately had three passions, of all of which her subjects disapproved: dancing, gardening and riding. Relating to the first, my great-grandfather gives the following account of a "grand ball" he and his wife attended at the palace. "On driving to the principal entrance, and mounting the grand staircase, a large anteroom is first entered. This leads into a

---

[1] Otho, b. 1815, second son of King Ludwig I of Bavaria, and uncle of the Mad King. Appointed King of Greece by the Great Powers in 1832. He married Amelia, daughter of the reigning Grand Duke of Oldenburg.

suite of three very lofty and well-decorated rooms with *parquets* of beautiful *marqueterie*. The first is the ball-room. The Queen, and all the ladies present, collect on one side,—the King and the principal members of the corps diplomatique approaching to speak to them; whilst the remainder of the male guests, crowded together, form a deep semicircle opposite. After a very formal half-hour spent in presentations, etc., the Queen opened the ball by a *polonaise*; she was followed by the King, but by not more than three other couples. . . . The King danced the first quadrille with Lady Albert. . . .

"There was a remarkable deficiency of female beauty, and not a single fresh-looking girl did I see; all looked like faded, married women. The Queen, who is thirty, appeared the youngest woman in the room: she was admirably dressed, danced beautifully, and it is impossible to do justice to the grace with which she spoke to those present. The male guests must have nearly quadrupled the women, for the Grecian ladies are not fond of dancing. Of the latter, but a few were in the costumes of their country, and these dresses had evidently seen much service. There was a great mixture in the attire of the men: some wore a mass of embroidery (especially the King's Greek aides-de-camp, who blazed in scarlet and a profusion of gold,—said to be the Queen's taste); others were in plain clothes, with black and even-coloured neckcloths, and wore boots. I heard that some of the guests present bore dreadful characters. One or two were pointed out to me as having been more than suspected of awful crimes."

Regarding her second passion, the Queen made the lovely garden of the Royal Palace in Athens, of which I shall say more in a later volume; a garden over which floats perpetually the scent of orange blossom from grove and avenue. But though it became subsequently the favourite place of resort in the whole city, at the time she was much blamed for her creation, because it was said that, in the summer, when water was scarce, she poured "vast quantities upon the palace garden, instead of allowing the poor to benefit by it."

Nor was she less disliked because of her third passion, for riding; and, worse even than riding in the eyes of the orientals that the Greeks still were, sometimes she even walked! Thus,

once, while returning to Athens from Megara, Lord Albert saw
before him at a distance of about three miles from the capital, a
carriage progressing at a foot-pace. His Greek courier, Dmitri,
"cried 'Milor, milor, please stop!' In front of the carriage were
two ladies and a gentleman, walking in line along the dusty
highroad; it was the Queen with two attendants, taking that
exercise for which she has a fondness quite inexplicable to
the Greeks, who, especially the women, detest any exertion
that is avoidable. . . . To the utter astonishment of those who
witness it, she drives out of Athens by one road, alights from
her carriage, and sends it round to await her in a road in an
opposite direction; then makes her way across the fields on
foot. The Greek maids of honour, unaccustomed to exertion
until they entered her service, can hardly perform the duties
of their office and keep up with her."

The chief cause of the unpopularity of the royal couple is to
be ascribed to the fact that no set of persons, no single person
even, in the whole country was used to their ways or, more
generally, to western modes of thought and enjoyment. Indeed,
almost the only resident in Greece who knew the world outside
was the eccentric and lively Duchess de Plaisance,[1] who had
originally come here to live in Athens, but had now designed
for herself at the foot of Mount Pentelicus a small gothic castle
of green marble; a building which still existed in 1939. Of this
lady, Lord Albert gives the following account. "Having the

[1] Sophie de Barbe-Marbois, wife of Anne-Charles, 2nd Duc de Plaisance
(1775-1859), a general and the son of the statesman to whom Napoleon gave
this title. She was born in 1785 in Philadelphia, where her father, a man of
decided character, was French consul. She opened her career of adventure
by making a voyage from Marseilles to London with Casimir Delavigne, the
poet, as her companion. She separated from her husband in 1824, and
eventually, suffocated by the atmosphere of the restored Bourbon court,
sailed for Greece with her daughter in 1830, and four years later set up
house in Athens, where she decided to abandon the modern for the antique
style in dress. Accordingly she took to wearing a white tunic that fell in folds,
and a hat of flexible straw, like that of a Tanagra figurine, often with a scarf
floating from it down to the waist. At her table, which was more delicious
than generous, she entertained the most eminent men of Athens. . . . After
the death of her daughter, she tried to surround herself with young people,
and when this effort failed, fell back on the society of animals, especially
dogs. She died in Athens in 1854, intoning, as she passed away, some lines
by Lamartine.
    (See an article from which this note is derived, by Constantin Photiadès,
in *La Revue de Paris*, 1st July 1908.)

misfortune to lose her daughter whilst travelling in the East, she caused the body to be embalmed, purposing that it should be interred with herself, and she kept it in her own room; her house catching fire, she offered a very large reward to those who would save the body,—but in vain, the case was too heavy for removal. She has now left her property to 'the most virtuous woman'; a committee of which the Queen of Greece is to be the president, having to decide amongst the competitors; English women are specially excluded from competing."

After his sojourn in Athens, Lord Albert visited Macropoulos, Port Raphta, Sunium, Marathon, Corinth, Argos, Callimaki, Megara, Nauplia and Mycenae, and then sailed from the Piraeus to Patras, and thence to Corfu; at that period a gay and well-ordered island, thriving under English rule. In the small capital town, the Lord High Commissioner resided in the Palace of St. Michael and St. George, a large stone mansion obviously designed by Nash or one of his disciples. (In its chief room, decorated with brocades of the period, there still hung before the outbreak of the present war a handsome portrait of King George IV, by Lawrence, or after him, and Lord Albert will no doubt have regarded this picture of his old friend with particular attention.) The atmosphere of the place was elegant and amusing, there was an excellent season of opera every year, and it possessed good English shops. "I thought", remarks Lord Albert, with his mind recurring, perhaps, to the "semi-penal settlement of Boulogne-sur-mer", "that were I to live out of England, no part of the world would offer to me such attractions as Corfu,—with its temperate climate and lovely scenery; as a sportsman, I should have first-rate shooting on the coast of Albania. . . . I should have the finest yachting, boating and sea-fishing in the world—all this, combined with the advantages of a good town in Corfu, and the protection of the British Government; regular communication with England, and, above all, very cheap living." The only drawback—as so often—to this paradise, was its inhabitants, some of whom were so little conscious of certain of their blessings that they wanted to throw over English rule; ". . . the population generally ape the Greeks, being as inferior to them as is the monkey to its human prototype".

From Corfu, the Denisons proceeded in turn to the islands of Paxos, Samos and Zante; Paxos and Zante also being in English occupation, though far from so desirable as Corfu; Zante, indeed, at the time being characterised as "a place of dreadful banishment" for its English Resident. They then sailed for Sicily, and, when they reached Messina, first encountered the backwash of the tremendous wave of the 1840 revolution, under which the island, and the whole mainland of Italy, were still reeling. The lovely city had just endured a twenty-four hours' sack, accompanied by atrocities such as "the imaginations of demons alone could have invented" at the hands of the Neapolitan troops, who had then moved on to enjoy three days' rapine in the neighbouring rich city of Catania. After the manner of all amateurs of atrocity stories, Lord Albert tells us, rather ambiguously, that these "statements were not merely assertions, for pains had been taken to render them capable of being proved". However, even such horrors could not make the population forgo the pleasures of grand opera; a company had just been performing in Messina, presumably through the sack of the city, and now came on board the vessel upon which the English travellers were sailing to Naples. "The first tenor was a very good-looking young fellow of about one-and-twenty: he was remarkably well dressed. The prima donna made a sad appearance without rouge, and in her slovenly travelling dress. These two were objects of worship to their companions, as well as to several mustachio'd, dingy-looking men, with satin stocks and collarless shirts."

Lord Albert found Naples much changed from the gay place he had known seventeen years before. It seemed as though the character of the people had become more grave and matter-of-fact: certainly, they were more discontented. King Bomba,[1] penultimate monarch of the Bourbon dynasty of the Two Sicilies, sat unwieldily upon the throne, and, because of the detestation in which he was held by the educated classes, had

[1] Ferdinand II of the Two Sicilies. He was twice married, first to a Sardinian, and then to an Austrian princess; both queens being his cousins. He began his reign in 1830, and died "of a loathesome disease" (say the democratic guide-books of a year or two later), but still king of his domain, in Lecce in 1858.

not dared to show himself in public for a year past. The Queen was scarcely more of a favourite: being a thrifty housewife, "the very tradesmen she employs, dislike her. . . . Amusing stories are told of her care for the durability as well as the price of her children's boots and shoes. She will, indeed, make an admirable wife, if the King should have to retire into private life." . . . The *lazzaroni*, however, were still royalist, as they had been fifty years before, during the Napoleonic wars, and were constantly threatening the liberals, or "constitutionalists". "Patrols of cavalry and infantry were continually moving through the streets, to show that the authorities were prepared."

This feeling, so well justified in Naples, of living on the edge of a volcano, did not, however, prevent the travellers from visiting the sights of the city and its suburbs. They made the accustomed ascent of Vesuvius: I have always considered this a boring enterprise, and can enter into the feelings of Lady Albert's English maid, who, the author tells us, on peering down the crater, remarked, "Lor, if it is not for all the world like looking down a London chimney." (Indeed, we do not have to go as far as that now for a simile, for civilisation has brought craters nearer to each of us.) They saw Herculaneum, and Pompeii, which even then seems to have been organised for tourists. More recent visitors to that dead city will remember the crowds of cripples and the beggars they see on arrival there, the singing of blind men, levying a pitiful blackmail on foreigners having luncheon, and the scraggy gaiety of the dancers of the tarantella, tottering on the verge of the grave. It was all, evidently, the same a century ago. "The railway station is surrounded by mendicants of every description, to torment and distract the attention of the unfortunate antiquary. Some are musicians playing the Tarantella, others are dancing to the music; some accompany their own singing by their guitars; there are blind and lame beggars; many compel charity by the disgust of their deformities, and others alarm women into it by their gibbering as idiots." . . . Lord and Lady Albert also made excursions to places further afield, to Capri, Sorrento and, south of Naples, to Salerno and the temples of Paestum. Indeed, they seem to have been most thorough, for they even drove to see the very remarkable early baptistery of Santa

Maria Maggiore, near Nocera dei Pagani, so neglected by foreigners in more recent years. North of Naples they visited Capua and the great Benedictine monastery of Monte Cassino. The palace of Caserta, which he must have passed on this journey, he seems to have liked no better than did my Hely-Hutchinson great-grandfather, whose opinion of it I have quoted in the last chapter, for he characterises it as "an unsightly brick building".

Of his departure from Naples for Leghorn, he writes: "I left Naples without regret. Though the most charming residence in the world, it is dreadfully unsafe; there would be an immediate insurrection whenever the Neapolitans saw the slightest chance of success; and the muzzles of cannon that are expressively pointing down the various streets, show how well the king is aware of the feeling of his capital. . . . The steamer was much crowded. Amongst the passengers was a Neapolitan church dignitary, with his staff of chaplain, secretary, etc., on their way to pay their respects to the Pope, who was waiting at Mola di Gaeta till foreign intervention could persuade his unruly flock to receive him back at Rome." At Civita Vecchia many alarmed fugitives came on board, as well as "three Roman patriots, who, dressed and bearded in true young Italy fashion, and finding themselves safe under the French flag, were loud in their regrets at having left their brothers in arms. One was the spokesman of the rest and boasted to all who would listen to him, of what they themselves had done in the gallant defence offered by the Romans to the French. My excellent short and sleek acquaintance, Count St. G——e, who was returning from Naples to Tuscany, upon some private mission from the Grand Duke[1] to his Austrian reinstaters, swelled and strutted as he passed their group, and cast them such melodramatic glances of hate, that, had they any feeling, they must have been withered."

Leghorn had lately been taken and was swarming with troops, twenty thousand Austrians and three thousand Modenese. Kolavrath was there, and a large number of people, supposedly disaffected, were being daily shot in the fortress. Florence was also in the middle of a revolution, so the English travellers avoided it and sailed for Marseilles, and home;

[1] The Grand Duke of Tuscany had fled to Naples.

though, still indefatigable, they first visited Nîmes, Arles and Avignon on the way.

"Lady Albert", to whom the writer so constantly refers, was not my great-grandmother, but his second wife. He had married first Henrietta Maria, daughter of the first Lord Forester, a very beautiful woman, and the original of Baxter's celebrated print, "The Bridesmaid". Her mother, Lady Forester, was the daughter of that famous beauty, the 4th Duchess of Rutland, who was thrice painted by Sir Joshua Reynolds. Augustus Hare, in his *Story of My Life*,[1] tells us that Lady Waterford, the gifted amateur artist, had known her well and recalled that the Duchess, as a very old lady, liked to describe the manner in which Sir Joshua had painted her, "how he would rush forward, and look closely into her eyes, take her well in, and then go as far away as possible, and look at the general effect in a distant glass, chiefly making his picture from that". Duchess Isabella, as she was known, was the daughter of the 4th Duke of Beaufort, a great patron of the arts and one of the three noblemen responsible for bringing Canaletto over to England and for paying his expenses while he lived here. His wife, only sister and heir of Norborne, last Lord Bottetourt, possessed unusual charm and character, as her letters at Badminton testify, and in the 1788 edition of *The Abbey of Kilkhampton*, an annual volume of imaginary obituaries, mostly of an insulting or jocose nature, Sir Herbert Croft, their author, goes so far, with a sycophancy unusual in him, as to say, "She had in her Veins the Blood of Berkeley and of Bottetourt, in her Demarche the greatness of the Queen of Sheba, in the Fire of her Eye, the Pout of her Lip, and the Bend of her Neck, the Majesty of Cleopatra, the Spirit of Margaret of Anjou and the Innocence of Joan of Arc". She lived to be an old woman, dying in 1799 at the age of eighty; and her daughter survived to an even more considerable age—in a period when sixty was considered to be very old. . . . Poor Duchess Isabella, the years told on her, and she became known to her younger friends and relatives as "Duchess Was-a-Bella". But her spirit never deserted her, the will to be beautiful persisted. A grand-daughter, Lady Adeliza Manners, once met in the park at

[1] *Op. cit.*, vol. vi, p. 501.

Belvoir a country girl who would have been exceptionally lovely save for the loss of a front tooth.

"How did it happen?" she enquired. "What a misfortune!"

"Oh, the Duchess had lost one of hers, so she forced me to have mine taken out to replace it."

Lady Albert Conyngham, her granddaughter, inherited none of this arrogance, being of the sweet and amiable disposition sometimes associated with the consumptive temperament. She died only ten years later than her grandmother, in 1841, after seven years of married life. Two of her sisters, Lady Bradford and Lady Chesterfield, survived to become in late Victorian times the equally beloved confidantes of Lord Beaconsfield.'. . . .Lord Albert married again in 1847, and had a large family by his second wife. My grandfather, Lord Londesborough, was the eldest son of the first marriage, and it is, perhaps, due to the fact that my grandfather so much disliked his stepmother, that I have been told so little of her or of Lord Albert. All I know of him, apart from what I have written, is that he is described as being very highly strung, and that, as he became older, all servants and gardeners had to be banished from his sight, or he would be menaced with a nervous breakdown! Though his various large houses required great staffs to work them, he liked to assume that the rooms, the carpets and furniture, the pictures and lamps, the flower-beds, terraces and clipped hedges of ilex, all looked after themselves, miraculously swept and tidied or renewed. It can have been no easy matter to quell the sounds of dusting, the rustling of dresses in the corridors, and to make sure that no clumsy garden boy blundered across his path when he walked in the grounds of Grimston or Londesborough.

Lord Albert died in January 1860, and to his rent-roll of £100,000 a year, and, it was said, two million in stocks and shares, my grandfather then succeeded at the age of twenty-six and set himself to its dispersal, itself the work of a lifetime, with zest and abandon. . . . Meanwhile let us note in passing that his grandmother, Lady Conyngham, was still living; though she was sixty when last we saw her thirty years ago! Thus I have been able to talk to—and discuss her with—many people who remember her well.

Long gone, now, were the days of piracy and power, and she had become a very strict, religious and dignified old lady of whom it was impossible to think evil. The Crown jewels she had worn, had—many of them—been long returned; it was whole decades since she had ruled Windsor and the Royal Pavilion, forty years since Princess Lieven played the piano to King George and wrote afterwards, ". . . he was overcome, and for five minutes could not speak. At the end of that time a flood of tears relieved his feelings. I have never seen a man more in love,"[1] nearly forty years since the Russian Princess had stayed at the Cottage[2] in Windsor Great Park, and had described how, after dinner, she had looked up to find "the King gazing at Lady Conyngham with an expression in which somnolence battled against love; Lady Conyngham was gazing at a beautiful emerald on her arm; her daughter was toying with a ruby hanging round her neck". How far away they must have seemed, those years when she and her friends dined on warm summer evenings in the Fishing Temple on Virginia Water, with a garden full of flowers, shut out from everything, while opposite on the smooth, light waters was moored a barge on which the King's band used to play. She found it a strange age now, this entirely different epoch into which her life had been projected by her iron constitution; the demure little hats, the little parasols, the huge crinolines, how different from the orchid-aceous fashions of the Regency or of her King's reign! The royal idyll that had endured for two decades was nearly over—(Lady Conyngham died at the age of ninety-one, two months before the Prince Consort, who was half a century younger than herself). The occupant of the throne was now more respectable than any of her subjects, and had increased immeasurably its influence, though art and humour had become continually further removed from it. Only the old Guelph passion for music—from which Lady Conyngham, who had not cared for opera or concert, had so often suffered—survived. How different England was, scarcely recognisable! And the old lady may sometimes have sighed to herself and thought that, if she

[1] *The Private Letters of Princess Lieven to Prince Metternich*, edited by Peter Quennell. (John Murray, 1937.)
[2] First called The King's Cottage; now The Royal Lodge.

had been younger, she would have migrated to Paris, where persisted at the court the sort of life to which she had been accustomed. She would have been more at home across the water in the gilded and *parvenu* empire that had yet inherited the ways of the old European monarchies. . . . But she was too old for such fripperies, religion was her chief joy, and she attended church every Sunday, a large and beautiful old lady in a vast black crinoline, walking with the aid of a small gold-headed cane that the King had given her; looking "very different", her granddaughter, Lady Treowen, told me, "from all those regrettably coarse and scandalous caricatures in the press".

My grandfather, who will figure later in the pages devoted to my childhood, married his cousin, Lady Edith Somerset, youngest daughter of the 7th Duke of Beaufort, a magnate who owned, in addition to estates in England, nearly three whole counties in Wales. These Welsh possessions descended to the Duke from the ancestress who, in 1477, had married the 1st Lord Worcester, Elizabeth, daughter and heir of William Herbert, Earl of Huntingdon, and, through him, of the Welsh Princes. An impressive portrait by Winterhalter of the 7th Duke hangs at Badminton. His mother was the sister of Granville Leveson-Gower, 1st Earl Granville—in whose eyes Lady Bessborough tells us she "dreamed her life away"—and he perhaps took after him, for he had great good looks and charm, and all his life, from the time when, as Lord Worcester, then a very young man, Harriet Wilson attached herself to him with ardour—only equalled in vehemence by the spite she evinced subsequently against him—, he seems always to have been greatly loved. He married, first, Georgina,[1] daughter of

---

[1] She has the distinction of being one of the few people of whom Greville spoke well, even touchingly. She died in 1821, and he wrote in his journal: "I have suffered the severest blow I ever had in my life by the death of Lady Worcester. I loved her like a sister, and I have lost one of the few persons in the world who cared for me, and whose affection and friendship served to make life valuable to me. She has been cut off in the prime of her life, and the bloom of her beauty. . . . I saw her so short a time ago 'glittering like the morning star, full of life and splendour and glory'; the accents of her voice still so vibrate in my ear that I cannot believe I shall never see her again."

Hume, the surgeon, told Greville that she died without pain, but Neumann, the Austrian Minister, who subsequently married one of her daughters, declared that on her death-bed she had said, "I never thought dying hurt so much."

the Hon. Henry Fitzroy and Lady Anne Fitzroy—afterwards Lady Anne Culling Smith—, the only sister of the Duke of Wellington. She died, after a few years, leaving two daughters.

A little over a year later, Lord Worcester married again—his former wife's half-sister, Emily, the daughter of Mr. Charles Culling Smith and Lady Anne. This match gave rise to endless gossip, for it was said to be within the prohibited degrees of affinity, "voidable though not void". Some echo of the excitement can still reach us. Princess Lieven wrote to Metternich on 2nd July 1822: "Society is all affairs of gallantry—there is a positive epidemic of them—and yesterday a clandestine marriage took place under the most extraordinary circumstances. What strange beings these Englishwomen are! Think of it, a little miss running away at nine in the morning from her parents' house, arriving at the church door, seizing two passers-by in the street and forcing them to be witnesses of the ceremony! The young man for his part had hired a parson and caught a passer-by too. They were married and left at once, meaning to cross to France. When they got to Rochester, they realised they had not a halfpenny; and there they are stuck, living presumably on love, for they have nothing else. The girl is own niece to the Duke of Wellington, and the young man is the Marquis of Worcester, future Duke of Beaufort."

The Marriage Act of 1835, by specifically forbidding all such marriages in the future, legalised those that had taken place in the past. Lady Worcester, later Duchess of Beaufort, was the mother of the 8th Duke and of several daughters. She lived to be an exceedingly old woman, and my mother used to describe her, a formidable figure still, but rather vague mentally, taking her pet parrot out for a drive in the New Forest. She always wished to go for a new drive, but the coachman invariably took her the same way; she was too old to be aware of the deception. The parrot, too, had long been dead and stuffed so as to give an illusion of life, and to prevent the storm that, even then, would have rained down on the heads of her retainers had she discovered that they had allowed this lovely creature to die. She was also too old, fortunately, to tell the difference between animate and inanimate.

Her father, Charles Culling Smith, Commissioner of

Customs, was the son of Charles Smith, Governor of Madras; but I know little of him or his family, except that Charles Culling Smith spent the latter years of his life at Badminton. . . . Of the Wellesleys, her mother's family, no account is necessary. The Duke of Wellington and his four brothers are now legendary and fabulous as the Paladins or the Sons of Hauteville. But perhaps it is permissible to stress the love of building that ran in their blood—as evinced particularly by Lord Mornington and by his son the Iron Duke—and, still more strongly, the love of music. Lord Mornington had learnt to play the violin when he was nine years old, and soon after was taking his part in difficult sonatas; at fourteen he could play both harpsichord and organ and, before long, could improvise fugues. He composed the glees "Here in cool grot" and "Come, fairest Nymph". The great soldier himself played the violin as a boy, and was so passionately attached to it that, the night before he joined the army, realising that he now must abandon the instrument, he broke it in half. This same love of music I have in my own lifetime watched developing among many of those descended from Lord Mornington.

But the quality which for the majority of these families I have mentioned counted more than any other, was the love of Sport. So famous have the Dukes of Beaufort been in this field for three centuries that I will not dwell on their passion for it, or their prowess in its exercise, but will only mention one detail connected with it: that John Wootton, appropriately enough the first great English delineator of horses, was page to Lady Anne Coventry, daughter to the first duke, and she brought his talent to the notice of her great-nephew the third duke, who accordingly paid for the artist to go to Italy and study in Rome. The large paintings of the four chief sports of this nobleman— including hawking on Salisbury Plain near the boulders of Stonehenge—adorn the walls of the stone hall at Badminton as a testimony to this patronage. . . . But now I will turn to other facts concerning them. I have already indicated that Glamorgan invented the theory of the steam engine; nor need I do more than allude to the famous descent of the Somersets, recalling to the reader that the first duke was given the choice of taking Somerset or Plantagenet for his surname, and that the dukedom was conferred upon him, the patent expressly states, "because of his noble descent from John of Beaufort, eldest son of John of Gaunt by Katherine Swynford".

Charles II appointed the first duke to be Lord President of Wales, and he made a splendid progress through the principality in 1684. Thomas Dingley's *Account of the Duke's Progress* is the most superb MS. of its epoch, retaining in its drawings of towns on hills, of castles and landscapes, something of the beauty of an illuminated missal of gothic times: perhaps the spirit and ways of that earlier period still persisted in that remote and mountainous country to inspire Dingley's pen.

Dryden, or more probably Nahum Tate, with Dryden's aid, presented him to the public under the guise of Bezaliel in *Absalom and Achitophel*—

> First Write *Bezaliel*, whose Illustrious name
> Forestals our Praise, and gives his Poet Fame.
> The *Kenites'* Rocky Province his Command,
> A barren Limb of Fertile Canaan's Land;
> Which for its gen'rous Natives yet cou'd be
> Held Worthy such a President as He.
> *Bezaliel* with each Grace and Virtue Fraught,
> Serene his Looks, Serene his Life and Thought,
> On whom so largely Nature heapt her Store,
> There scarce remain'd for Arts to give him more.

Of the way of life of this ancestor, and of his wife, we know as much as of our own contemporaries, so full is the account of it in Roger North's *The Lives of the Norths*.[1]

This family has also two earlier associations with great poetry. One is to be found in Spenser's "Prothalamium", with its enchanting refrain of

> Sweete Themmes, runne softly, till I end my song;

this is described as "A Spousal Verse, in honour of the double mariage of the two honourable and vertuous ladies, the Ladie Elizabeth, and the Ladie Katherine Somerset, daughters to the right honourable the Earle of Worcester", and in it the two sisters are called

> The World's faire ornament
> And Heaven's glorie.

[1] Reprinted as Appendix B, p. 258.

The other link resides in the fact that Katherine Swynford, our ancestress, was the sister of Philippa, Chaucer's wife. They were the daughters of Payne Rouelt or Roet, whom some authorities hold to have been a Herald, seeing in "Payne" a corruption of *Paon* or Peacock. Chaucer himself was in the household of John of Gaunt, whose marriage to Katherine was legitimated by Act of Parliament on the condition that their descendants should not occupy the throne. From them, however, was descended, it is said, every monarch who reigned in Europe in 1914, except the King of Spain. Moreover the Tudor claim to the throne of England was based expressly on this ancestry.

There, reader, you have, in any case, the converging roads down which three travellers came, to meet, and thence start on a new journey. And as I am, perhaps, the most earthbound, it is fitting that I should describe its beginning.

I do not know that it is easy to deduce much from these diverse pre-natal tracks lying behind us. Out of the sixteen great-grandparents, there seem to me to be three strains of original talent, Wellesley, Heber and Sitwell; one of music, Wellesley; two of religion, Tait and Heber; two of marked practical capacity, Wellesley and Hely-Hutchinson; and many of the spendthrift, a trait which most certainly I inherited and which, though by now repressed of necessity, still troubles me. In every, or nearly every, direction there is, too—especially during the last century—a frenetic attention to sport. Above all, and from every source, my ancestors have for generations been used to getting their own way. Further, common to all four of my great-grandfathers is one other thing I have not mentioned, but have most specifically inherited: gout.[1] Of this illness, mysterious in origin and manifestation, the late Dr.

---

[1] One member of the family, Francis Sitwell of Renishaw (1682-1753), was peculiarly the victim of it. I have always been told that his sufferings were so great that, it being believed at the time that an open wound was good for gout, allowing "the humours to dissipate", he accordingly made an incision in his leg and for many years propped the wound open with an orange pip, an object then known for its curative properties!

A portrait of him hangs in the dining-room at Renishaw. It shows him in a short white wig and sepia coat, but though his expression is severe, as one might expect, he betrays no real sign of his partially self-inflicted martyrdom.

Havelock Ellis wrote[1] that it "occurs so often, in such extreme forms, and in men of such pre-eminent intellectual ability, that it is impossible not to regard it as having a real association with such ability", and again that it would be impossible to "match the group of gouty men of genius, for varied and pre-eminent intellectual ability by any combination of non-gouty individuals on our list. . . ." He adds that they have frequently been eccentric and irascible, and in the eighteenth century were termed "choleric" by their contemporaries. Another earlier writer and most famous physician states that gout kills "more rich men than poor, more wise than simple". But Havelock Ellis supplies a reason for the connecting of this pathological condition with mental activity. The poison which causes it, he declares, acts as a stimulant to nerves and brain, while in addition the periodic fluctuations of it from the blood to the joints and back again, afford the victim the benefit of two different points of view, almost, as it were, of two different brains: one, when the poison is in the joints, melancholy and over-clouded, the other, when it is in the blood, unusually clear and vigorous.

So, as I lie in my bed, from time to time, comfortable, as Horace Walpole writes of himself, during an attack of gout, "as St. Lawrence on his gridiron", I try to soothe my pains with the personal implications of this theory. Certainly gout stimulates the brain, influencing it at the time of an acute attack, almost as though a drug were at work: (during one such short period of torment, I was able to make drafts for seven short stories). Groaning, afraid to move an inch upon my rack, I say to myself angrily that the decay of great men, the disappearance of consummate generals and statesmen, is in reality only due to a decline in the numbers of gouty subjects. Bound together by the tie of an agony that brings its own reward, this small but privileged community of victims to which I have the honour to belong knows no boundary of faith or creed; Kubla Khan and Talleyrand, William Pitt and the Bacons, father and son, Wesley and Darwin, Gibbon and Fielding, Milton and Newton, and many another name as famous, go to compose the roll of honour of this martyred

[1] *A Study of British Genius,* by Havelock Ellis. (Constable & Co., 1927.)

D

but happy band; and of Ben Jonson, Drummond of Haw-
thornden[1] tells us that the great poet "hath consumed a whole
night in lying looking to his great toe, about which he hath
seen Tartars, Romans and Carthaginians, feight in his
imagination".

[1] Drummond's *Conversations with Jonson.*

Book Two

LET THERE BE LIGHT!

"You never enjoy the world aright, till the sea itself floweth in your veins, till you are clothed with the heavens, and crowned with the stars: and perceive yourself to be the sole heir of the whole world, and more than so, because men are in it who are everyone sole heirs as well as you . . ."

THOMAS TRAHERNE'S *Centuries of Meditation*

CHAPTER ONE

Rags and Bones

ON the 8th of December 1892, at Scarborough, my Aunt Florence,[1] whose earlier journal I recently edited, entered in her diary the following words:

"Yesterday morning a telegram to Mother announced the birth of a son to George and Ida. Rejoicing in the town, and bells ringing. Today, in a letter to Mother, Lady Londesborough describes the little boy as healthy, lively, compact and plump—also pretty." And, three months later, she notes: "Wednesday the eighth of March was the day when little Francis Osbert Sacheverell was 'received into the church' here at St. Mary's. I was so sorry, not being well, to be unable to attend the service. Such a crowd, I heard. . . . Mother says the baby kept his blue eyes fixed on the coloured glass window, or on the lilies that decorated the font. When the service was over, one woman in the crowd rushed forward and kissed him before anyone could prevent her."

The preceding account of my christening, together with the fact that, so I have been told, I gave during the ceremony a violent tug at the beard of the Bishop—he being the inevitable "dear Archdeacon" of my aunt's earlier journal—contains all the precocious indications of appearance or character of which I have been informed. Even now, however, were I to sit for long in church, my eyes would wander toward the coloured glass or the decoration of flowers round the altar; and no

[1] Miss Florence Sitwell, my father's only sister. Her journal, under the title of *Vestals and Vestries*, forms the Second Part of *Two Generations*.

wonder, besides, that I rebelled and tore wildly with my hands
at the iconic countenance of the Bishop, for, being a delicate
infant, I had already once been baptized, by the son of the same
dignitary, in London, so that "the pomps and vanities of this
wicked world", which have always been so dear to me, had ere
this been forsworn on my behalf, and were now doubly prohibited. . . . As for the crowds of people, and the general and
pleasant attitude of welcome recorded, this was, alas, in no
way due to infant merit or virtue, but the result of my father
being Conservative member for the old borough of Scarborough
and of the popularity of my mother and himself in a day when
personal enthusiasm still supported party politics. For my
names, too, my father was responsible, Francis being, like
George, a name borne by the Sitwells in succeeding generations
for many centuries, and that, in addition, of my uncle and
sponsor, Lord Raincliffe;[1] I was called Osbert, after an ancestor
through the Reresbys of whom we are the heirs, Sir Osbert Fitz
Osborne, and Sacheverell to celebrate another ancient family,
now extinct, from whom the Sitwells are descended, and whose
portraits and many of their belongings they inherited. The name
Sacheverell is a corruption of Saute de Chevreuil, the home of
the Sacheverells in Normandy.

I had come into the world in London, rather unexpectedly
and with nothing prepared for my reception, on a very cold
December afternoon, and the place of my birth was 3 Arlington
Street, opposite to where the Ritz Hotel now stands; described
contemporarily, I find, as a "nice house with electric light,"[2]
which my father had taken for a year or two in order to attend
his parliamentary duties. My arrival, I think, cannot have
impressed my parents so much as I would have liked, for they
forgot to register my birth until six years later, in 1898, after
my brother had been born. . . . Perhaps London, a year or
two subsequently, is the first place I remember. Exploring dim

---

[1] Viscount Raincliffe, afterwards 2nd Earl of Londesborough.

[2] Electric lighting was apparently still rare. . . . In a horrible, chatty,
spiteful little book of personalities, published in 1885, seven years before
the date of my birth, I found the other day a reference to Lord and Lady
Randolph Churchill's house: "Matters are arranged on a princely scale, for
Lord Randolph has all the inclinations of a *grand seigneur*. His house is one
of the few which possess the electric light. It costs him about fifteen times
as much as any other mode of illumination. But what of that?'. . . '

recesses of memory, I seem to have a recollection of being wheeled down Piccadilly, of the trees of the Green Park and the old wooden gates of Devonshire House opposite, and of my mind being occupied with the polysyllabic music of the word "Piccadilly . . . Pic . . ca . . di . . lly", which seemed to me then, as it does today, a very strange and beautiful name. . . . But London did not then occupy an important place in my existence; the two backgrounds of my childhood were Renishaw and Scarborough. . . . In any case, though, being a slow rather than a quick child, it is places more than people, and words more than thoughts, that remain to me from my earliest days. The first words I learnt were "Rags and Bones".

At Scarborough the night nursery was at the top and back of the high old stone-pillared house we then occupied, and looked out above a narrow alley. When the rushing and bellowing winds of the winter ceased for a moment to roar down this passage made for them, tearing the words from the throats of the speakers right away into the void, and only the background of tumultuous seas remained, you could hear very distinctly what was said below. In the winter dawn, before it was fully light, these houses resounded with the loud cry, "Rags and Bones! Rags and Bones!" And so it came about that these words were the first I learned, and who knows that such countersigns to mortality, pronounced at an impressionable age, may not have influenced my mind, making me seek behind the flattering disguise for the mortal and immortal core? It served, maybe, as a warning not to take too seriously the comfortable life of the senses developing round me, and emphasised the same lesson to be learnt in my favourite nursery rhyme—

> Hark, hark, the dogges doe bark,
> The beggars are coming to town

though these had been not the outcasts of the industrial system, already tottering, but the great armies of starving men caused by the nationalisation of the monastic houses, which for so long had distributed food for the needy; men as lazy, desperate and tattered, as ready to laugh or kill, as the *lazzaroni* of Naples in the late eighteenth and early nineteenth centuries. We, however, have seen during the last few years the contemporary armies of the persecuted and dispossessed increase until they seem to fill the whole horizon of the world.

"Rags and Bones!", the old man used sometimes to shout, sometimes to insinuate slyly, in a voice that was between a song and a whine, into the frozen air, beneath where the fleeces of the sky were now showing their flayed and bloody edges, "Rags and Bones!" . . . And so, since I associated him with the first words I had taught myself to utter, I took an interest in him and can still see very clearly his figure as he was a few years later, his bearded face crowned by a battered top-hat— the survivor, it seemed, of innumerable orgies, just as it had been the witness, too, of countless interments—, vacant and smiling eyes full of an ineffable crankiness and guile, his whole impression and his jerky movements as he pushed his barrow along, giving a little the flustered yet inanimate air of a scare- crow subjected for many seasons to the force of an intolerable wind. My curiosity concerning him made me, too, watch the other gesticulating figures on the perimeter of the circle, so that my eyes in their observation of people moved from the outside toward the centre, towards those nearest me, rather than in the usual and contrary direction; torn figures in grotesque and appalling attitudes, like those of Callot's etchings, with a sinister and legendary panache, who stand on walls under the fierce short polar light of white foam from enormous storms and of the immutable, shadeless, cold flashing of seagulls' wings. The struggles of the winter sky, of towering, dazzling clouds and utter darkness, are reflected in the faces of the beggars, the tramps, the pedlars, the clowns, the organ-grinders, the contortionists, the company of the crazy and of the street- singers, who,

> With faces of wallnut
> And bladder and small gut,
> . . . come scraping and singing to rouse ye;

their lips moving, their voices soundless under the plunging and roaring of the distant sea, which now engulfs with a wide halo of thin-spun spume the whole town.

Of such human beings, feckless, unable to extricate their weighted limbs from this terminus in which they found them- selves, Scarborough in those days offered an inexhaustible supply: the negro, locally known as "Snowball", who limped with a pitiful exoticism through the winter streets, trying to sell flowers, bunches of violets and button-holes, a figure from a warm Italian picture strayed into these trim, northern streets, with their frozen gutters and their roofs saw-edged with icicles; the bearded and witless tramp, known as Lousy Peter, ever tormented by various gangs of small boys, who would hit him when he fell asleep, warm in his rags, in the deserted squares at the hour which for everybody else was the dinner hour, or throw buckets of water over him—and then run away; or experiment upon him daily with a new booby-trap of their own skilful invention; the Cat Man who mewed to himself on the sands; the cretinous cherubs, children of the rich, but no less fantastic than the beggar contingent, and the more ordinary, but yet alien, players of the hurdygurdy, now extinct, with their pleading, broken English, and their coated and capped attendant monkeys, decked out in the remnants of a brighter age. (How well I remember being allowed to throw down coppers to them, as they played, from the nursery window: two or three pennies, I recall, were always screwed up in a piece of paper, whether to secure them or to disguise the smallness of the gift, I do not know.) And there were the more subtle and rare specimens of whom I will write in their proper place in this book, though the observation of them, albeit it belongs to a later day, when I could more fully remark and comprehend, was nevertheless the fruit of this cry that I learned so early, "Rags and Bones, Rags and Bones!"

At the time of which I write, people still scarcely existed for me; the cry, the song, the tune on the barrel-organ, but not those who uttered or produced them. Indeed it is a question whether I did not see and remember a ghost before I could pin down any human being in my mind, since a giant and spectral figure was seen one summer morning, just as it was growing light, a figure, immense, gaunt and grey like a shadow, that rushed round the room, its rhythm faster and faster, but making no sound. . . . We all saw it, my nurse, my sister and myself—or so it was supposed, for I first called the attention of my two sleeping companions to it, by yelling, loud and long. Our nurse got up, and the figure, nine or ten feet high, rushed like a wind through the door, which it must have left open, into nothingness, no sound, no trace, no sign. There was no one there, and I have no solution of the mystery to offer. The event, or the hallucination, or whatever it may have been, remains inexplicable. Yet I will not dismiss it from its early place of honour in my life for fear of not being believed. . . . So was it, as far as the three of us could tell.

When next I woke, it was full daylight, and I was saying "Rags and Bones, Rags and Bones" to myself. It was a cry that announced the day, and I welcomed it, for it kept me safe from the beings that had escaped out of the darkness of which they were part and had, thus isolated, assumed a visible substance until the light drove them back. . . . Perhaps partly it was the memory, a faint stirring of memory, of that ghost which made me look forward to hearing the words spoken outside in the bitter green light of the next day. The hours of sleep would be finished. Nowhere as well as here, in the wintry north, situated in a frozen white cocoon of spray and fog and rain and cloud, could one watch the unending and gigantic battle that swayed, though its rhythm was undeviating, first this way, then that, between day and the victorious night. The night was hollow. The night was hollow and of immense size. Nor was it invariably unfriendly, though it was always sad, and always frightening. It possessed two faces, one kind and one unkind. Very occasionally, when the day had been a disaster, the hollow night offered its numberless caves as a refuge into which you could creep, and hide the voice that spoke within you—that voice which was the enemy of all authority—and wherein you could hide yourself too, and not be found. But more usually, on the other hand, it would unleash against you the dead, and its army of the monstrous, giants and dwarfs, contorted faces that floated past, who made their lair in these derelict dark quarters.

"Rags and Bones" was thus a cry of delivery, and I repeated it rather indistinctly but none the less to the continual dismay of dear old Davis, who always tried to prevent these particular attempts at articulation and would no doubt have preferred me to lisp more reputably "Gentle Jesus, Meek and Mild", than such words of ominous suggestion.

With the mention of Davis we come to the first person who can be seen clearly through the vanishing darkness. Gradually from the chaos of wide-eyed incomprehension and blind instinct, various figures begin to present themselves in the pale green light, cool as the sound of a hunting horn in the first hours of the morning. I see a group, Davis and Edith and myself, beneath a tree bearing golden fruit, gleaming in the bright armour of the sun; an apricot tree, I imagine, but I know not where it grew. Davis is in her grey alpaca dress and straw hat, and has her usual expression of kind and puzzled patience, while Edith is dressed in blue, pale blue, and under a hat like a mushroom, her curved eyelids, lank golden hair and sweet, musing expression, all give her an air of dreamy determination.

We must pause now to examine the most important member of this small group, both because of the force of her personality even at such an early age, and because of my affection for her. Five years older than I when I first remember her, in this respect unlike most other members of her sex with whom I was acquainted in my infancy, and who are today younger than myself, she has remained so ever since. . . . She first comes on the scene when just over two years old, in an entry in my grandmother's diary: "George's little daughter paid me an early visit, and was wildly excited when I offered her a bit of garden, exclaiming 'E dig and plant flowers. E go to sleep, and wake up and flowers all grown.'" And, from the later journals of my Aunt Florence, I am able to give a more detailed and vivid picture of this unusual child and of her surroundings at the age of three and a half. In June 1891 she writes: "Baby is just like a child in a story book in appearance, with fat cheeks, sometimes like pink campions, blue eyes and fair curls, a dear little person, touchingly devoted to her dog, Dido. She seems very young . . . to have visited Venice, but has quite a memory for her tour abroad." Three weeks later, she gives us a delightful family group at the station, rather reminiscent of an Academy picture of the period. My grandmother had gone to see them off by the night train to Scotland, and had subsequently described the scene to my aunt. "She told us of George at the station, with his many books of historical research under one

arm, and the *Spectator*, *Lancet*, *Athenaeum* and the architectural journals under the other, embracing her, regardless of
onlookers, of Baby, who declared 'No little "gell" has had so
many night journeys as I've had—but, oh, how I've had to
sing and repeat things to amuse the grown-up people!', and of
her little dog, Dido, waking the station with her cries, thinking
she would be parted from Baby and left behind—but she went,
too, with the family."

Here—for this is a group, and the other figures in it require
attention, so that we see the child in her proper perspective—
I must interrupt the account of my sister, as she was at that
early age, in order to amplify one particular detail of my father's
outfit as described. He always carried with him in the train
many journals of diverse technical interest, and also a small
black bag into which he put them sometimes, and which bore
on it, nearly obliterated, the words "House of Commons",—
since he had bought it, when a member, to carry his various
notes in. It is, in fact, fortunate that my aunt alludes to his
numerous papers, because it enables me to mention them in my
turn; I believe that it is possible that with these papers and his
black bag he has made his only bow, so far, from the literary
stage—regarded from the outside, that is to say, and not through
his own numerous publications.

George Moore,[1] writing of a time some seven or eight years
later, and describing how the Boer War and its cruelty and
stupidity had both exacerbated and numbed his feelings,
proceeds: ". . . Not only books and pictures had lost interest
for me, but human characteristics; opinions were what I
demanded, and from everybody. I remember coming from the
North of England with a prosaic middle-aged man who had
brought into the carriage with him for his relaxation three
newspapers—the *Builder*, the *Athenaeum* and *Vanity Fair*—
and in the long journey from Darlington to London I watched
him taking up these papers, one after the other, and reading
them with the same attention. At any other time I should have
been eager to make the acquaintance of one who could find
something to interest him in these papers and should have been

---

[1] In *Hail and Farewell!* vol. i, *Ave*, p. 231. (Heinemann, Ebury Edition,
1937; first published 1911.)

much disappointed if I did not succeed in becoming intimate with him by the end of the journey. But, strange as it will seem to the reader, who by this time has begun to know me, I am forced to admit that I was only anxious to hear his opinion of the war, and, my curiosity becoming at last intolerable, I interrupted his architectural, social or literary meditation with the statement that the *Daily Telegraph* contained some very grave news. Two eyes looked at me over spectacles, and on the phrase, Well, the war was bound to come sooner or later, we began to argue, and it was not until we reached Finsbury Park —he got out there—that I remembered I had forgotten to ask him if he were a constant reader of the three newspapers that he rolled up and put away carefully into a black bag."

This, I think, must be an attempted portrait of my father. He could, it is true, scarcely at any age have been called "prosaic", for he was too tall and fair, resembling a portrait of Caesar Borgia, altogether too late-Gothic or early-Renaissance in style for such a description to be apt. Moreover, he would be scarcely forty at the time, nor can I see why he should have got out at Finsbury Park (he might well have been travelling from Darlington); but then George Moore often, in spite of his talents, missed the physical character of those he sketched, or bestowed upon them his own, which he saw through spectacles with a special fault-minimising focus. (Indeed, he never possessed any conception, I think, of what he himself looked like, distinguished writer and observer though he was. Sickert, I remember, used to relate that Moore would often tell him how Manet had loved to paint him as a young man, because of the pale, golden corn-colour of his hair, upon which the artist liked to expend all of his technical achievement—whereas the truth was merely that the young George Moore at that time bore an accidental resemblance to the Emperor Maximilian of Mexico, on the great picture of whose execution Manet was then at work.) But notwithstanding these points, the rest of the detail, the papers and the black bag are unmistakable—save only that I suspect that *Vanity Fair* was in reality *The Lancet*—a journal which my father was fond of reading, so that he could recognise every fresh symptom as it occurred. . . . Yes, it must be George Moore's sketching of him.

To return to the group my aunt portrays to us so vividly.
Dido, the other living being, was a *griffon*, to whom my sister
was particularly devoted. . . . But let us now read another
account of Edith in my aunt's journal. In November 1892,
the month before I was born, the diarist continues: "Mother
and I are alone together, and have been for some time, with
the exception of dear little *E*, who inhabits the room above the
Far Library with her nurse; and is a great pleasure to us.
She is now five years old, a most interesting and dear little
person. . . . I have been giving her tiny lessons after tea. Last
Sunday, I began the life of Our Lord with her, and she is
learning by heart 'Ye know the grace of our Lord Jesus Christ
that though He was rich yet for your sakes He became poor'.
Then, after the lesson, we—her Granny and I—sing, this
time 'Once in Royal David's city'." . . . And on the last day
of the month she adds:

"Dear little E has grown round one's heart, and it was sad
parting with her. I missed saying a real good-bye to her, though
I had glimpses of her and little talks with her in the morning.
All of them, she and George and Ida, started for London in a
saloon carriage with Miss Milne in the afternoon. . . . Yesterday
morning I had vases in the library to arrange with evergreens—
we had no flowers for that room. The child wanted to help—I
handed her the leaves, and I think she did four vases with her
dear little hands, taking great pains to make them pretty, and
making quaint remarks, such as 'We must make the best of
things', 'We mustn't "carol" [quarrel] with what we've got'.
In the evening, when she was playing with her little friend
Robin in the drawing-room, she spoke feelingly about the
serious illness of his father, explaining that, if he died, his wife
would be a widow, and ended 'And even if she married again,
it wouldn't comfort her'. . . . Last Sunday we again had our
short Sunday lesson. We had the story of His being found in
the Temple amongst the doctors. When I talked to her a little
about His crucifixion for our sakes, and what we might do for
Him who loved us so much, and told her about being loving
and kind to people, even to those who were not always quite
nice to us—specially with regard to Martha, her nursery-maid,
with whom she has her little feuds, the child said of her own

accord that she would try to do so. . . . Poor Martha! Mother's version of what E said of her a little time ago, was 'She does nothing to amuse, and everything to displease me'. . . . It is wonderful the way in which the child is getting on with her reading—really teaching herself—, asking the meaning of unknown words, and remembering them. Fairy tales have been her especial delight. She is very reflective and at the same time full of fun and mischief, delighting in a joke. . . . Once she got one of her frightened fits, and clung hard to me."

In these curiously expert sketches, so truly and simply drawn, of my sister, a few things stand out, her precocity and love of reading, for instance, and her memory for the places she had visited abroad.

. . . The "frightened fits" to which my aunt alludes were inexplicable attacks of unbounded childish terror, during the first of which she saw an enormous and bloody head rolling round the room. And as for the love of fairy tales, this predilection bore fruit, no doubt, years after, in her long poem *The Sleeping Beauty*, and in its lovely songs; for example, that "Song of the Soldan"—

> When green as a river was the barley,
> Green as a river the rye,
> I waded deep and began to parley
> With a youth whom I heard sigh.
> "I seek," said he, "a lovely lady,
> A nymph as bright as a queen,
> Like a tree that drips with pearls her shady
> Locks of hair were seen;
> And all the rivers became her flocks
> Though their wool you cannot shear,
> Because of the love of her flowing locks.
> The kingly sun like a swain
> Came strong, unheeding of her scorn,
> Wading in deeps where she had lain,
> Sleeping upon her river lawn
> And chasing her starry, satyr train.
> She fled, and changed into a tree,—
> That lovely fair-haired lady . . .
> And now I seek through the sere summer
> Where no trees are shady!"

The account, then, of her character is singularly congruous, and I especially like, and recognise, the story of her description of the shortcomings of Martha, the nursery-maid. The physical description of her alone, though I see from contemporary photographs how accurate it must have been, I fail to identify, for, by the time I first remember her, when she was seven or eight, there was no sign of the small child of a year or two before, the butterfly had already emerged from the chrysalis, and she was thin, tall for her age, with the budding profile of a gothic effigy or a portrait by a Sienese master; she was already the same person I know today.

My father considered sons, especially elder sons when they were small, as a valuable extension of his personality, and my mother preferred small sons to small daughters, and the newest arrival to the earliest, and so my birth caused Edith to be relegated to a second place in the nursery, a position which her very nature forbade her to occupy anywhere, even at that tender age. It never altered, I believe, her feeling for me, but all the same it must have constituted, like an inoculation, a first experience of the cruelty and fickleness of men and women. . . . In consequence, it was only a few months after my birth that this little creature tried to run away from home, making an escape from our house in Scarborough so far as the outskirts of the town. Only the fact of her being as yet unable to lace her own boots, and of their being, as a result, so loose that further walking became impossible, was responsible for her capture and enforced return after an outing of three or four hours. . . . Davis herself was angry with her. As for my parents, they were furious: for where she was concerned, a sense of humour, usually so noticeable a trait in both their natures, entirely deserted them. They had produced, instead of what they had expected—a "charming" toy reproduction of themselves in fifty-fifty proportion—, a changeling, a small being with an intensely individual character and appearance, quite unlike those nearest her, with an aquiline nose instead of the straight one for which my father had been prepared, and (it became clear in time) with no love of sport, as my mother had hoped—worse, a small creature with an alien and immortal soul, difficult to bend or mould to the comfortable, late Victorian conventions of her class. . . . No, their sense of humour, and even of pity, completely vanished when in contact with her

I doubt whether any child was ever more mismanaged by her parents; they failed entirely to comprehend the sort of being who was in process of flowering before their eyes, they mistook nervous sensibility for awkwardness, imagination for falsehood, and a capacity for throwing the cloak of drama over everyday events—often the sign of an artist—for "being affected". As she grew older, instead of allowing her to find her own range, in the same manner that she had taught herself to read, they tried to force her to comply to their own measurements. Her seriousness, and an attitude of criticism which gradually developed in her concerning current class beliefs (such as that the poor deserved to be poor, and the rich, rich, or that sport was of more value to life than art), terrified my mother, albeit she enjoyed, and always more with the passing years, the immense sense of fun that my aunt had noticed in the child so early, and which continually developed. My father, on the other hand, insisted on her admiring the things which he, with a taste he held to be infallible, himself admired. If she wanted to play the piano, no, it must be the 'cello instead, for he, profoundly unmusical though he was, had in his own mind decided that the 'cello was the finest of all instruments. Then, where poetry was concerned, Swinburne must be bad for her to read, for he had not read him, and therefore could not like him: she ought to be content with Tennyson for beauty, Austin Dobson for charm and Kipling for strength. Besides Swinburne was not the sort of poet to read; my mother agreed. "Morbid", she pronounced, with some lack of conviction, for she never read a line of poetry of any sort—or, rather, "morb", for she clipped her words.

But I am going too far ahead. . . . The other member of the group under the tree with the fruit of gold, was Davis, our dear nurse, who had been nursery-maid to my mother, and who remained with us until I was nine. Placidity and a comforting trust in the beneficence of God and man were her chief characteristics. Her wisdom was of the blood, not of the mind, and she possessed a great understanding of young people, young animals, and of birds and wild flowers. She regarded the rest of the world with a kind bewilderment that deepened with the years, for the whole globe was altering and she liked things to be stable. Black bonnets, for example—which she always wore in the winter—were going out, and bananas, a common fruit, had made their appearance, even in the best fruit shops. . . . And so, in the evening, as she sewed, with the aid of a shiny black, rather obsolete machine, wide pink or pale-blue satin ribbons on to a white material, covered with lace, to make the high caps that she wore indoors, she deplored the tendencies of the time to the nursery-maid, who adopted an attitude of formal but dutiful listening and acquiescence. The perambulator which she wheeled was very ancient and wide, belonging to a period at least half a century earlier than herself, and her cure for bruises was Butler & Crisp's *Pomade Divine*, a magical ointment of the early-nineteenth-century nursery, which still retains in its general presentation, no less than its scent, soothingly and—if it be not a contradiction so to phrase it— aromatically *fade*, the impress of past times, for the bottle is of individual form, and done up in a bright green pyramidal box that resembles a metronome in shape. This certainly constituted the most modern specific of any kind of which she was aware. She lived for children and their love, which she always obtained, but Edith was her most prized and cherished charge: though she was to lose her in a few months, for by the time I was first fully reconnoitring my surroundings, Edith was already in the care of a governess, with whom Davis carried on for years, with force and ingenuity, if not with absolute enjoyment, the usual nurse-versus-governess feud; (a feud that perhaps has its origin in the same sort of state of tension that exists between man and monkey, where each sees in the other a slight resemblance to itself.)

Davis and my sister, then, compose the first group. But, soon now, the background becomes recognisable, the figures clearer and more plentiful,—Edith, Davis, the nursery-maid, Martha or Emily or Mary, Mother and Father, aunts and uncles, grandfather and grandmothers, ranged one behind the other in their generations, building themselves up into a concrete image of the past; and servants, above all in those days, servants.

The traditional upbringing of children in a family such as mine, implied, before the present nursery days of vitamins and orange juice and the use of Christian name between the employed and the children of the employer, a frank acceptance of the situation. Parents were aware that the child would be a nuisance, and a whole hedge of servants, in addition to the complex guardianship of nursery and schoolroom, was necessary, not so much to aid the infant as to screen him off from his father and mother, except on such occasions as he could be used by them as adjunct, toy or decoration. Thus, in a subtle way, children and servants often found themselves in league against grown-ups and employers. The female child sought shelter with nurse and housekeeper and cook, the male in the pantry. Certainly I learnt more, far more, from talking to Henry and Pare in the pantry, from their instinctive wisdom and humour, than from more academic sources. They prevented the atmosphere from becoming too rarefied or refined. Their expressions nourished the writers hidden within the children, just as the food which Davis favoured on special occasions, when my father was, for some reason or other, not likely to interfere, nourished our bodies. For though she held boiled mutton and rice pudding to be the correct everyday food, and though she thought bananas "common", she often added winkles, bought as a treat on the sly (because of my father's fear of ptomaine), to our diet for tea, or shrimps, measured out in an enamel mug at the fish-shop or dragged, sandy and recalcitrant, from the pools along the shore, by ourselves. It would be vulgar for ladies and gentlemen to indulge such tastes, but children were children.

As for Henry, in after years, himself recognised the part he had played in the development of Sacheverell and myself, for in a letter I received from him, in retirement at Scarborough in 1938, he says: "There is often a bit in the newspapers about you and the members of *my club* rush up to me and show me. I see in Monday's *Scarborough News* a bit in about your hobbies, saying your education was not got at school or college,[1] but during your holidays. Well, Sir, I make bold to claim some of that, because whether you were at Scarboro', Renishaw or

[1] This refers to a comment at the time in some of the newspapers upon a phrase in my current entry in *Who's Who*; it ran "Educated during holidays from Eton".

abroad, if you or Master Sachie wanted to know anything about things on the earth, the sea under the earth or in the air above you generally came to me, even when you had a tutor, and often the tutors came too."

In the days when I first remember the pantry, it contained as its permanent figures Jones, Henry and Pare. Jones was in charge, a lean individual, who had been my father's scout at Oxford, and possessed an extraordinary physique, thin and long-chinned as the meagre type favoured so often by Rowlandson: it was, really, a memorable chin, all the more so because, contrary to the usual reading of such a feature, it spelt indecision and a lack of organising power. Under him served Henry, who later became butler, and Pare, while a few friends or ex-retainers like James Broadbent, my grandmother's fat and jovial coachman, then retired—or, rather, discharged—would look in, especially late at night. But Henry Moat, even before he superseded Jones, was always the chief personality there. How often he used to imitate for me some guest, to whom I had taken a childish dislike, or talk to me about "Sir George's latest idea", or tell me stories about the sea, or sing in his handsome bass bellow, which resembled the singing of a whale —could a cetacean be induced to sing—, that won him, I found out later, so many female admirers; his atmosphere was always of the sea, for he came of a long line of sailors, fishermen and whalers. His humour was in no way esoteric, but belonged to the genius of the race. Stephen Pare was his foil, intensely appreciative of Henry's jokes and general character, but sad himself—and not without reason, for his wife, whom I only remember dimly—though she was often mentioned in my hearing with a lowering of the voice—and to whom he was devotedly attached, had gone mad, and he was losing his sight through having been struck by lightning. Thus he introduced a contrary and biblical element of Job-like patience into the happy and robust eighteenth-century atmosphere of the pantry.

Henry first came to us as footman in 1893, as his signature, cut with a diamond on a window-pane of the pantry at Renishaw, still testifies, and remained with us, on and off, for forty-two or forty-three years. His absences were caused by his giving notice to my father, usually because of the introduction of some new idea of which he disapproved. But, as Henry used to complain to me, you "never knew what Sir George would do next". He lacked continuity, it seemed, in the smaller items of behaviour, though, regarded in another light, each fresh contradiction seemed hall-marked with his personality. "There's only one certain thing, and that is, you can't do right." Thus, at the age of one and a half to two years, I had unknowingly provoked a crisis, for while if Henry broke anything, or allowed it to be broken, he was always severely taken to task for it, yet on this occasion, when he had grabbed a valuable wine-glass from me, just as I had smashed one, and was evidently going to smash another, my father's esthetic theories were disturbed, and he reproved him sternly, in the words, "Don't do that, Henry! Leave him alone, or you will spoil the boy's sense of touch." . . . And there were his innumerable other theories, or "Sir George's fads", as Henry called them. New ideas or, indeed, ideas of any sort, were a great trouble, for servants, even the most unusual, always like their master to be conventional. In spite of his antiquarian attitude towards life my father, for example, was fond of reading the latest scientific treatises and of trying to keep up with modern inventions. (He considered he had made some discoveries himself on occasion.) "Henry," he called one day to the great man, "I've a new idea! Knife-handles should always be made of condensed milk!" (I must explain that a substance derived from milk, a sort of paste in various colours, had lately made its appearance.) Henry looked particularly disgusted at the idea and very worried at its application. Then, with emphasis, and with an unusual air of correctitude, he countered, "Yes, Sir George. . . . But what if the cat gets at them?"

At other times he left because it was a tactical move in the lifelong strategic game which he and my father played together, or, again, he disappeared in a trail of mystery and disapprobation, because his enjoyment of sensual pleasures had been too pronounced.

Sometimes Henry would ask to come back, sometimes my father would invite him to return; but one thing was certain, whatever the cause of the break had been, however permanent it might have appeared for the moment, or for the month, back he always came in the end. He and my father, though mutually critical and at the same time appreciative, never failed to gravitate towards each other again, as if influenced by the working of some natural law. My father always referred to Henry as "the Great Man", and Henry for his part, mixed with feelings of the utmost disrespect, cherished towards him, as well, sentiments approaching veneration. He realised his quality, both mental and physical, and that he was an uncommon, if difficult, character. This singular mixture of regard and ridicule,—which for the understanding of both of them as their figures gain substance in these books must be comprehended by the reader at the outset—, is best illustrated by the following very typical letter which I received from Henry many years later, describing experiences abroad. This is a literal transcription:

HOTEL BRISTOL, BERLIN
Sept. 23, 1929

DEAR CAPTAIN OSBERT,

We have been travelling a good deal in Germany since the 12th of August and very interesting it is Sir George taking me and sometimes Miss Fowler[1] with him to see the Castles, Palaces, Museums and ~~Pubs~~. We have become well-known in Germany Ginger[2] visiting the above places over and over again and giving the attendants a hell of a time so that when we enter a door and they see him they scatter like scalded cats some through doors, some through windows and others up the chimneys one fat old woman wanted to take his umbrella from him and then commenced a vigorous tug of war result the fragments of the umbrella has been sent to the Castle[3] to be put away in the armoury. At present he is looking remarkably well and looking well after himself—and after us too. He has docked us all of soup, meat and sweets for our dinner, for fear that we get fat—her Ladyship too—and of course pays half-price for us where he has to eat double portions to get built up again, himself.[4] But joking apart Sir George is very good to me and took Miss Fowler and me to

[1] My mother's maid.

[2] My father had, during the war, had an altercation with a taxi-driver over the amount of the fare, and the taxi-driver, looking at his red pointed beard, said, "After the war, Ginger, I'll get even with you!" Thence this sobriquet.

[3] Montegufoni, my father's home in Tuscany, of which he had very much emphasised the medieval aspect, building up clumps of stone cannon-balls in the courtyard, and opening up oubliettes and armouries.

[4] "The doctor says I need building up" was a favourite phrase of my father's.

Potsdam. Very interesting. The palaces and gardens are truly beautiful. In the ex-Kaiser's private palace in Berlin we saw the table on which he ordered the mobilisation of his Army and Navy "I.VIII.XIV. at 5 o'clock" the table is made from the oak taken from Nelson's ship the *Victory* and for the writing paper, envelopes etc to stand in there is a model of the *Victory*[1] the stem and the stern and small enamel flags showing the famous signal "England expects that every man this day will do his duty". There was also a beautiful atlas globe of World in the Kaiser's study and I showed Sir Geo where you was in Spain.

We went the other day (friday) to the Hohenzollern Museum (Sir Geo and I) of course I marched behind him and really I think and others say so too that if possible Sir George looks more distinguished than ever and the attendants eyed him intensely the head one especially and we had all of them bowing and scraping. The head guide ordered a special catalogue to be brought and given to Sir George and then he came and asked me his (Sir Geo's) name I felt very proud of him.

Now dear Master Osbert, take great care of yourself. We leave her this Wednesday for Munich stay there at the Continental Hotel until the 3rd October then H.L. departs direct for Florence and G.R.S. and self for Verona. I remain your obedient servant, HENRY MOAT.

Henry claimed that he was descended from Italian jet-cutters, called Moatti, who had settled in Whitby in Queen Elizabeth's reign, and certainly his family had lived for well over two hundred and fifty years in the house, which later he inherited, in the fishermen's quarter of Whitby; a delightful old house, built into the rock, its front concealed in a passage as narrow as a medieval street. Whether or not of Italian ancestry, nobody could have looked a more complete Yorkshireman than Henry. He stood well over six feet, and, with his high colour, gave an impression of great physical strength; in character he was robust, original, vigorous and audacious. He thought things out for himself, and maintained a respect for learning, in spite of his matter-of-fact attitude toward life, so well exemplified by a remark he made, a few years ago, to my sister. It was a beautiful starlit night at Montegufoni, and he was in the garden contemplating the stars with the interest of both a sailor and a philosopher. . . . He said nothing until my sister passed, when he observed suddenly, "All the same, miss,

[1] This is accompanied by a good rough drawing of the model of a ship.

let's stick to the eggs and bacon." It was perhaps his respect for originality, but more especially for learning, that induced him to return so often to my father's service. When Henry had grown old, Walter Cooper, my chauffeur, who thoroughly understood his character, asked him what he most regretted, and Henry replied, "If I had my life over again, I'd go in for scholarship and deep-thinking". He had, as his letters show, a natural gift for a turn of phrase, and, when he retired, I repeatedly offered him sums of money if he would write his life, which had been of a most entertaining order, just as his ideas had always been his own. But he was then too tired and ill, I think, to undertake it.

A letter of Henry's—also a literal transcription—written to my mother in 1919 during one of his absences from the family, gives a good picture both of himself, and of the pantry as I first remember it:

To The Lady Ida Sitwell

MY LADY,

Big thanks for the beautiful letter you sent me, it was like a ray of sunshine. I was very sorry just to miss Captain Osbert last Saturday, if I could just have seen him before I left I would cheerfully have cancelled my visit to Stokesley and Stockton. . . . all being well I will come over to Scarboro' tomorrow (friday) when I hope to find your ladyship in the best of health and spirits although it takes a mighty effort these times but it is worth it to try. My lady if I had gone to Scarboro' last Saturday it would have been the 26th anniversary of me entering your service (Oct. 26th 1893). You were a fine young lady then full of high spirits and fun I would not have missed the career for the earth. The first night I arrived at Belvoir House[1] Sir Geo was expecting a Committee meeting of 18 and so we only had 3 chairs in the dining room. The electricians had not got wired up, Lords, the caterers, had forgot to send, poor old Jones could not get his razor to sail round his chinn (I thought I had better put 2 n's to chin, my Lady) and poor old James Broadbent[2] sitting sighing on a

---

[1] At Scarborough. My father and mother had just moved into it.

[2] My grandmother Sitwell's former coachman, who had been in her service for many years. He was of a jovial disposition. My Aunt Florence's diary for 23rd November 1892 has the following entry: "Poor Mother has many troubles just now. Aunt Minnie and Aunt F., ill: Aunt Puss, very, very far from well; the anxiety about Uncle Charlie,—the constant trouble of seeing Mr. Dale in his sad state and having had to give notice to J. B. under such sad circumstances: and other anxieties such as a girl at the Home having gone out of her mind. . . ." After being dismissed by my grandmother, he continued to work for my father and mother.

chair *very tired* repeating "I wantsh go 'ome." I know you will pardon me for the above my Lady I never feel lonely when I just think of my past life the cinema is not in it. Wishing you well my Lady, I remain, Your obedient servant, HENRY MOAT.

Though, as I say, all these persons played so large a part in my childish life, and though I saw more of them than of my parents, yet the atmosphere for all of us was distilled by my father and mother; by my mother's unusual beauty and strange temperament, her kindness, indulgence, and furious, sudden rages, my father's cleverness and determination, and a view of life, a plotting of detail, of each move in the countless games in which he was engaged, which seems to me more Chinese than European. The atmosphere they provided was unmistakable.

I was in the happy position as a small child of being my mother's favourite. I played on her bed, and upset everything with impunity. I adored her. Yet there were two things about her which I could not understand. The first time she lost her temper with me (I forget about what, but now I deeply sympathise with her), the whole world temporarily assumed a more tragic tone. I had been so sure of our relationship, now growing out of darkness into light, in which neither could do wrong for the other. I would not have believed that such a thing as this could happen, that so radiant and lovely and considerate a creature, always gay and gentle, could contain so dark a shadow within her. Moreover, though we were on such equal terms—for she treated every child as a friend and contemporary, never let him see that she was laughing at something he had said (and this no doubt was the secret of the easy influence over children, the affectionate intimacy with them, which all her life she was able to establish)—I had not until that moment suspected its existence. . . . But the dreadful day at last ended, and by morning, time had restored the old relationship.

I used to wander in and out of my mother's room as I liked. I upset everything, as I have said—that was my privilege. I used to lie for hours in the morning on her bed, which was a drift of every newspaper published, of letters, and of cards, for she had been playing patience. I knew so well every familiar object, the flat, folding, leather card-tray upon which she had arranged her game, the clock like a huge watch in a green morocco case, the vases of flowers, the bottles of scent, the handkerchief laid on top of one of them ready for the day, the pincushions, with every size of hat-pin in them, always with black shiny tops, pins that had continually to be rescued from me by my mother's prim and patient maid, who would edge into the room, holding a newly arrived or newly brushed dress at arm's length, as though it were a corpse, instead of an object of pride to her. But she would always have to drop it, and remove the pins from me before irretrievable harm was done. I recognised the use of all the detail on the table, the diamond and ruby horse-shoe brooch, the gothic pendant that had been made for Lord Albert to give his wife, with its fantastic shape and its black pearls, the silver hair-brushes, the innumerable photographs, the bottles and jars: but I did not understand one thing, a loop of thick rope, a foot or two long, twisted in a knot round the head of the bed. . . . Eventually, after many implorings, I was told what it was. "It's a bit of a hangman's rope, darling. Nothing's so lucky! It cost eight pounds—they're very difficult to get now. Old Sir William got it for me." . . . And, suddenly, I was back again in a world, instinctively comprehended, of Hogarth and Gay.

Now a barrel-organ struck up outside a tune called "Queen of My Heart", and the sunshine was pouring in at the three wide windows, which showed an expanse of light-blue sea, of a sparkling gaiety that was imbecile. A German band, also, was playing at the corner of the Crescent, and a voice somewhere was singing "Linger Longer, Lucy, Linger Longer, Lou!" The gardenias my mother had taken off the previous night were lying on the dressing-table and were scenting the room, and competing with the fragrance of tuberoses and sweet geraniums that stood in a vase. It was nearly noon, and she must begin to get up, for she was going to play a game of croquet before luncheon, and at the same time to rehearse with her partner and opponents a conversation—for a man, who had the reputation of being "most amusin' ", was going to show her and three friends how to make a phonograph record, and they were to pretend to have a quarrel over a croquet match. The record itself was to be made after luncheon: but already the vibrant tin trumpet, and the virgin cylinder, that looked as though fashioned of cheap brown chocolate, soft and smelling of oil, stood ready to catch the impress of their voices, and fix their tones, it seemed, their inflexion and laughter, in the throat of Time. No need now to depend upon a signature, glittering like rain, incised upon a sheet of brittle glass with a diamond ring for a particular kind of immortality: this was a much more secure method. And the phonograph was a new invention— not that my mother took any interest in scientific progress for its own sake, but it was a novelty, and it was fun. She left the theoretical side to my father.

Shut up in his study that smelt of strong Egyptian cigarettes, of which he smoked from twenty to thirty a day, my father was meanwhile, though quite unaware that an expensive phonograph had been imported into the house, reading a paper that had just appeared in a scientific journal upon the more recent discoveries of Edison, with especial reference to a machine— apparently called a phonograph—which recorded voices. (It was an interesting idea, but what a pity, he reflected, that he did not know Edison; he might have offered some valuable suggestions to the inventor, if only he had been consulted!) Then, he must run through a thing in the *Athenaeum* on "Modern Modifications of the Theory of Evolutional Survival". But, alas! he could not spend so much time upon it as he would have liked, would have to leave making notes on the subject until another day, for he had also to think out a scheme for the discomfiture of "the other side", and he must work, too, at the pedigree of the Sacheverells, the origin of part-singing (a subject in which, except that it *had* an origin, he was not really much interested), make notes for a speech that he was to deliver to a large audience the following evening, ending with the quotation of a couple of lines from Byron, and consider the decorative motives employed in the leaden jewellery of the Middle Ages. The household bills were again too high—such a mistake to entertain all these friends, people never did it in the thirteenth century, but were content to live modestly and quietly within the castle except on some great occasion! He must send for the cook about them, and also explain to her about the making of that sauce, she did not do it right. Henry polished boots the wrong way, and he must show him how to set about it. He must enter in his architectural note-book what he had found out about the origin in the East of Romanesque architecture. He must write to Turnbull, to say that the yew hedges were not being properly planted, and that he wanted all the levels taken again in the Eckington Woods for the new twelve-mile drive. He must send a letter to that new shoe place, pointing out that he refused to pay more than 18s. 6d. for a pair of shoes, and send a cheque to an architect, whose name he had temporarily forgotten, for £346 : 6 : 11. He must revise, since seeing that last exhibition, his notes on "Greek Sculpture of the Golden Age". The editor of the *Scarborough Post* ought to bring the leading article to him every day, so that he could approve it: he must think out a letter to him at once. (Sometimes he felt he would never get all these things done!) He must also enter his endorsement about the tints of spring foliage. "I have been trying to formulate my ideas as to the Spring Tints in planting. The 'old gold' which some oaks assume in May seems to me the finest colour in that month, especially when against a background of Scotch Fir. The contrast between apple trees in bloom and yews is fine, though too strong for most positions, but I have on several occasions been pleasantly surprised by it in the right place." . . . He must drop Sir Henry White a line to tell him his law was incorrect where the sale of copyhold coal was concerned, and write to Ernest, the gardener, about the proper way to plant roses (they understood these things much better in medieval times). In a note-book entitled "The Wisdom of Life" he wrote down an aphorism, or a caution, "Never open a letter from a correspondent known to be troublesome, until after luncheon". Now he corrected the date of "Hugh Fitz Osborne, called Blundus" from 1084 to 1086, and entered in their right place some discoveries he had made about the art of heraldry. In the pages devoted to gardens, he added that the Byzantines used to gild the trunks of cypress trees up to the height of a man, before proceeding to read over to himself a small account he had written of "Domestic Manners in Sheffield in the year 1250".

Then he shut his note-books and went to his solitary

luncheon, with Henry in heavy and dignified attendance. He always had luncheon by himself except on special occasions. People distracted him, and their company prevented "the gastric juices from following their normal course". . . . An hour later, my mother and her friends would have an enjoyable meal, full of laughter and fun, and I would be in attendance under the table. Several of the guests were staying in the house, others came from the town or the country houses round. (There were sixteen to luncheon, but my father did not know that, and I was not to tell him. He made such a fuss about the household bills. "But whatever one may say about him, there's no one else like him," she would add.) Some friend would admire a bracelet, and she would say "Take it, darling" and give it to her. She would also give away, in the same manner, several dresses after luncheon. Ada, or Ethel, or Amalia or one of my mother's other devoted friends, would try to prevent her from this folly. But it was no use; if anyone liked anything she had, she must give it to her. . . . Now, if they were all to go down to the Spa at four, that record must be made on the phonograph, at once. . . . So those who were to take part, and their coach, drank down their coffee, and went into the next room. I was allowed to accompany them on condition that I kept quiet. The needle ground out the sound of its progression, and there was scarcely a hitch in the making of the records. Only, perhaps, here and there, a voice waited a fraction too long before coming in. . . . And somewhere, in this house, the records still exist; some are smashed, and even those that are whole cannot be played, for my father's favourite Law of Evolutional Survival has relegated the instruments for which they were made to that same limbo to which dinosaur, dodo and our own anthropoid ancestor have at the end of their respective periods been consigned. Nothing remains of that golden hour, which was to be handed on so surely to posterity, except the oily, rather unpleasant scent of the records, that yet takes me—but alas! me alone—back to that gay interval between luncheon and going down to the Spa, as clearly and as surely as would the sound of the voices themselves. . . . It was time to go on to the Spa.

In the evening my mother and father would both come to

say good-night to me: it was the high moment of the day; a reception! My father would tell me a story, but his attitude was very different from that of my mother,—it was thought-out. He was considering my good, not my pleasure. It would be something about the Crusades, though he was in no way stiff with children, but they existed to be improved, and in the meantime to amuse and interest him with their curious point of view. . . . My mother stayed on with me while I fell asleep, which even then, when I was a very small child, I found difficult because of a fear of not sleeping. . . . She kissed me, and I remembered nothing more until morning came and I heard the cry "Rags and Bones, Rags and Bones!" But the full tide of spring was washing the town, and the urgency and meaning, tragic and implicit, of the cry was lost beneath the surge of flowering trees in backyards, hawthorn and apple and pear and lilac and laburnum, and the brilliance of the sky, a hard northern brilliance reflected in the sea.

CHAPTER TWO

Gemini Rising

LOOKING at a horoscope drawn out for me last year, I read: "The chief defect of Gemini is an inclination to worry and fret. Your sun is another restless sign, Sagittarius. Jupiter is the ruler of Sagittarius, and he is in Aries, a very free sign. You would not be tamed, you like to dart here and there, both in space and thought, like a dragon-fly. Gemini rising gives you a dual impetus, you will find your left hand nearly as easy to use as your right, you will like to read two books at the same time, or, if you are a writer, as I suspect, you will often work at two books. You will have two backgrounds for the life you lead, and you will be very sensitive to them. You will like old customs as much as new things that you discover for yourself, and the position of the moon in your sky will make you fond of your home."

To me, my home always meant Renishaw; and the summer took me there, so that it meant the summer, too; summers that from this distance all merge into one. . . . I remember, every year, directly I arrived, running through the cool, pillared hall to the low, painted door a little taller than myself, opposite, and standing on tiptoe, so that the smell of the garden should come at me over it through the open window; the overwhelming and, as it seemed, living scent of stocks and clove carnations and tobacco-plant on a foundation of sun-warmed box hedges, the odour of any component of which to this day carries me back to infancy, though never now do I obtain the full force it drew from that precise combination. . . . I remember, too, the pleasure with which I always arrived at the house, and my sorrow at leaving it, for though we spent much time in Scarborough, and paid long visits to London and to grand-parents, Renishaw was my home. I felt this with peculiar intensity, experiencing a curious attachment to the soil, a sympathy with the form of the country, with its trees and flowers, the frail blue spires of the bluebells in May, or the harebells and toad-flax of August, which has never left me and has made me wonder at times whether my ancestors, in the building-up of an estate through so many hundreds of years, and by the hunger and passion for this land which must have inspired them—for it was an estate gradually accumulated, not obtained by huge grants or the purchase of Church property —had not bequeathed to me something still very real and active in my nature; this love seemed to me so much older than myself and so much part of me.

Again, it may have been due to the sombre but vivid charm of the country, so unusual in its appeal. On one side is Hallam-shire, from which we spring, once a kingdom stretching across England, and from which during the passing of the centuries— for coal was dug here in Roman times and iron was exported to the Bahamas, Bermuda and Virginia before the Civil Wars —has been born a great industrial district, a conglomeration of cities, Sheffield and Rotherham and Chesterfield, situated in wild and splendid scenery of which the famous crooked spire of Chesterfield Church, whether bent by wind or lightning, or, as a legend says, kicked by the Devil as he flew over it, is the soul and symbol; on the other, the hills and dales of Derby-shire, with their druidical remains, with their quarries of blue-john and of grey marble, with their gushing mineral waters and petrifying streams, with their thousand lingering traditions of Sherwood Forest—which not so long ago extended into our countryside as far as Chatsworth—and of the Peak, where the playing of the bagpipes lingered on until the sixteenth century.

In this wide country the most typical feature is the splendour of its houses, Hardwick and Welbeck, Bolsover Castle and Chatsworth, Wentworth Woodhouse and Haddon. Sutton Scarsdale,[1] with its grand façade, Corinthian columns and elaborate coats-of-arms, was, at the time of which I write,

[1] The façade of Sutton Scarsdale was designed by Francis Smith of Warwick. Originally constructed for a former English Ambassador to the Holy Roman Empire, the house was sold at the close of the eighteenth century to a member of the Arkwright family. Tradition maintains that it is the house to the plan of which the old nobleman in the periwig is pointing in Hogarth's *Marriage à la Mode*. All the detail was exquisite; the marble chimney-pieces were by the hands of the best Italian craftsmen, and the plaster-work was executed by the most famous Venetian stuccoists of their time, Artari and Bagutti, who also worked at Houghton for Sir Robert Walpole. Indeed the decorations of the rooms here were finer in quality and design than any to be seen in Venice.

still lived in, whereas today it has been reduced by the greed
of the native speculator to an eyeless and roofless ruin in which
the foxes nest, and from which they have to be dislodged before
a hunt. Today even the lake is sightless and lies drained.
Scarcely less imposing than the mansions are the remains of
ancient industry, the huge derelict buildings as well as those
that are new and efficient. On the Renishaw estate, one mill,
formerly used for the iron trade,[1] bears the date 1641, and
within a few miles stand mills where sickles are still made by
hand (and exported to Chile and Peru), after the same pattern
and in the same place in which they were wrought in the reign
of Queen Elizabeth.

Here things endure. The old tides of rural existence survive
beneath the indications of industry, new and old. Even though
the furnaces blaze and belch, and the smoke sullies the very
sky, men still measure the seasons by the facts of rural life.
Summer comes with the ripening corn, autumn with mists and
the picking of mushrooms in meadows and blackberries in hedges,
winter with the falling snow, which lies long, often for two
months, upon this high, cold country, but the advent of spring
is heralded, not by the choirs of birds or the opening flowers,
but by the passing of a black horse. Along the roads, along the
lanes to the farms, a man will see a fine stallion pass, glossy and
strong, led by an attendant, its mane plaited, its tail tied with
blue and yellow ribbons, and will remark to his friend, "Why,
spring must be here. There's the Dook's[2] stallion going by!"

The dialect of this potent and contrasting landscape is
characteristic as its stone hedges and cliffs and crags, its great
stone-built churches, Norman or Gothic, with their stone
spires, its stone-built farms, windswept on their little hills, and
bearing such names as Spitewinter, Toadpool, Shady Hall,
Hagg Hall and Clod Hall, Johnnygate and Highlightly. It
possesses words unknown elsewhere, but few are of French

---

[1] I once consulted a local ironmonger about the cleaning of a breastplate
that had belonged to an ancestor of mine. He showed a knowledge of armour
that astonished me; when I enquired why he was such a master of this
subject, he replied: "Well, my family have been in the iron trade since the
fourteenth century. They used to make armour in Sheffield. And we all
know a bit about it."

[2] The Duke of Devonshire.

origin (blue-john—*bleu-jaune*—is, though a local product, an exception, as is an adjective quoted in a moment). There are names, of course, from France, like Beauchief (Beechif) Abbey; but most of the language hails from the North, from Denmark and Norway. This district retains the use of "thou" and "thee" in all their pristine vigour and freshness, without any suggestion of Quaker affectation, while the word "the" is pronounced "t'", and so easily differentiated from the second person singular. Other Biblical grammar still lingers on; for example the use of "I" and "me." The miner, grimy from his work, calls out "I'll wash me" or says "I'll buy me a new whippet"; "Yes" and "No" have not yet banished "Yea" and "Nay", which are common forms. Less ecclesiastical is the use of D. H. Lawrence's "mardy"—a word of obvious derivation for those who swear in French—, here meaning silly or soft; there is, too, "nesh", which has almost the same significance. "A luv a-ricking" means a chimney smoking, "Sithee!" is used for "Look here!", "strind" (rhyming with "blind") for stride, "sup" for drink, "lathe" for barn, "mistil" or "shippon" for cowshed—(but that is the Yorkshire side)—"wiggin" for mountain, "laking" for "idling", and "marlaking" as a more emphatic form of this same word. In the winter you are never "cold", you are "starved" or "clammed". As for local idiom, "I'll pize thee one" is what the angry mother says to her child; if you are born left-handed, you are a "keggie-hander"; if you must wait your turn, you "mus wairt thee kale"; and, if you hurry, a farmer calls out "Are t' thronged?" "Gate" is still the word for road, that very late invader, unheard of until Elizabethan times, whereas "gate" survives from the uses of medieval agriculture, when the paths between the fields were known as "gates", a meaning still to be detected in the common names of places in the district, Southgate and Moorgate and Norgate, or in the angry tones of a waggoner who bids you to get your motor "out o' t' gate". If a field suffers from lead poisoning it is "bellund".[1] And all these words, and many others, are

[1] To show the influence of past times upon the present, when my father in 1915 cut down a wood which belonged to him, in order to turn it into arable, it was found to be "bellund", the reason for this being that the Romans had established a place for the smelting of lead there, bringing the metal from a mine near Chatsworth.

only to be found in Hallamshire, and are not to be discovered in West Derbyshire, twenty miles away; just as, for example, "cloud", the West Derbyshire word for a hill, is never to be heard here.

Moreover, at the time of which I write, when the light first sculptured for me the outlines of ridge after ridge, misty and tree-tufted, stretching away toward the heights, distant and unattainable, the lansdcape and its inhabitants possessed even more character than they do today. Then, as now, in the distance beyond the park, the great plumes of smoke would wave triumphantly over the pyramids of slag, down which, every now and then, crawled writhing serpents of fire, as the cinders were discharged from the trucks. After dark, this process at conjecturable intervals lit the whole night with a wild glory, so that, my father told me, standing on the lawn, he could read his watch by the light of Stavely flares three miles away, and in the woods this sudden illumination gave an added poignance to the sylvan glades that it revealed, causing the rabbits to be frozen for an instant into immobility, their eyes reflecting the glare and the terror within them, showing a shape, which might be that of an otter from the lake below, scudding through the long wet grass, and making the great owl hiccup uneasily in the trees where formerly he had hooted with assurance. As the golden surge diminished, so did the uneasy stirring of the minute but multitudinous life beneath the tall bracken. . . . All this is the same today—except that the immigrant small owl has made his way here and adds his clamour to the summer night; indeed, the flares are brighter. But in those times, during the hours of daylight, the very starkness of the little houses, and the blackness of them from the smoke—of which there had been no attempt at amelioration —, added their own quality of outrageous contrast, even, as it were, of colour. In this *chiaroscuro* world, the gangs of miners returning from their work would tramp along the roads, wearing stuttering clogs, cord trousers and scarlet tunics, the cast-off tunics of a happy army, then still dressed in musical-comedy uniforms, which the colliers bought regularly; a costume which set off the blackness of their faces and their scarlet lips. Where else could you see such colour in the clothes

E

of the working people at this period? Even the roads were
different, bordered with tall trees, now cut down by councils
eager in their triple quest of tidiness, uniformity and standard-
isation, and the lanes of the countryside, and the drives through
the park, were more vivid, I believe, than others anywhere—
for their surface was laid with clinker, a vitreous substance,
turquoise-blue, marine-blue and sea-green, which, if it had
been a natural product instead of having been cleaned out of
the vast furnaces of the neighbourhood, would rank, such is its
beauty, as a semi-precious stone. (What exquisite mountains,
temples, trees and fantastic animals in miniature, Chinese
craftsmen would have carved from it!) Fragments of clinker
can still be found best after a very rainy day when the down-
pour has lifted the surface, along the drives; but no new
substance of the same kind can be obtained, for improved processes of industry now leave only an ugly grey stone behind them.

In the hot summer the house, standing above the world on
its wide table-land, threw its battlemented and spired shadow,
uncompromising and stark for all its fantasy, as far as the tall
beech trees at the hills' edge, while down below, in the north
park, the golden mist still lay melting. On this side, the house
makes no gesture to the graces, but is a stout-built, machicolated
screen with but a few shallow breaks in the hundred yards of
its façade. Here is no garden, only the grass and the old trees,
of great girth; in spite of its austerity, it is rustic and pastoral,
cows and horses come out of the Palladian stables into the park,
and in their seasons buttercups and mushrooms grow among
the green tufts of the turf. But on the south side, the atmosphere
changes dramatically, is no longer pastoral but romantic. The
house with its deep recesses, the fountains and pools and hedges
set so fast among their surrounding woods that in the distance
from the south the building appears to rise from a forest, the
vistas to which lead every alley and every green court, are all
part of the great romantic movement; and water provides the
link which binds them together, water dripping from fountains
and flashing from pools and culminating in the expanse of lake
below, that swoons in a summer ecstasy of sun-born mist and
still green leaves to the nostalgic rhythms of Mendelssohn,
Weber, Chopin and Tchaikovsky.

People, except those very near me, were still strange and stiff from first sight as those figures, full of latent movement, seen in a pointillist picture, female figures in wide skirts and angular sleeves and straw-hats, resembling those portrayed by Toulouse-Lautrec or Beardsley, figures just learning to ride bicycles, men in round caps and cricket blazers and white trousers. . . . Sometimes I would look up from the garden, hearing my name called, and see my father, talking to an architect or a landscape specialist upon the roof, far above. And I could never make out by what magic they achieved those heights. . . . Then there were the rustics, bearded or bonneted. But, more easily, I remember *occasions*; those aquatic afternoons for example.

How delicious were those long picnics on the lake, in the wide, flat-bottomed boat, blue-painted, that yet rots somewhere in the disused stables; those long, hot, calm, drowsy, sun-spangled afternoons of childhood spent on that mirror-flat, cool surface, the slow movement and the sound of the rowlocks as Davis listlessly plied the oar, the hours in which we drifted, yet never wasted our time, for if Edith and I leant over the thick blue wall of the boat, we could watch the fish flickering in their chequered mail through trailing avenues of weeds. And sometimes my father would appear and carry me off for a swift darting journey in a canoe, while his spaniel flopped and splashed after us in the water or, after shaking himself in the sun on the bank, until his dangling ears flapped wildly and a smell of hot wool ascended from his steaming body, then tried, if we were near enough, to jump upon our prow, and, missing it, fell into his other element again.

Edith and Davis would be watching us from the boat, now moored by the island under the light shadow of a grove of young trees. At four-thirty a footman would come down with a hamper, and we would begin collecting dry wood to make a fire upon which to boil the kettle. The twigs crackled and burst, and the kettle began soon to hiss. Presently my mother and her friends would join us, and their grown-up laughter— laughter at things hidden and beyond our sight—would sound among the tea-cups. But my mother, with her own children and with others', but especially with her sons, was like a child herself, absorbed in their interests. Her friends, however, were thinking of themselves and how they looked; their air was patronising in its unnecessary and false kindness (this stricture of course, in no way applies to the several we loved, and who treated us as equals). Soon my mother would light a cigarette to keep the midges away. (In those times, women who smoked usually did so to be daring, but she smoked for pleasure. But time was passing, and soon we would climb the steep sun-baked hill to the house, entering the garden, sweeter than ever in these hours of dwindling light.

In the lamp-room, under the heavy fumes of paraffin, the sightless Stephen Pare—with his vast and hollow eyes, that now I understand resembled the gaping eyes of an antique mask of tragedy—was already lighting the wicks, which, by an unhappy irony, were to make clear for everybody else the exterior world, to him so dim, and indicate the shape and corners of chair and table, blurred to him and fading. Indeed he was the only person to gain no benefit from the process: he could not read at all, even, and he felt his way by instinct through the lofty, darkening rooms. But never, during the many years I knew him, did he make a mistake; he placed things down more softly than would any man who could see. Many of the rooms were now beginning to glow with a light forgotten today, for we belong to the last generation of children brought up by candlelight, and the smell of snuffed wicks lay heavy on our nostrils as we went to sleep. There was, however, though it was already time for bed, still a grateful hour or two before we must go to sleep, for I hated darkness here, was frightened in this large, rambling old house, haunted and haunting, and counted every moment until my mother came upstairs after dinner to bid me a second good-night—a custom strictly forbidden by my father—, bringing with her the comfort of her warm and, to me, loving presence, and the scent of the gardenias and tuberoses she was wearing, and usually—which was also prohibited—a peach, strawberry water-ice, or some delicacy of that sort. She would bend above me, standing close to me, talking to me as to one of her own age, telling me how her cousins, who were staying with us, had behaved at dinner, of how Henry, still a footman, had suddenly laughed at something that was said, and of how difficult my father was being, with all his new ideas—probably he would alter them all again, tomorrow. . . . But though I was so frightened of the night, there was never a moment when I would not rather have been here than elsewhere. I loved the impalpable essence —what later one learns to call the "atmosphere"—of the house, a strange prevalence, laden with the dying memories of three centuries, pervading the mind like a scent faintly detected, the smell of wood-smoke, for example, that seems to colour a whole room with its fragrance though a year has passed.

My mother, who looked so beautiful in her light-coloured evening dresses, pale pink or yellow, would say good-night, and unless already I was in an almost trance-like condition of fatigue, I would struggle to prevent her going. With her, as she walked out of the door, she took the last remainder of all the light that the day had held. The lingering breath of strong scent she affected, and of the warmth of a physical presence that, as with other members of her family, was Italian in its radiance and, at first sight, apparent simplicity, only made the night still darker than it had been before she arrived. There was nothing now except darkness, out of which substance ghosts are spun and torn. Through the door, however, left open on purpose, I could, if I removed the sheet from over my ears, hear the monotonous, grating tone of Davis's voice as she talked to the nursery-maid in the day nursery. It was a dull sound, but I loved it, because it supported me on its safe wings, even the smell of cheese and beer which accompanied it—for they were having their supper—, though at other moments it made me feel sick, now seemed pleasant to me, exhaling a human warmth and animal coarseness. A piece of garlic hung outside the window, says the folklore of South-East Europe, secures a sleeper against vampires, and, equally, I can testify that the scent of beer and cheese can dispose of ghosts for children. I would listen to the voices, and then, the next thing I knew, it was morning and the blinds were being drawn up in our room level with the highest tree-tops.

At Renishaw, then, the background was less complex than at Scarborough. The atmosphere of political excitement for

one thing—and in those days it was marked—was lacking,
there were no gifts of chocolates from enthusiastic supporters
of my father and the Primrose League, no circuses, and neither
bands nor nigger minstrels. The climaxes were more artless
and traditional: a donkey ride with Edith in the morning to
where the toad-flax grew on the banks of the now deserted
canal (part of which had been constructed two centuries before
at the expense of my ancestors, so as to help to improve trade),
or to one of its pretty stone bridges, elegant in span as are those
shown in paintings of Canaletto's, or a drive in the pony-cart,
shining with paint and with brass and patent-leather, drawn
by the buxom piebald pony who pulled us along the roads for
so many years and had enjoyed a romantic past, having been,
it was alleged, the former star equine performer in a circus
(indeed, at Scarborough, it was noticeable that certain tunes
played by a barrel-organ or a band would strike some chords
of memory, for first he would stand still, then prance and try
to take us in a fast and sweeping circle). Usually we drove
through the Eckington Woods, under the banks of dog's-hair
—flowing Alpine grass like the hair of nereids, and a speciality
of the Derbyshire hill country—, and hunt among it for wild
rasps and strawberries, here where my great-great-grandfather
had hunted the tiger. (These glades had no doubt often sheltered
Robin Hood—and indeed the tallest man could stand unseen
in the bracken which flowed up and down the hills—, and, at
the time of which I write, his bow still hung, as it had hung for
three centuries, on the staircase at Barlborough, three miles
away.) Sometimes, again, we would only walk, in the wood
called the Settings, as far as the ice-house, a strange, forbidding
cave, seemingly ancient as the beehive tombs of Mycenae, to
peer down its shaft full of a century's drifting of dead leaves, a
place still set apart for winter even in the midst of summer.
Then we would spend the rest of the afternoon in the company
of my mother, making butter under the guidance of Mrs. Hunt,
who presided in the dairy. In the centre of the floor was an
Italian vase of marble from which water spouted, and to its
octagonal sides were fitted slabs of Derbyshire marble, grey and
showing sections of fossils, things, such as the razor-shells, that
I knew in the life of this age from the sands at Scarborough.

It was deliciously cool even in the hottest hours of August, and I can still hear the wooden clatter of the "Scotch hands", as they are called, see the liquid running out of the butter as the print is pressed on to it, and smell the sour odour of the butter-milk. Sometimes, again, I would be taught to fish in the lake, the hook being baited with a maggot, chosen by an attendant, with the eye of a connoisseur, from a loathsome tin box that contained all writhing hell within its putrid compass, or I would watch my mother fishing for pike in Foxton Dam (Foxton, the Wood of the Little Folk, is near by, through meadows full of dark-blue scabious a-flutter with small blue butterflies). After fishing in the Dam, there was always tea with old Mrs. Stubb, wife of a farmer, who lived by the edge of the wood in a large stone cottage hidden behind a huge espalier apricot; and when we had eaten home-made scones and cakes and jams, she would, on being pressed, favour us with— in, if the truth is to be told, a rather cracked and hollow voice— part of the Hallelujah Chorus. She loved to display her gift, but it was a treat that always reduced my mother, partly, perhaps, because of our obvious enjoyment of it, to helpless though carefully hidden laughter. And finally, towards the end of August, came the climax of the summer, a flower-show, held in the park on the highest ground where there is a flat stretch bearing the biggest and oldest trees. Here was every possible attraction. Besides the tents—filled with a crowd that surged round mounds of fruit and vegetables, in an atmosphere laden with the heated scent of prize flowers and of prize onions mingled together—, besides purple potatoes in their Assyrian armour, besides giant cauliflowers like rustic faces and mammoth dahlias, and huge gooseberries, over-ripe, sticky and melting like cheap sweets, there was a military band playing Waldteufel waltzes, simple tunes pursued by fat, moustached bandsmen down serpentine instruments into an eternity, an infinity, in which nevertheless every vista was clearly defined and obvious. At the gallop, green-clad Lancers would tilt at wooden Turks'-heads and there were Punch-and-Judy shows within the natural stage formed by the seven branches of a vast old elm known as the Seven Sisters, there were marionette shows and displays by midgets, while in the hot seclusion of small, red-lined tents rustic professors foretold the future from the lines of sweaty hands. I was held to be too young to consult them, though several times I ran in a determined manner towards the entrance.

Alas! from this moment the progress of the year downhill was within sight, we were near the autumn, which, to my chagrin, always took us back to Scarborough, electric light, and to children's parties, those fearful ordeals imposed upon the young by their elders. Before us stretched long autumn, and then winter, months, blustering winds and wreck-strewn seas.

At this season the town reverted from a gay, holiday-makers' paradise to a borough with a life and tradition of its own, and the tradesmen would stand gossiping in their doorways or come out to talk to us as we passed. The market was full of the smell of apples and the sunlight hung in tattered autumn streamers from roof-top and tree. This condition went on throughout the golden autumn till Martinmas (a local festival, but one which—for it fell on 11th November—I was to celebrate in the future with great fervour and more cause). On the day in question the ox-eyed ploughmen and the maidservants from the neighbouring farms would walk round the market to be hired, a custom that has now everywhere died out; though, before the days of general advertising, it was common. (In Eckington we hired our ploughmen on Guy Fawkes Day, known as Eckington Stattis—a corruption of statutes—, when there was a small fair, gypsies and coconuts and roundabouts— but here no diversion was allowed except that, to countrymen, of walking round a town.) It was also a favourite day upon which ploughmen chose to marry their round-faced rustic brides, and many was the procession we watched climb up the hill to the old inn in Newborough, where the wedding breakfast would be held; flushed countenances, seemingly carved out of turnip and then coloured, stolid, listless and good, large red hands crammed into cramping gloves for the occasion, white favours and white flowers.

The town, however, was in no way dependent on such arbitrary connection with the land as these customs would indicate; it derived its scaly, glittering harvest from the waves that could be seen rolling their long lines in exemplary formation. By the fruit of the sea it lived all the autumn, vying proudly with Aberdeen. The quays would be lined nearly every morning with ships, their brown sails furled, and often fleets would be seen under full sail, approaching. Nets bursting with fish, and empty barrels stood upon the stone platform, and the air was strong with the smell of salt and rope and fish, and tar and wood-smoke. The fishwives roared to each other across their tables, slimy and running in the morning sunlight, and the paving itself was slippery from the catch, soon to be smoked and dried. It was such a sight as this, perhaps, the memory of which inspired Thomas Nashe to write, in his *Lenten Stuffe*, "In Prayse of the Red Herring". It must certainly have been familiar to him from a childhood spent in Lowestoft and Yarmouth. Doubtless he is laureate of fishes. "Homer of rats and frogs hath heroiqut it; other oaten pipers after him in praise of the Gnat, the Flea, the Hasill nut, the Grashopper, the Butterflie, the Parrot, the Popiniay, Phillip sparrow, and the Cuckowe; the wantonner sort of them sing descant on their mistris gloue, her ring, her fanne, her looking glasse, her pontofle, and on the same iurie I might impannell *Johannes Secundus*, with his booke of the two hundred kinde of kisses. . . . To recount *ab ouo*, or from the church-booke of his birth, how the Herring first came to be fish, and then how he came to be king of fishes, and gradationately how from white to red he changed, would require as massie a toombe as Hollinshead. . . ." I have written of these scenes elsewhere, and so will only recall to you the vivacious tarpaulin faces of the fishwives, as they sat over their baskets and called to us, and spoke in their broad tongue, for they knew us, and our parents and grandparents before us. A democratic freedom of speech prevailed, and they spoke their idiom, so fine and expressive, with none of the Berlitz School accent that has since become popular in novels. . . . The courage of these women, no less proverbial than that of their men, was hereditary, for fishing was a profession closed by custom to all those not born to it, and the old inn, near by, open in the early hours of the morning especially for sailors setting out, was said to have been built in the days of Richard the Hunchback.

When the great storms of December began to break, and the

rolling, gigantic waves bellowed and roared far out to sea and shook the whole town as they battered and pounded, and the houses seemed caught, themselves, in a net of finely spun spray from the breakers, snowy and mountainous or creamy with sand, I have seen the impassive faces and stoic endurance of these women, waiting for their husbands and fathers, and themselves so well able to value the dangers run, since not one woman in the fishers' quarter but had lost during the passage of the years some relative. I have, too,—to anticipate—been in later years able to compare it—this northern bravery, this waiting and watching, without ever a hint upon their faces of drama, or ever a word suggesting it—with a scene I witnessed in Sicily, when the immense volcano floated, light and iridescent as a bubble upon the horizon. There suddenly one night, when the fishing fleet was out, a storm broke of such tempestuous violence that waves gathered and rolled even through the land-locked harbour of Syracuse. In the purple dawn, loud above the outrageous voice of the sea, could be heard the lamentations of the women as they rushed through the streets to the Cathedral, that had once been the Temple of Neptune, so that the chapels had been fitted in between the Doric pillars of the Sea God, and implored the Madonna to protect the men they loved. They knelt, many of them, with arms lifted horizontally in supplication. Their posture repeated the shape of the Cross, and their mournful, dark-eyed faces streamed with tears. Unforgettable and moving as was this scene, it was not more impressive than the trust and calm reliance on everyday of the Scarborough fishwives, and so let us set the herring, the cause often of tragedy, above the sardine, for all its excellence. "The puissant red herring, the golden *Hersperides* red herring, the *Meonian* red herring, the red herring of red Herrings Hal, euery pregnant peculiar of whose resplendent laude and honour to delineate and adumbrate to the ample life were a woorke that would drinke drie fourscore and eighteene Castalian fountaines of eloquence, consume another *Athens* of facunditie, and abate the haughtiest poetical fury twixt this and the burning Zone and the tropike of Cancer. . . . But no more winde will I spend on it but this: Saint Denis for Fraunce, Saint Iames for Spaine, Saint Patrike for Ireland, Saint George for England, and the red Herring for Yarmouth"—and, let me add, for Scarborough.

The frequent storms gave, indeed, an awful and vivid excitement to life in the winter. For days and nights at a time you could hear the pounding shudder of the vast forces throwing themselves upon stone walls and cliffs, and above it, the distress signals that sounded dull and vague, but infinitely sad, in this upheaval of air and water, these wastes into which the avenging spirit had descended, and in the morning I would listen to Martha telling Davis that the lifeboat had been ordered out seven times in the night, but that once it had been too rough for it to put to sea. (The lifeboat played a chief rôle in our estimation, because, apart from its achievements, the skipper, John Owston, was a great friend of ours, and we would often visit him and be shown round the boat.) But, for all the terror it carried in its tremendous power, I loved the sea passionately then as now, this immense and tragic blind force which seemed somehow, as you stood near it, to change and renew the feeling in every cell of the body; I loved all its moods, but especially the storms and the fine, blown-out mornings that followed them, when the sands at the waters' edge were tumbled, laden with inexplicable treasure, sea fruit and weed and strange shapes in wood and bone and in a substance black as jet and weighing as light.

When the days grew shorter and darker, though, they became for me more miserable. At the age of eighteen months I had a very serious illness, from which I was not expected at the time to recover. Though I contrived to hang on to life, it had left me a rather delicate and nervous child, and I suffered from attacks of that now fortunately extinct, but very terrifying disease, croup. Damp, and in my case especially sea-fogs, mainly induced it, and being, albeit rather backward for my age, by no means stupid, I could detect, some fifteen to twelve hours beforehand, its approach, though still too young to be able to explain the nature of the symptoms and that I recognised them. Thus, since I could only indicate that I expected an onslaught, when it came, those in authority over me, instead of being grateful for the warning they had received, would denounce me for "bringing it on"; a sin visited upon me, when the attack occurred, by extra strong mustard baths that flayed the victim alive as though he were an early Christian martyr, and by doses of the indescribable ipecacuanha, that searing drug which even its name, with, implicit in its mournful but fascinating rhythm, all the lilting tangos of South America, can never redeem. But Davis belonged to a generation which believed in old-fashioned remedies, as did our doctor, with his frock-coat, top-hat and coral-pink stethoscope,[1] that seemed, when he used it, to be an exteriorisation of the breathing apparatus within the body. Both the doctor and Davis immediately quelled any instinctive tendency on the part of an invalid to eat things—such as oranges, for example—which would have cured the malady. The patient must be choked with fortifying delicacies, sago pudding and blancmange, and calves-foot jelly, made of melted hoofs and horseshoes, it seemed. Yet on the whole, I must have obtained a good deal of my own way in the nursery, for I can still hear Davis's favourite cry, where I was concerned: "Anything for peace, Master Osbert." For Edith, her refrain consisted of the words, laden with a burden of repining, "Even slaves have an hour for their dinner."

The light all this time is growing stronger. Nevertheless from my infancy in Scarborough, I can remember incidents more easily than people; incidents better forgotten. Thus I recall only too well how I stole an apple at the age of three from the market —not so much "stole" perhaps as "took," for all children are born communists. It was a lovely autumn morning; within,

---

[1] This instrument, now suffering a decline in glory, was once the outward symbol of a doctor's calling. . . . Thus in "A Scandal in Bohemia", the first of *The Adventures of Sherlock Holmes*, which came out in the year of my birth (1892), I find the following dialogue, though I have had somewhat to condense it, between Holmes and Dr. Watson; which shows how invariable was once the ritual of both top-hat and stethoscope for a medical man:

" 'Wedlock suits you,' he remarked. 'I think, Watson, that you have put on seven and a half pounds since I saw you.'

'Seven,' I answered.

'Indeed, I should have thought a little more. Just a trifle more, I fancy, Watson. And in practice, again, I observe. . . .'

"Then, how do you know? . . .'

'It is simplicity itself . . .,' said he. '. . . As to your practice, if a gentleman walks into my room smelling of iodoform, with a black mark of nitrate upon his right forefinger, and a bulge on the side of his top-hat to show where he has secreted his stethoscope, I must be dull indeed if I do not pronounce him to be an active member of the medical profession.' "

the cool and shadowy lanes of the great stone temple were lined with mounds of rosy fruit, which scented the air, impregnated it with a sweetness almost like decay. The whole world was my apple, and I was tempted. I managed, as the saying goes, to "get away with it," though how my furtive munching escaped Davis's attention, I cannot imagine; presumably she was talking about life and death—her favourite subjects—to one of her friends. The apple-woman waited until we had left, and then stumped up the hill to see my father, acquaint him of his son and heir's disgrace, and to demand five pounds as the price of her silence; otherwise, she hinted, he might find himself at the bottom of the poll at the next election.

The next episode is hardly less discreditable. On a hot summer day I was taken down by Davis to the sands to bathe. I very much resented the squalor of the old bathing machine (I can still remember the feeling of sand upon the warm wooden floor under my feet), poised, one of a long line, upon its high wheels: but when I stepped out, and was led into the water, my fury knew no bounds. I hated crowds, communal life and obedience as much as I do now, and regarded the whole proceeding as unnecessary and undignified. Accordingly, when for a moment Davis looked behind her, I lay down resolutely under the foot or so of receding water and with determination held my breath, until I was hoiked out, dressed, and began to roar at the top of my voice as I was conveyed home in a cab.

During the long winter evenings there were fairy stories— of which my father strongly disapproved, holding that they developed the imagination in the wrong channels—to be followed by the usual childish terrors of cupboards and dark places. On the other hand, when tardy spring at last arrived, when the bands played and the barrel-organs, I would dance to them with abandon. And, about this time, when I was three or four, my mother in an inspired moment decided to arrange with John Owston, the captain of the lifeboat (whom I have mentioned before), to give me lessons in dancing the hornpipe. He used to come to Belvoir House twice a week to teach me. How much I looked forward to those mornings, and enjoyed talking to the old fisherman with his mahogany face and fringe of white beard, and asking him endless questions about the sea and his rescues! . . . I made good progress, too, and was soon willing to give displays of my prowess in nautical cory-bantics on the slightest provocation. . . . On other occasions I would dance to a very different tune, for I used to dance from temper, and one or two of my cousins liked to make a point of annoying me on purpose, in order to be treated to this spectacle.

In a moment I will tell you of my cousins and of the life of which they were part; but I am only just beginning to see them, or to range beyond members of our own household. Indeed, I can remember, with the utmost distinctness, an animal, almost before I can remember human beings. Henry Moat's brother, Bill, was a fisherman, and used to bring over to see us from Whitby a tame seal. He had caught it during a whaling cruise, and it now lived in the backyard of his ancestral house at Whitby. It can be imagined with what mingled pride, pleasure and interest my sister and I made the acquaintance of this new friend, who flopped about the sands after us in the most flattering way, used suddenly to come up and poke his nose at the back of his master's knee so that he would nearly fall down, and would then bellow loudly for fish. . . . The reader may wonder how such a slippery customer was con-veyed to us. . . . Unlikely as it sounds, by train, and then by cab. Bill was a well-known character in Whitby, and was allowed to take his seal with him in a third-class carriage. He would have charge of its head, a porter would help him by pushing from below, and the sleek creature would ride beside him, giving a delicious breath of the ocean—and of fish—to the whole of the compartment. Once arrived at Scarborough, they would take a cab, sent by my mother, the seal again sitting beside him, and looking round with interest at place and people.

It seemed fitting, and in no way strange to us—or to any that knew either of them—that the brother of Henry, who belonged, like all his family, in his very essence to the sea, coming of a whole dynasty of sailors and fishermen, should possess such a pet. . . . Many years later, just after the First Great War, I went over to Whitby from Scarborough and called on Bill, then an old man. He was at work in the paved yard of the old panelled house, concealed in the narrow alley that ran along the hillside, engaged in making a dummy, in the likeness of the Kaiser—I forget why, since Guy Fawkes Day was past —, to be burnt by the children. The seal—or perhaps a successor—was flapping languidly and watching the proceedings with appreciation. . . . It was an extraordinarily traditional scene, in the style of one of the episodes from Hardy's *The Dynasts*; the old fisherman, the dummy (taking the place, no doubt, of others made by his ancestors of Napoleon and, before him, of Louis XIV), the seal, the very emblem of his former calling. And over all, in his speech and in his movements, was to be felt the rhythm and vigour of the dynamic northern seas.

This was all my experience of places and people, so far, except for two excursions into the outer world.

When I paid my first visit I was three years of age. Davis's father was a cobbler in a small village near Newbury in Berkshire, and she was going home to spend a few days with her parents, who were both very old. Since I refused to be parted from her for an instant, she—though it must have spoilt her holiday—nevertheless, in accordance with the principle of appeasement which she had adopted where I was concerned ("Anything for peace, Master Osbert!"), arranged to take me with her. How clearly it comes back to me! Perhaps I remember it so well because that the visit took place at all, constituted, I even then realised, a personal triumph; my mother was jealous, my father disapproved, my sister would like to have gone too, and the governess was frankly furious; by the sheer power of my plaguing I had obtained, almost for the first time, my own way.

Certainly every detail of my stay lives in my memory: our arrival, very tired, at the cottage on an evening of timeless June, the long shadows of the trees on our way there, and how I woke up the next morning, very early, because of the excitement of the change, and how at that hour the light of the sun still lay flat as feathers along the ledges of the windows. Presently the rays slanted downwards, and there were signs of activity. Life seemed very intimate and enclosed here, after the larger houses to which I was accustomed; warm and compact and lacking in any sense of fear. There were no creaking boards, no inexplicable rustlings, no feeling of interruption if one ran into an empty room. Every noise here made explicit

its meaning. I heard now, as I lay there beside Davis who was
still fast asleep, the sounds that accompanied her father's getting-
up, the washings and splashings and crinkling tug of clothes
being put on, then his going downstairs, moving about, lighting
the fire and washing the dishes. Soon after, I heard the sizzling
of bacon as he crisped it on a fork before the fire for my breakfast—for, I do not know why, he, not his wife, did this part of
the cooking—, and then there reached me the talking of rustic
voices below.

From contrast with the surroundings I had left, the primi-
tive conditions of this cottage existence seemed to offer a new
kind of idyllic comfort, composed of warmth and simple ease.
Everything I saw, I touched, I ate, possessed a new value for
me. Even the waking-up so early was in itself a joy, I comprehended, as I lay there in bed, touching the warm reality of
Davis's body, for I stretched out a foot against her leg. The
shafts of light now entered the windows, and I watched happily
the gay vibrations of their dancing motes, which seemed,
because of the intensity with which I gazed at them, to contain
an augury, if not a revelation, of the future, though I could
never fully grasp it. (I think all children are superstitious, even
when very young, and I was exceptionally prone to omens.)
It was difficult to trace the precise patterns formed by these
glittering constellations; but the light itself brought joy with
it. . . . Always I see the light, the quality of light in which
things existed, light, which is the immaterial side of material
objects.

After I had been dressed and had eaten the bacon, so crisp
and delicious, I was allowed to sit in the workshop, full of the
smell of leather, and watch the old cobbler hammering at his
last and listen to him talking through the din to his friends.
. . . Then, after that, there were the walks, accompanied by
the angelic host—fair-haired and round-eyed—of Davis's
numerous nephews and nieces, through the flat, flowery
meadows so different from the abrupt, dramatic country to
which I was used. As a rule shy of other children, with these
I was at my ease, for I loved all beings and all things belonging
to Davis. Indeed these promenades retain in my memory an
idyllic and pastoral note that I was only momentarily able to

regain, thirty years later, among the broken columns, dry river-
beds, and green hillsides of Olympia, albeit I was never able to
identify the common denominator between the lanes of Greece,
bossed and honeycombed with flowers, and these Berkshire
meadows; probably it was the scent of some particular blossom.
. . . Many flowers here did not grow at Renishaw or near Scarborough; the brown and yellow pansies, cornflowers and large
crimson pimpernels were all new to me and fascinated me, as
they glowed and expanded in this moment of high summer
which, looked back on, seemed to hold all eternity in its golden
and hazy light.

In wild flowers, the names of which Davis taught me—
and how much more of value I learned from her than from any
governess or tutor!—, I took, after the fashion of most infants,
an extraordinary pleasure. And the reason of this delight is
perhaps worth tracing: to be sought, it may be, not only in the
child's innocence and freedom from other sources of gratifica-
tion, but in a more obvious cause; the beauty they see in such
common things as buttercups and daisies may be due, not only
to their lack of sophistication and the comparative newness to
them of these flowers, but because, in addition, they are, while
they play, so much nearer to the ground, to the impeccable
yellow glaze of the buttercup bowls and the complicated, rosy
design of the speckled daisy centre and the manifold radiating
petals, to the infinite, bloomy complication of these simplicities,
set against their background of grass, that enormous wood the
blades of which point to heaven as if they were the spears and
lances of a great army, and the green depths of which are full
of crepitation and the whirring of wings, while through them
move fearful monsters, comparable to those painted by Hier-
onymus Bosch, armoured beetles, spectral green grasshoppers
chafing their legs, and caterpillars with vast protruding eyes.
Above these writhing and terrifying creatures, far above them,
tower the flaming forest trees, sorrel or flowering grass, and the
huge moons of the ox-eye daisies seem to them to hang down
from the sky itself.

I see, still, the faces of the children who played with me, as
we peered into the green depths, looking for new flowers. . . .
But this brief pastoral episode was soon over. My next, my

second, visit was of a different kind, accompanied by my entire family and paid to my grandfather and grandmother at Londesborough. And it must have taken place, I think, in the late May of the following year, for I remember that the hawthorns, grafted pink on white or red on white, were carrying their chequered banners, exhaling their curious and alluring perfume—not so much sweet as enticing, making you want to smell the blossom, so as to make sure of what it smells—over the hilly, beautifully shaped park.

There were whole continents apart, these two houses; this was a different world, given over to those pomps and vanities which, in their own day so overwhelming, notwithstanding, leave no shadow behind them—unless they are fortunate enough to catch for a moment the attention of a Rowlandson or a Constantin Guys, and so remain fixed in the eye of time—; a world of horses, carriages and liveries, an immense machine, producing little, unless it were the love given it for its own sake, scarcely, even, rewarding with smooth working, still less with any pleasure, those to whom it ministered. Here there were major-domos, grooms of the chamber, powdered footmen, wearing velvet knee-breeches on the right occasions, grooms, gamekeepers, the cool and ordered processes of the dairy, and stables full of haughty and glossy gods, well tended. In their fragile glass cases were caged the steamy fragments of Africa and Asia, orchids and rare, strong-smelling flowers, while, in their seasons, ripe peaches and grapes and nectarines and melons flourished within their crystal orchards.

The park, I remember, contained groves of immense dead trees, as well as living, for my grandmother, though in other directions of by no means so soft a disposition, would not allow them to be cut down, because to see an old tree felled always made her cry. In consequence, these gnarled, gigantic skeletons, standing in groups, seemed to preserve, within the general leafy paradise, their own bony deserts of winter, and in their antique desolation, contrasted with the well-drilled, even ranks of trees of the younger plantations which soared up the hillsides, and then swept down again as sharply. Every branch in them seemed to shelter a cock pheasant that, giving its Chinese cries, flew whirring like a rocket out from it as we passed. A whole army of

men looked after the domestic life of these birds until the time
came for their slaughter. We used to stand below the plantations, with my grandfather and uncle, while eggs or young
chicks were brought up to be shown to us. . . . How tall they
seemed, both trees and men; for my uncle—my mother's only
brother—was six foot six inches, and my grandfather was but
an inch or two shorter.

As a rule, however, all day long the men of the party were
out, only returning for their meals. In the mornings, Edith
and I would wait with some trepidation for our summons to an
audience with our grandmother—not so much that we were
frightened or had cause to be, as because it was plain that our
parents, our governess and nurse quailed before the ordeal. . . .
Then, afterwards, tension having relaxed, we would spend the
rest of the sun-streaked hours before luncheon sitting with
Davis in the pleasure-grounds, as they were called, which lay
some distance from the house. They, together with the avenue
of cedars which led to them, had been planted by the great
patron, Lord Burlington,[1] who had also made the lake. Davis
would read to us, or tell us ghost stories (which she was strictly
forbidden to do by my father). I remember she told us that a
Cavalier, carrying his head under his arm, haunted the cedar
avenue. I never much believed, even at so early an age, in
ghosts of that romantic sort, but was impressed when she told
me—what subsequently I found out to be true—that old Mr.
Wilton,[2] the parson, had seen this headless Cavalier not many
months before. Mr. Wilton had long been rector here, and had
constantly, during the course of twenty years or so, walked
through the avenue on his way to dine with my grandparents.
But one Sunday, a year or two before, in the dusk of a summer

[1] Richard Boyle, 3rd Earl of Burlington and 4th Earl of Cork (1695-1753).
A patron of many architects, especially Colin Campbell and William Kent,
and the creator of many palaces and gardens including the old Burlington
House, and Chiswick House, as well as Londesborough. He was really
responsible for the continuance of Palladian buildings and taste in England,
when the whole of the rest of Europe had adopted the Baroque or the
Rococo, or both. He was himself an amateur architect, designed parts of the
various buildings for which he gave the credit to others, and profoundly
influenced the professional architects he employed so liberally. The old
house at Londesborough had been taken down in 1819, and the present
building, without any claim to beauty, was erected in 1839.

[2] The Rev. Richard Wilton, M.A.

day, he had suddenly seen—or was under the impression that he saw—this Wardour Street anachronism walking towards him. Just as he drew face to shoulder—one cannot say face to face—with it, the spectre disappeared, and he never saw it again.

In these sunny hours, such things were not frightening, though at night the stories had a habit of returning to the mind. But the days of childhood are very long and the night lay so far ahead. In the afternoon we walked by the side of our grandmother's bath-chair, accompanied by our mother and her tall sisters, in slow progress round the red-walled kitchen gardens full of every sort of sweet-scented leaf, myrtle and geranium and verbena. And, at tea-time, we fell back into the rhythm of the nursery. . . . This life went on for some time, until I let my parents down by developing that mysterious "summer cold," an ailment which so frequently afflicts children, and which, in the houses of relatives as opposed to one's own home, always carried with it a suggestion of disgrace. . . . No doubt in my case this *congestion*, as it would aptly be termed in France, had been caused by over-indulgence in the most delicious chocolate-cake in the world, a speciality of the house. The taste of it, as I write, I can still recall vividly as the varying flavours of the old-fashioned remedies made in the still-room, such as black-currant tea, to which my consequent indisposition and confinement to bed rendered me for some days subject.

It is all very clear, and the light, still growing stronger, shows me many figures beginning to emerge with sharp outlines. . . . Thus, during this visit, my mother took Edith and me to see many friends of hers, and I especially remember the aged and devout Mary-Anne, who tended the birds on the lake. She lived in a small cottage, entirely furnished with patchwork, on an island, and her image crystallised for me about thirty years later, for I never saw her again: and the interest that perhaps attaches to the working of creative processes must be my excuse for introducing this portrait here.

> Mary-Anne,[1]
> Wise, simple old woman,
> Lived in a patchwork pavilion,

[1] From *England Reclaimed*.

Pitched on an island,
Feeding the piebald and the tartan ducks.
Flotillas of ducks
Lie low in the water,
And Mary-Anne seems
The Duck-King's daughter.

The floating ducks crack up in their arrow-pointed wake
The distorted, silent summer painted in the lake,
And the days disappear
In a leaden stare.

Then Mary-Anne waddles
Through the evening cool,
And a smell of musk
Lingers by the pool,
For the trembling fingers of the honeysuckle
Wring out the blue and the dew-drenched dusk.

At night the pavilion
Is hung by a silver cord
That the nightingales plait
With their intercoiling song.
Within Mary-Anne mutters
The Word of the Lord,
Till the candle gutters,
As the summer sighs outside
And taps
At the shutters.

CHAPTER THREE

Sacred and Profane Love

THE world of relatives I have just described recurrently
expanded, in the late, or less frequently, in the early
summer, when the members of my mother's family would
arrive in Scarborough for a sojourn, in large numbers and with
quantities of children. Usually we would go to Renishaw before
they returned to their homes; but even in the few weeks or days
of our being there together, there would be all kinds of new
amusements for us.

My grandfather Londesborough was devoted to children
and had a fascinating manner with them. He liked to take
Edith or me—or sometimes both of us, though there was
scarcely room—for a drive in his buck-board, a then fast and
dashing equipage (there were of course no motors in those
days), balanced precariously on two enormous wheels and
drawn by, one would have said, a permanently bolting horse.
My grandfather chose this vehicle, because it could be driven
over the countryside, without following a road, and could
actually cross ditches without its occupants incurring any mis
hap worse than a severe shaking. But he was a famous whip
the president of the Four-in-hand Club, and we trusted him
implicitly even when the drive became unusually exciting
As a rule we first went through Raincliffe Woods, to the beauti
ful and celebrated Forge Valley, where a groom would be
waiting to take the reins. My grandfather would give him
orders to meet us in some other valley, while we walked up one
of the steep hills, thickly covered with trees, and down the
other side. (Here, in their season, you could discover the
beautiful burnet-coloured wild columbine, tangles of the
sweetest honeysuckle, and many rarer flowers.) The woods
were large, however, and the meeting-places difficult to find as
in the Forest of Arden, and if the arrangements he had made
went wrong, as most frequently they did, my grandfather's
language—famous, like his son's after him, for a wealth and
warmth of imagery that, perhaps, suffering a metamorphosis
is to be traced, identically, in the poetry and writings of three

of his grandchildren—for a moment echoed far and wide. Suddenly he would remember our presence, and hush his voice for the sake of the young, so that only very occasionally we glimpsed the real works of art at the end of these fascinating and unfamiliar vistas. Sometimes, again, he would carry us off to the cliffs, to show us where the Grass of Parnassus flourished, a delicately veined, pale flower, uncommon in England, half sorrel, half snowdrop, swaying on a wire-thin stalk, to near-by dells, nigh hidden in their rocky clefts, where grew the yet rarer Herb Paris, a green flower with a monk's cowl to match and hanging head, or to Cayton Bay, where we would walk from the high cliffs down to the deserted shore, on which the waves, always the fiercest in the neighbourhood, washed up quantities of shells, nacreous or rusty or rose-pink, shaped like the spires of Wren's churches, or like ears, or like the very shells from which Venus arose on the Paphian shore. Or he would take us to see where the sea-birds nested, or to some other of his domains, for the cliffs belonged to him as well as the woods. Indeed he was still in those days one of the largest landed pro-prietors in England—Scottish land-owners possessed, of course, bigger estates, but they were usually somewhat barren. He could ride, it was said, from Scarborough to Londesborough, sixty miles away, without leaving his own ground; and the estate included whole towns, such as Selby.

In appearance he was, as I have said, very tall and rather dark, with a longish, pointed beard. In repose there was a certain air of Spanish dignity about him, and he possessed a combined distinction and ease of manner which enabled him to get on well with everyone. In his clothes, too, he displayed a very personal style. When he took us out driving, he always wore an ulster with, at the back, a hood which, after the fashion of a monk's cowl, he could put over his head if it rained. Many years previously he had lost an eye, as a result of a shooting party (though no one had yet dared to tell my grandmother the name of the friend responsible for the accident). Thus, in addition to the particular charm he undoubtedly exercised, his glass eye, with its fixed and lucent stare, proved a great source of attraction to his grandchildren and promoted him in their regard to the legendary and heroic status of a Nelson.

It is difficult, extremely difficult, to present the peculiar essence of the charm that someone long dead exercised half a century ago. Times change, and charm changes with them. W. B. Maxwell, the novelist, and his mother, the celebrated Victorian novelist Miss Braddon, lived near my grandparents in the New Forest and knew them well. Maxwell felt the spell of my grandfather, and so I here reproduce an account[1] of him and his daughters as they were some ten years before the time of which I write; for it gives an idea of his character and surroundings.

"Swell, I love that word for a person of extreme excellence and splendour. I don't know what young people call them nowadays—not bucks, bloods, or nuts. . . . Our permanent local swell,[2] and a big one at that, was Lord Londesborough, the well-known person I have mentioned before as being a lavish patron of the theatre. He possessed many houses— Londesborough Park, The Lodge at Scarborough, and later Blankney, as well as the largest house in Berkeley Square, into which Lord Rosebery moved when he gave it up. But I think he and his family were fondest of the home he had made for them in the New Forest. He had one son, Francis, who succeeded him, and four daughters. I had a great liking for Francis Denison, but we had more to do with his sisters. In the summer they used to come to us at Richmond for a happy day, and those visits gave us the greatest pleasure. We took them for drives to Bushey Park and Hampton Court, and played games of hide-and-seek indoors, and cross-touch in the garden. They were charming, attractive young people—the eldest, Lady Sybil, nearly grown-up, and the others, the Ladies Lilian, Ida and Mildred, following her fast. . . . Lady Ida had brown hair, a bright complexion, an impulsive manner, and was really the most delightful girl imaginable."

The houses which Maxwell enumerates at the beginning of this passage were luxurious but contained little of interest. My grandfather had long ago disposed of Grimston and had from

---

[1] W. B. Maxwell in his book of memoirs, *Time Gathered*. (Hutchinson & Co., 1937.)

[2] I notice the writer of a book called *Society in London*, by a foreign resident (Chatto & Windus, 1885), begins, too, his description of my grandfather, "Lord Londesborough is a typical specimen of the English Swell".

time to time—to meet, perhaps, the calls made upon his purse by some particular act of extravagance—parted with the various remarkable collections of *objets d'art* which he had inherited from his father. . . . The furniture from the Petit Trianon, for example, which I have mentioned, had been brought up to London some years before, in order for it to be offered under the hammer at Christie's. It had been stored for one night, preceding its removal to the auction rooms, in a famous warehouse and had, during those few brief hours, been burned. . . . Pictures, armour and missals, china and furniture had gone; everything except the jewels and plate. The rooms were empty of things of beauty: though his house in London,[1] in which my mother was born, had a certain intrinsic charm, derived from the L-shaped dining-room of George II's time, looking out on to a garden, and to the several later apartments designed by the brothers Adam, and with ceilings decorated by Angelica Kauffmann.

Londesborough Lodge, his house in Scarborough, which had been bought and "improved" by Lord Albert, had no large rooms in it, but was an enchanting place for seaside *villeggiatura*—if such a phrase is not a contradiction in terms. The rooms, small but numerous, were set in their own world of strange trees. Cut flat at the top, these were grotesquely bent by the winter winds, so that they resembled a whole grove of Daphnes frozen in permanent flight from the cool waves below. The state, the organisation of household and garden and stable, that prevailed, even in this comparatively small house, would seem remarkable to-day—would, even, have seemed remarkable yesterday. When the family descended to the Spa, by way of the private bridge which crossed the main thoroughfare that led to the sands, red carpets, literal as well as metaphorical, had to be put down for them; almost a mile of red carpet. It was, indeed, an atmosphere of the hill-tops—though not mentally, I am afraid: but it was pleasant, welcoming, luxurious, and the thought never occurred to any of those living in it that it might

[1] Formerly it had a plain stucco front of the eighteenth century, but the late Lord Rosebery, when he bought it, added a façade of red brick, and turned the old laundry at the back—it was the last London house to possess its own laundry—into an Italian ballroom. This house existed almost until the war, being pulled down before the Germans could get at it, in 1939.

not be deserved. Moreover, the genuine good-feeling which lay under what some people might have thought the sycophancy evinced in various directions, had, in truth, been earned by the kindly qualities of the principals.

No: my grandfather's houses—and in particular, perhaps, The Lodge—depended for their quality not upon beauty, but upon *fun*. He was still dissipating his fortune in a thousand different directions. It seemed as though the special money sense which had enabled earlier generations to build up their prodigious fortune had, in their descendants, become hyper-trophied, so that they could exercise no restraint in spending it. And this extravagance, which all who come of our blood share, produced results which were sometimes as unexpected in their fantasy as, at others, they were tragic. Of the lighter consequences, I recall, for example, a remark of one of my grandfather's younger sisters, who, when I grew up, often entertained me in her large and hospitable house. Tall and thin, and like all her sisters, with a beautifully cut profile and turn of head, she looked astonishingly young for her age, and had kept her vivacity. She loved seeing people, and at luncheon there were always a great many guests. The food was good and plentiful, but one day, when I arrived early, she said to me, "Dear boy, I fear you'll find these luncheons rather monoton-ous, but they're ordered by the trustees"; for the lavishness of the household bills in the past, obliged them now, in order to prevent expenditure in this direction, to supply her with salmon and chicken and garden produce from her country estate.

Nobody, however, dared to interfere with my grandfather. Occasionally, I am told, he would suffer from hours of exag-gerated depression over his money affairs and exaggerated abnegation, hours in which he believed himself to be utterly ruined, and would refuse to spend a farthing: but they were quickly followed by a reversion to his normal lavish moods of spending money, and of his intense pleasure in doing so. A great deal had, of course, already gone. Yachts, races, coaches, carriages, sport of every kind, especially shooting, speculation and the stage were the chief channels he had found for ridding himself of his earthly burden. His houses, as I have said, teemed with servants, and his first act in 1861, on inheriting the fortune, had been to provide all his chief servants with cheque-books so that they could draw on his funds at the bank without worrying him for his authority: after a year or two, however, the remonstrances of his angry bankers induced him to cancel this comfortable and original arrangement. Stables and gardens were decorative hives of idleness. His carriages had long been famous for their smartness, the horses for their gloss, speed and style.[1]

All channels for waste, then, were welcome, but the most rewarding in sheer expense, and certainly his favourite, was the theatre. In this connection, again, W. B. Maxwell[2] describes the sort of company my grandfather enjoyed, and various of his activities.

"It was in this year that I went to the first of two or three quite entertaining Henley parties. These were given by Lord Londesborough, the local potentate of the New Forest. Their scene was a houseboat, named *The Ark*, from which, however, we could issue if we wished and take a little tour in punts or canoes or skiffs on the crowded river. But the company it was that so greatly delighted me . . . theatrical stars of both sexes, with the very prettiest of the actresses, together with a selected band of our host's innumerable friends, for the most part, like himself, of noble rank. . . . Lord Londesborough was a patron of the stage, and was reputed to have lost thirty thousand pounds in one production—*Babil and Bijou*, a musical spectacle. For some years he ran the Olympic Theatre, with Henry Neville,[3] in legitimate drama. It was on *The Ark* that I consolidated my acquaintance with dear Mrs. John Wood, the comedy actress, and Lionel Brough, the comedian."

[1] Repercussions of any feature of life in the nineteenth century are apt to occur in quarters that are unexpected. Thus, in the second volume of that charming, unworldly book, Kilvert's Diary (*Selections from the Diary of the Revd. Francis Kilvert*, edited by William Plomer: Jonathan Cape, 1939), I find the following entry for the 7th of April 1872: "Colonel Pearson . . . said that in his capacity as chief of Police, he was applied to, to let four carriages draw up within the rails at Buckingham Palace. Strictly it ought not to have been allowed but he permitted it. The four equipages were faultless, acknowledged to be the finest in London, and had been pitted against each other. They were Lord Derby's, Lord Sefton's, Lord Londesborough's and Lord Craven's.

[2] In *Time Gathered*.

[3] Henry Neville was the lessee and manager of the Olympic Theatre from 1873 to 1879. His productions included Byron's comedy *Sour Grapes*, Mortimer's *School for Intrigue*, the *Two Orphans*, Coppée's *Violin-maker of*

W. B. Maxwell, it will be noted, mentions thirty thousand pounds as the sum my grandfather was currently supposed to have lost over a single theatrical venture: but I have always understood from others that it was a hundred thousand. And it can be well imagined how eager I had been, ever since I first heard of it, to find out more concerning this fascinating financial escapade of my grandfather's. Nor, now that I have come to know more of it, do I consider it as by any means merely financial. It was, in the true sense, an escapade; for, though by no means a clever man, he was no doubt more than usually susceptible to atmosphere and emotion, and his backing of *Babil and Bijou* constituted an attempt on his part to *escape*, to deliver himself from the settled, foggy, humdrum air of mid-Victorian London, and regain for the evening the less conventional, flaring ambience of a Paris that had only just died so violent a death in the siege and Commune, a Paris that had only three or four years before been the pleasure centre of the world, numbering not least among the joys it offered the always skilful and often inspired comic operas of Offenbach, with Hortense Schneider as their chief ornament. The very essence of that gilded, contaminated city, where life had been pleasant, free of every duty except dissipation, had been distilled by such entertainments as these that he hoped to introduce. . . . The reader, therefore, will allow me again to step out of my childhood for a moment, so that I may take him to look for a few minutes at a forgotten episode in English theatrical history; an episode that, it is true, led to none of the ends anticipated for it, but, notwithstanding, attracted at the time enormous attention.

When I first possessed the leisure wherein to make these enquiries—which was directly after the last war—, the early 'seventies of the past century already seemed so distant, that it

Cremona, Wilkie Collins' *The Moonstone*, and Gilbert's *Ne'er-do-Weel*. His chief success was as Lord Clancarty in Tom Taylor's *Lady Clancarty*. He was born in 1837, the twentieth child of a twentieth child, John Neville, manager of the Queen's Theatre, Spring Gardens, and was first brought on the stage in his father's arms as the child in *Pizarro*. All the members of his family went into the army, and his refusal to do so estranged him from his father. "Though he lived for the theatre," says the *D.N.B.*, ". . . he painted, carved and modelled with taste, took a keen interest in sport and was . . . a crack rifle shot . . . a man of sound business capacity". He was, it adds, a "romantic actor of the old flamboyant school". He died in 1910.

appeared almost impossible to find out anything concerning *Babil and Bijou*. Certainly I never expected to be given an account of the entertainment by an eye-witness, far less by a member of the first-night audience.

It must have been one night in 1925—for, alas, he died the following year—that A. B. Walkley,[1] for many years the dramatic critic of *The Times*, came to dine with my brother and myself. I had met him first at the house of Mr. and Mrs. Somerset Maugham in Wyndham Place, in the large, beige-painted, barrel-vaulted drawing-room of which delightful eighteenth-century mansion their friends were privileged to meet all the most interesting figures connected with the worlds of art, literature and the theatre, both here and in America. A remarkable character, he belonged to a traditional type which inevitably has something in it of the dandy's attributes; the Englishman with a passion for French culture. Short, rather stout, with a little black imperial and very black and shiny hair, and with an eye-glass attached to a broad black ribbon, he could easily have been mistaken for a French literary man of the 'eighties or 'nineties. It would have been with pleasure, no doubt, that he would have welcomed such an instance of mistaken identity. And yet, the fact that he was an Englishman came through the French polish, to give him, in addition, just something of the air of a stage Frenchman. He sprinkled his conversation, always interesting and often witty, with French phrases and allusions, and he also modelled the style in which he wrote upon that of the French critics of his youth. Though we knew that he had been connected with the theatre for very many years, it seemed improbable that he had seen *Babil and Bijou*. . . . Idly I asked him if he had ever heard anything about it, and the delight of my brother and myself can be imagined when he replied that he had been in the audience on the first night. Perhaps the French tinge of its name may have been responsible for his presence there, but he stated that he had enjoyed the performance. Further, he declared that, if it had

[1] Arthur Bingham Walkley, 1855-1926. He was originally a clerk in the secretary's office of the General Post Office. He became the dramatic critic of *The Star* in 1888 and *The Times* in 1900. His articles were very carefully written and full of personal style. The *D.N.B.* talks of his "fearless gaiety in attack".

been produced half a century later, its success would have been tremendous, so much was it in the taste of the revue-ridden times in which we were at that moment talking. The curtain, for example, he told us, had been made of drops of water (if it had been made of champagne it could scarcely have proved more costly) and, to persuade the audience of the stark reality of the scene before them, which represented the ocean bottom, live lobsters—not pantomime lobsters, but genuine, black crustaceans—had gambolled and waved friendly claws from among the rocks at the back of the stage.

As a theatrical convention, I thought, at the time he told me, that it had been a mistake to allow the lobsters to face the limelight in their own black shells—because these remain to the conditioned mind of the consumer peculiarly unconvincing. It was, in fact, a technical error, comparable to allowing the chorus of a musical comedy to come on without make-up. . . . Perhaps I mistook what he said, or perhaps Walkley's memory misled him in this instance, for he can only have been seventeen or eighteen years of age when he saw *Babil and Bijou*. Certainly the programme, now in the possession of my brother, of "This New Fantastic Musical Drama", as it is described, makes no mention of *real* lobsters, though, in the third act, on the other hand, it specifies a chorus of "Oysters, Crabs, Cockles, Seals, Sea Lions, Sea Horses, Sea Anemones, Sharks, Alligators, Swordfish, Devil fish, Starfish and Lobsters".

Babil and Bijou was first produced at Covent Garden on the night of the 29th of August 1872 and ran for one hundred and sixty performances. The programme tells us that Mr. Dion Boucicault was the lessee—and had written "The Drama", as opposed to the "Lyrical Part" by Planché—and Lionel Brough,[1] who also appeared on the boards, the stage-manager. The feast provided for the theatre-going public must have been extensive as well as expensive, for it began at seven, and was not over, one paper states, until the audience, having pelted Mr. Boucicault and the principal artists "with the last bouquet in Covent Garden", dispersed finally "on the stroke of midnight". The piece possessed an enormous cast, which I will

---

[1] See footnote on pp. 260 and 264 respectively for details of Boucicault's and Brough's careers.

not detail here because the names of the chief performers will occur, as though casually, in a moment. The scenes were very varied, being extremely numerous and fantastic in their invention, and I may mention that a large ballet company also took part.[1] Its chief star was the captivating Mademoiselle Henriette D'Or in the part of *Iris*, while Madame Espinosa danced the rôle of *Maxaia, Chief of the Tartars*, and her husband, Monsieur Espinosa, acted as Ballet Master throughout, and made his second appearance on the English stage, this time in the capacity of *A Dancing Dervish*.

To return to our lobsters, and allow them to act as *compère* and *commère* to the evening's show, let us read what Clement Scott has to say[2] in this connection, for he offers us his testimony concerning both them and their producer, Dion Boucicault. "I saw very little of him", he writes, "after that strange and unaccountable disappearance to America on the night of the outrageously costly spectacle *Babil and Bijou* at Covent Garden, when, having been asked by that devoted and loyal patron of the drama—Lord Londesborough—to write a play or comedy, he of course did neither, but literally made ducks and drakes of his friend's money, and produced a quite unnecessary spectacle, with reckless extravagance.

"He engaged Helen Barry for a stately Amazon, which, indeed, she was, and of the most remarkable beauty; introduced Henriette D'Or, one of the most graceful dancers of the old ballet school ever seen in this country; gave commissions to the veteran Planché to write verses for the music of Hervé and Fred Clay; asked Rivière to compose songs and choruses, amongst which was the celebrated "Spring, Spring, beautiful Spring"[3] for boys' voices, one of the unexpected successes of

---

[1] In Appendix C, on p. 260, I have assembled for any reader who may be interested in the subject, information concerning the *Féerie* in general, and contemporary accounts of *Babil and Bijou* and its magnificence.

[2] Clement William Scott (1841-1904), dramatic critic of the *Daily Telegraph* for many years, in *The Drama of Today and Yesterday*. (Macmillan & Co., 1899.)

[3] This constituted what would now be termed the "smash-hit" of the piece, and was sung, whistled and ground out on street organs in every town in Great Britain for several years. It was apt to come to life again now and then, after a period of quiescence. The boys who sang it were selected chiefly from the choir of the Brompton Oratory.

the play; gave us Mrs. Howard Paul, Mrs. Billington, Lal Brough, J. B. Howe, Turtle Jones—called so on account of the creature of calipash and calipee he represented; served up scarlet boiled lobsters at the bottom of the ocean, committed himself to innumerable anachronisms; and then made tracks for America....'

It can, then, be deduced, that whether or not real lobsters, boiled or unboiled, appeared in this production, a number of genuine—and, if one may be permitted such a phrase,—hard-boiled sharks were connected with it. . . . Yet in spite—or perhaps because—of this, the opening of *Babil and Bijou* seems to have been awaited with positive expectancy and impatience, and when, at last, the first performance took place, to have caused a prodigious stir. . . . Indeed for many reasons it was a notable evening, full of attempts at novelty, great and small, though all alike in their failure: while these efforts were not confined to the stage, but were forced upon the audience as well. For example, a journal remarks, "It will be extremely interesting to watch the results of Mr. Boucicault's daring innovation in allowing ladies to wear their bonnets wherever they are seated".

Though *Babil and Bijou* did not, as I had formerly thought, run only for a single night, though it endured for one hundred and sixty performances and even enjoyed occasional revivals, notwithstanding, Clement Scott was able to brand it[1] as "the most scandalous waste of money on record". But whether the figure of thirty thousand pounds or one hundred thousand pounds, given variously as the cost to the backer, is correct, the reader may wonder how so long a run could end in so grave a loss. No doubt the answer is that the theatre did not shut its doors until the money put up had been exhausted. Even longer runs have ended in disaster to the "angels" of the piece.[2]

Most of the papers were in agreement concerning the strict propriety of the performance. The *Daily Telegraph* declared it to be "unexceptionable", and said that "from one end to the other, there is not a trace of indecency, fastness, vulgarity or bad taste".

Others there were, however, who held contrary opinions. An echo of another sort, this time by way of a book, reaches us

[1] In a footnote to *The Life and Reminiscences of E. L. Blanchard*, edited by Clement Scott and Cecil Howard. (Hutchinson & Co., 1891.)

[2] *Florodora*, for example, enjoyed a run of four hundred and fifty-five performances.

faintly from the distance. Augustus Hare, writing[1] in February 1877, four years after *Babil and Bijou* had been withdrawn, tells us that he had recently met Mr. Knowles, ex-editor of the *Contemporary Review*, at luncheon. Knowles, in describing how he had once taken Tennyson to see a ballet, and how "when the ballet girls trooped in, wearing *'une robe qui ne commence qu'à peine, et qui finit tout de suite'*, Tennyson had rushed at once out of the box, in an agony over the degradation of the nineteenth century", had added that "a general improvement in the stage had dated from a climax of impropriety in *Babil and Bijou*". (Special half-price terms, I note from the programme, were reserved on Saturdays for "children and schools"!)

That all-time low record in morality was, however at the time of which I am writing, some twenty-five years in the past. The very name *Babil and Bijou* had died out of memory, and I have only given so full an account of it in Appendix C,[2] in order to show the delightfully extravagant and capricious tastes of my grandfather. Now, though still no form of enjoyment came amiss to him, he was growing old, and the cup of life was nearly empty. It is true that we sometimes accompanied him and my grandmother to the theatre called after them in Scarborough, but it was the Cricket Festival, which he had founded, that now claimed his chief interest here. Certainly, he had grown more domestic. He took increasing pleasure in the society of his daughters and of his numerous grandchildren, upon whom he liked to play the most ingenious and elaborate tricks. . . . Thus I recall that during one of the first church services I attended—a Children's Service—a photograph of a peculiarly hideous and ill-disposed little girl, a year or two older than myself, and whom, though I met her at every children's party to which I went, I much detested, fell out of my prayer-book, as I opened it, with a clatter that focussed all eyes upon me. The whole incident produced an effect of childish pining which was most embarrassing, and my grandfather had, of course, arranged it, taking infinite pains to secure the photograph and secrete it in the best place, whence it was sure to drop out at the most stupefactive moment.

[1] In *The Story of My Life*, etc.   [2] Appendix C, p. 260.

F

His daughters adored him, and my grandmother was in her own way, a protective way, devoted to him; while he—I think there can be no doubt about it—was terrified, even though fond, of her. Hitherto I have mentioned her little in the course of this chapter, but that is, as I hope to show, in no manner because she lacked character. The whole world trembled when she spoke, for her words, which she could inspire with an infinite and indefinable charm, partly from the sound of her voice, warm and luxurious, could also perform the most expert incisions upon conceit and self-importance grown dropsical. . . . Even my father, I think, was frightened of her, though he would never admit it. But each of them, being worthy of the other's most ingenious schemes and best retorts, perhaps enjoyed rather the battle, and it may be as a result of this, that, in the end, towards the final years of the old lady's life—she died in 1915—a real and most unexpected friendship had come to exist between them. . . . It was not always thus, however, and I recall one occasion—two or three years after the time of which I write—when she came to stay at Renishaw. My father had recently bought in Italy some painted hangings of which he was very proud. These he caused to be spread on the ground, to an inaudible flourish of trumpets, for his mother-in-law to inspect. Standing back, with a self-congratulatory air and indulging in a gesture that implied his assured expectation of receiving a compliment from her upon his powers of bargaining, he remarked:

"I paid the owner forty pounds for these."

"How pleased he must have been!" she answered, in tones that implied a tribute, sure enough, but rather to his charitable disposition than esthetic discernment.

To her young grandchildren she was invariably charming. Well shepherded by—in the background—a circle of nurses with restraining hands and cautioning voices, we would raid the breakfast table at The Lodge at about 10.30 every morning, to be rewarded or bought off with a peach or nectarine (and fruit seemed particularly delicious in those days). Our tall uncles and aunts would be sitting round the table, trying to eat a little—and breakfast then meant cutlets and cold grouse, as well as such things as fish and eggs—in order to fortify themselves against the fatigues of the hours before luncheon: but this, owing to the bullying and cajolery of their young relatives, who, now entirely out-of-hand, worried them after the manner of so many gypsies or the whining beggars of Spain and South Italy, was a difficult process. The pack of children was numerous, composed of Raincliffes, Codringtons, Westmorlands, Ogles and Sitwells. Behind us the nurses looked pale, showed in their features clear evidence of strain: for my grandmother with her compact, feminine adaptation of the Wellington profile, her features powdered very white, almost floury, and revealing through this make-up a small blue vein above the bridge of the nose, and one on each temple, with her deep-set, tragic eyes of brown velvet peering from this mask, and with her velvet voice, so slow and emphatic, with her beautifully-shaped, decisive hands—which carried on their fingers, besides the wedding ring, only one other, bearing an enormous square-cut emerald —was, most clearly, not a person to be trifled with. That much, at least, was plainly to be read in everything about her. They all knew it, but none so well as Davis, formerly a nursery-maid in the house. To her, down to the day of her dying, the mystic syllables "Her Ladyship" meant, and could mean, one person alone, a figure in black, with a white eagle's face, and a white fringe above it, who appeared always as an apocalyptic figure in a storm, her quiet voice sounding through the thunder for which she was responsible.

But what else did we know of her? She expressed little of her feelings. . . . Her remote and impersonal air seemed in contra-diction to the strong temperament it plainly covered. To me, it always seemed as though a whole age had passed since she was young, though, on the other hand, my grandfather's youth appeared to have been obscured but yesterday. I admired her as an object, but to this day how little I know of the mainspring of her inner life, how little of her intimate history—though her face, with its tragic aspect, seemed to signify so much. . . . I know, for example, that as a girl, the Emperor Napoleon III had wanted to marry her;[1] and that she loved opera with such passion that she had made my grandfather take her to Egypt,

[1] Her father, the 7th Duke of Beaufort, and her brother, had been the only people of their sort to receive this rather *louche* and penniless adventurer. Prince Louis Napoleon was then supposed to entertain disreputable liberal

so that she might be present at the first performance of *Aïda* in the desert. (This opera had originally been commissioned by the extravagant Khedive for the state opening of the Suez Canal, but the outbreak of the Franco-Prussian War held up the delivery of the costumes and scenery which were being made in Paris) . . . Such details, circumstantial, but at this distance elusive, lead to no trail; they are negative, particularly for a woman with so impressive an individuality.

Most people, then, were frightened. But fortunately the atmosphere of the round table in the round, red, pillared dining-room, was calm and pleasant this morning. The sun poured in at the French windows, which revealed an expanse of flat, mown tree-tops that seemed to form a closely-cropped aerial lawn slanting down to the sea, a racing-ground for the winds of summer. Beyond, the waters of the North Sea presented the blue and imbecile smile which they hypocritically reserved for summer visitors, who left the town never suspecting the winter rages that occurred when their backs were turned. In the room itself, my grandmother's two Pomeranians had begun to yap, a sound which always appeared to induce and assure a continuance of good-humour in her, and, from their cages hung just outside the open window, the parrots and cockatoos, feathered in pink and grey and in white and yellow, were talking and squawking to each other in fussy French. "Tais-toi, chérie! comme tu es méchante! Laisse-moi tranquille!" they would cry, and then dissolve into ardent, amorous giggles, varied by snatches of Tosti's most sentimental songs, rendered sometimes in high falsetto, sometimes as though by a warbling Italian tenor. The homely bullfinch and thrush joined in the uproar caused by these versatile and exotic fowl, and by the expert there could be detected, too, in this medley, the incessant chirrupings of small birds—the name of whose species I never could remember—, very rapid in their movement, with red crests and streaked and striped wings. . . . In

ideas, yet he stayed a great deal at Badminton, where for the most part he will have found exiled princes of the more orthodox type, fugitive and repressive Dukes of Parma or Lucca or Modena, and heavy German sporting princes, shortly to be driven from their dominions. And when Napoleon had made himself Emperor, the 8th Duke of Beaufort and the Duchess visited him, and a review was given in their honour at Compiègne.

the distance, on the town side, a barrel-organ was grinding out its tunes, so mechanically debonair. . . . To-day everything was all right, for she liked her grandchildren, especially the children of her adored only son (he spent the summer here, with his wife and sons and daughters, in a separate house in the grounds). Thus, however much her daughters and—above all—her sons-in-law may have been obliged at times to put up with from her, to us she was invariably the quintessence of sympathy. "Poor boy, poor boy," "little owls," "neat little things," she would say, allowing herself to be amused by the children, even while she was thinking out new ways of dealing with our recalcitrant parents. . . . Meanwhile her other favourites, my aunts Sibyl and Mildred, would be seated at a piano in the next room playing duets, a Strauss waltz or a selection from musical comedies of the time, *Florodora* or *The Geisha*.

My grandmother seemed pleased at these sounds, though the operas of Verdi were what she really enjoyed. All the famous executants, including Liszt, had performed at the house of her parents, the old Beaufort House,[1] but she liked most of all to hear the great singers. . . . Even while she was listening with this appearance of contentment, she also gave the impression of watching, waiting like an eagle to swoop. Soon it would be time for her to drive to the Spa, or up and down the Esplanade, through the summer crowds of fashionable people, who lined so thickly these two places of promenade that to walk along them in the height of the season would be an impossibility, while, overflowing from the roads that led to the station, the jostling crowds of holiday-makers, the women in straw hats, the men in bowlers and caps, could be seen spread over the wide light sands like confetti, and gathered in knots round the glittering, painted stalls of the hokey-pokey sellers. From where she drove, the nigger-minstrels, far below, upon their platform of planks, balanced upon barrels—like rafts washed in by the waves—gesticulated soundlessly at the sea, for the breezes snatched their voices, and only the recurrent breaks of laughter, hoarse, irresponsible, that came from the crowd after some particular sally, would reach to the top of the cliff. Here, where she was driving, and everywhere up and down the steep hills

[1] Later Wimborne House.

lined with shops or with tall, thin houses of plaster, or more
typically, of yellow and grey and blank white brick, rattled and
bounced the jockey-carts, which were the especial charm of
Scarborough: shell-like, brittle vehicles poised upon two immense back wheels, and, in front, two small, and drawn by a
smart pony ridden by a boy armed with a jockey's whip, and
dressed in a jockey's cap and clothes; white silk breeches,
boots and spurs, and striped silk shirt. A few people, my
mother among them, possessed their own jockey-carts with the
boys dressed in their own colours, but for the most part the
clothes of the drivers seemed always to present those particular
combinations of tints that are supplied to a May garden by its
columbines; maroon and saffron, lemon and rusty pink, sapphire blue and water white, colours gay yet drowned by time
passing and gradually immersing them. And like the spurred
columbine, these riders to the sea in their striped clothes imparted to the scene an air that was almost gothic, giving it something of the chequered and slashed beauty of the Palio in Siena.

Meanwhile my grandfather would be thinking out some way
of amusing himself and us. . . . The treats provided for us—
that is to say for his grandchildren—were many and diverse:
and, though I was rather too young as yet to show any prefer-
ence among my cousins, most of us had our chosen companions
for these occasions. My sister's chief friend and confidante, for
example, was Veronica Codrington,[1] our cousin—indeed, our
double cousin, for her father's mother, Lady Georgiana Codrington, was half-sister to our grandmother in common, Lady
Londesborough—, and this friendship continues as firm today
as it was then.

Chief of the treats (though never, alas, for me) was the
Cricket Week, when Scarborough broke out into its greatest
display, and there was feasting in the hot tents of the rich at the
ground's edge. My grandfather, the founder and president,
delighted to entertain—I was going to write the hungry, but
though he loved, too, to do this on other occasions (for he was
very kind and charitable, and in particular the trusted friend
of the fishermen and their wives, who in those days at times
found themselves in great distress), here it would be more

[1] Now Mrs. Frank Gilliat.

correct to say that he fed those who possessed a regular and recurrent appetite. The tents blazed with the ties of the cricketing clubs and the port-wine-coloured faces of the *aficionados*, and between the rounds of cold salmon and cold chicken that were dispensed, we would have to sit solemnly and watch the progression—if such it can be called—of this, to me, always unattractive and lengthy game. But my grandfather loved it and, guided by intuition, had formed, from the first moment of my appearing, extravagant expectations of my future prowess at it. In myself, out of all the family, he had divined the cricketer, and so had arranged with "W. G." to enter my name for the M.C.C. on the very day of my birth.

Alas, already, at the age of four, I was disappointing him, and early afforded, indeed, some evidence of the devil within me by falling asleep during what was, for others, one of the most thrilling moments of a County Championship match, and hurtling off my chair with a crash like a falling meteor. I shall never forget the sense of shame when I woke up bruised and on the ground, and realised by the wooden repartee of bat and ball, and by the expressions of shock and displeasure on the faces of my elder relatives and attendants, the execrable taste of the manner in which I had failed them. This was an experiment in slumber which I only surpassed in later years when, after the example of the great Napoleon, I went to sleep on horseback during a yeomanry exercise (though, unlike what is said of the Emperor, it was never quoted in my case as an indication of military genius)—and was deposited by my horse with needless ostentation at the very hooves of the Commanding Officer's charger.

But, to go back, as I grew older I was enrolled in a children's team, formed chiefly of my cousins, to play in a friendly game, for the amusement of my grandfather and grandmother and aunts and uncles, against the members of the Yorkshire Eleven, which, at that time, included in it Hirst and Rhodes. They played, left-handed, against us—and, as for that, I played left-handed against them, it being my natural bent. . . . Unappreciative of the game though I was, I derived much pleasure from the company of Lord Hawke, for many years captain of the team. A man of great charm and character, I often as a child reflected how apt was his name, for, indeed, his features, his shrewd, sharp eyes and dark brows and sunburnt face, made him, by some process of name-magic, resemble a hawk; but further than that, no likeness could be traced, for he was very tall and broad, with a slightly shambling gait, and the whole atmosphere round him, and for which he was responsible, was genial and human. Year after year he returned to Scarborough with his team, and when it was not actively engaged he would watch the other matches, and in the intervals of play wander round the ground, seeking out his innumerable young friends and admirers—among whom, in spite of my lack of interest in cricket, I was proud to count myself—and distribute to them peppermint humbugs of an especially vast size out of an enormous paper bag. His personality provided a background for the team, and together with my grandfather's universal presence, gave to the whole week a certain quality, an atmosphere of kindliness that, I believe, distinguished it from other festivals of the same kind.

Though I enjoyed part of the proceedings, there were other treats I preferred. . . . . Sometimes we would be permitted to stay up to see the fireworks which accompanied "Gala Nights" at the Spa, and from the windows of The Lodge would watch the rockets proffering their golden or tinsel-starred bouquets towards the empty and uncaring heavens, the lines of their stalks, before they burst into flower, momentarily incised in gold upon the darkness. Or, best of all—for the strain of staying up to see the fireworks was considerable, the excitement flagged and one was apt to grow sleepy—, word would be brought round in the long summer evenings, just as we were preparing for an ordinary and unexciting end to the day, that "His Lordship was going to the circus". Tremendous excitement would ensue in the various houses that we occupied, as all his grandchildren were hurriedly decked out in their best frocks and suits, before congregating at The Lodge and driving thence to the circus. There, in the pointillist mist created by the clouds of sawdust and the miniature explosions of the arc lamps, we would find a quarter of the circus reserved for us, and the gangs of tufted and conventionally painted and powdered clowns waiting specially to sell us the programmes and to give my

Uncle Raincliffe a welcome, for he was a patron and amateur of the circus.

Indeed the visit would probably prove to be an idea of his rather than his father's, for this giant, with his side-whiskers running on to unite with his moustache, and his rather melancholy blue eyes, had all a child's need of being amused, and all a child's power of being entranced by the tumbling of the clowns, their tricks and retorts, and could watch them for hours with just as much enjoyment as did any of his young relatives. And, if he evinced this urgent need for amusement, he possessed, too,—and to a greater degree, even, than his father—the gift, so rare that it is always endearing, of being easily and furiously amused, so that it was always a pleasure to be with him and make him, or see him, laugh. And so it had come about, no doubt, that he was the friend of many of the clowns, especially of Whimsical Walker.

His chief interests, however, centred in music and in machines. This musical strain, I suppose, was derived from the Wellesleys—a recurrent trait in them, and many of those descended from them, that I have mentioned in an earlier chapter—, but it was a taste in which his wife did not join with him, though she, too, shared this blood. To her, music was divided into two main bodies, "tunes" and "no tunes": whereas he approached the new and complicated with as much sympathy, and as little fear, as the old. But he liked every kind of music, popular or for the musical; barrel-organs, brass bands, orchestras, all offered him their joys, peculiar to themselves, and when he was annoyed, and swore with the terrible and vivid imagery, the use of which he had inherited from his father, the sound of music would soon make him forget his rage. He liked to spend an hour or two a day, with the door locked, so that he could not be disturbed—in whatever place seemed to him most suited for it—, conducting with a baton an imaginary orchestra in some familiar concert-piece or the overture to some opera.

As for machines, we shall, I hope, meet some of them during the Christmas parties in his house in the next volume, glass-fronted cupboards full of revolving, self-banging drums, and self-smiting cymbals, self-sawing violins and self-blowing trombones; forgotten machines that the radio and gramophone have now made as obsolete as the motor has made the horse. We shall meet, too, some of the early motor cars; but we must mention here, for it is so essential to the comprehension and development of his character, that he was an enthusiast and adept in the art of the fire-engine, and that, even when he entertained large parties at Blankney, and had probably been hunting all day, if he were summoned to some conflagration within, let us say, a thirty-mile radius, he would abandon his guests, however many and whoever they might be, and, to him what was more important, the dinner itself, to career into the night on the screaming, red-painted engine, only to return exhausted hours later with blackened face and torn hands. . . . I think his wife's relations, many of them, considered these exploits as more comprehensible than his passion for music, but foreigners—and there were always some present at these parties—were fascinated with his strange conduct, and amazed at this fresh instance of English *milor* courage and eccentricity.

In the fullest spring, when the tardy flowers of Yorkshire decked every hill and garden, my other grandmother[1] would come from Gosden to stay at Hay Brow, a small property she now owned about three miles outside the town. (Her house in Scarborough stood empty during these years.) Bringing her daughter, my Aunt Florence, and various retainers, she would spend a month or two there every summer, in order to be near both her eldest sister, Lady Hanmer, and my father. By no means a rich woman, with little more than her jointure to support her, she possessed a remarkable head for business, and her enterprise and power of organisation enabled her to extract an almost incredible value from every pound spent. She maintained in Scarborough at her own cost a small hospital (there was then no public hospital), a home for fallen women, and a club-room. All these were under the care of trained sisters, and everything was most methodically controlled. Even her smaller charities were imaginative—including, in former years when she had resided in the town, a breakfast of great local

[1] Louisa Lady Sitwell. An account of her by Dame Ethel Smyth is printed as Appendix D on p. 268.

celebrity, given in her house to the Scarborough postmen during the early hours of Christmas Day before they started on their rounds. In addition to all this, she ran her own two houses, which were usually full of people, friends and relations.

As evidence, then, of the different style in which people with a comfortable income, but who were not supposed to be "well off", lived, even so comparatively short a time ago, let me quote an entry from my Aunt Florence's journal, of about this period—indeed a year or two later—relating to the annual summer exodus from Surrey to Yorkshire. It affords, as well, a key indication of character, and of the interests of her mother and herself.

"*Gosden. Thursday the 22nd of May*. Yesterday was so busy, but at last, about 6.30, I got out to say good-bye to our people on the Common. The old woman of 100 was very dear and deaf and nice, and says she cannot remember the Battle of Trafalgar. Old Potter still unwell. I wonder if several will not have passed away before our return? . . . Up about 5.30 this morning, desperately busy nearly to the last. We travelled by a special arrangement of Mother's with the G.N.R. Company, starting from Shalford Station, and going, via Dorking, London Bridge and King's Cross to Scarborough without changing. I say 'we': it is necessary to explain the party. Mother, myself, our maids, and Bessie, Wilkinson, Florence, Frank (the butler) and his wife, Hill the coachman, George the footman; a carriage, horses and six Samoyede dogs. We travelled in a saloon and another carriage. Leckly remained behind, as she is very far from well and ought to undergo the Nauheim treatment."

How well I remember the collection of old servants! Leckly, who at the time of her death had been with my grandmother for sixty-three years, a gnarled and characteristic figure from the background of a piece of Flemish tapestry, keys at the waist, and on her wise but not agreeable face, somewhat fanatical in a common-sense way, a tinge of blue (her jaws fumbled always, as though one were trying to meet the other, in some indigestive prayer); Wilkinson, the cook, grey-haired and good, whose life passed in a dream of orange jelly, and who was with her sixty years; Hill, the coachman, who insisted on mending and, if possible, re-gilding the furniture in his spare time, which, so slow a driver was he, one would have deemed insufficient for the task; Jane, who had been there twenty years, the delightful, lanky housemaid from Suffolk, so kind and rustic, with a bump on her forehead, about which she often used to confide to me, as though it were a treasure, that "the doctors wanted to take it away"; Frank, the grave, humorous, grey butler; and the hot, white, furry Samoyede dogs—one of which had been the first of its kind to be brought to England.

Hay Brow charmed its every visitor. The garden, with its little lake and rare trees—a lake so still and deep, so embosomed in its trees, that it seemed to reflect them better than any water I have seen—imparted a sense of infinite, remote, yet well-ordered peace, a little comparable, perhaps, to that which must have prevailed in the Garden of Eden; all men and women who entered here, it seemed, were innocent, all creatures tame, all birds engaged solely in the practice of their choirs. The clusters of blooms seemed ever in full flower, and smelt of honey. Even in the height of summer, a deep peace and eternal coolness dwelt here, as dew dwells, even on the hottest day, in the heart of the rose.

The beauty of the flowers was in part due to my grandmother, and the interest she took in them in part to the gardener, Ernest de Taeye, a Fleming. . . . Ernest was the son of one of the chief gardeners in a famous azalea nursery near Ghent; the old man, when over seventy, had been given notice by his employers, and the shock of the prospect of being separated from these plants which he had so long tended was such that he had committed suicide. My grandmother heard of this curious tragedy, for she knew the nursery in question, and was informed, too, that his son, a boy of twenty or so, wished to find a place abroad. Feeling very sorry for him, and thinking, too, that the great love of flowers to which this suicide testified might be hereditary, she engaged him for Hay Brow. Thus this quiet, clever, sensitive man, a born gardener, with the secret of growing things in his hands, large but delicate, came to England, and remained in her service for many years until her death in 1911, when he came to us at Renishaw. When first he arrived at Hay Brow from abroad, he was still depressed by the death of his father, and for several years the only English word he knew was "No": which rendered conversation difficult and non-conductive, though it did not prevent him from courting and marrying the daughter of a neighbouring farmer. . . . In appearance he was a huge man, with the look of a portrait by Van Eyck; a similarity heightened, singularly enough, when in middle age he caught a rare disease from handling a plant in a hot-house, and lost in consequence all his hair, becoming completely bald, even of eyebrow and eyelash: after which he laid it down as a condition of his employment that he need never take off his hat of fine, amber-coloured straw in an unusual shape (in winter he wore a cap); so that even when arranging flowers or watering large-leaved plants in the house, he wore it, a badge of his green office.

Mrs. de Taeye was, physically, the perfect complement to him, though as typical of Yorkshire as he was of Flanders, bold, decided, generous, understanding, prejudiced and extremely careful in money affairs. She never seemed to have an idle moment, except the hours in which she entertained us children, and sometimes our cousins, to tea. Everything in the house was made by her, or by a member of the family; not a speck of dust sparkled in the beams of light that entered through the latticed windows, but every now and then, once or twice, perhaps, in the year, she would catch sight of a spider, unfortunately always out of reach, and it would become a fixation in her mind: she would be able to think of nothing else but ways of decoying it, ruses by which it could be captured and destroyed. It was to her no ally against corrupting flies, but a mortal enemy, clever, skilful, able to drop down here and run up there on magical ladders of silk. I shall never forget the expression with which she would regard its scuttling. . . . There was nothing common about Mrs. de Taeye; she possessed an innate dignity, born of centuries of freedom, freedom to think and to speak. And this freedom, again, was translated into her speech, for she would not only deprive a word of an introductory aspirate, but, much more arbitrarily, would impose it on a word that did not need it, or place an *h* indeed, wherever she liked.

Old Mrs. Hague,
The Gardener's wife,
Was not to be enclosed in any formulas.
She seems to stand upon a little mound
Of pansies,
      Primroses,
           And primulas.
Outlined against the pale blue eye of northern spring,
Heavily planted in this printed muslin beauty
Of clumps and spots and dots and tiger-stripes,
She swelled with ideas and ideals of duty,
Emphatic,
      Rheumatic.

If not upon this flower-sprinkled mound,
Then Mrs. Hague stood
Pressed in the narrow framework of her door
And fills it to our minds for evermore.
Out of the slender gaps
Between the figure and its frame,
Was wafted the crusty, country odour
Of new bread,
Which was but one blossom of the hedges
That Mrs. Hague had planted.

For Mrs. Hague was childless,
And so had wisely broken up her life
With fences of her own construction,
Above which she would peer
With bovine grace,
Kind nose, kind eyes
Wide open in wide face.
For
    Monday was Washing Day,
    Tuesday was Baking Day,
    Wednesday h'Alfred 'as 'is dinner h'early,
    Thursday was Baking Day again,
    Friday was a busy day, a very busy day,
    And Saturday prepared the way for Sunday,
    Black satin bosoms and a brooch,
    A bonnet and a Bible.

Nor were these all:
There were other more imposing barriers
Of Strawberry Jam in June
And Blackberry Jelly in October:
For each fruit contributed a hedge
To the garden of Mrs. Hague's days.

These fences made life safe for Mrs. Hague;
Each barrier of washing, mending, baking
Was a barricade
Thrown up against being lonely or afraid.
This infinite perspective
—The week, the month, the year—
Showed in the narrow gaps
Between her and the door,
As she stood there in the doorway,
Narrow as a coffin.[1]

In later years Ernest shed his allegiance to the solitary
English negative monosyllable and became a master of phrase.
At Renishaw, after the manner of all professional gardeners,
and in spite of his artist's mind, he yearned for hot, strongly-
coloured, real horticulturists' blossoms,—I suppose because of
some technical perfection he saw in them, invisible except to
the eyes of experts—just as fervently as my father, with his
theories (for he held that vivid hues conflicted with vistas and
lay-out), insisted on small, quietly-coloured flowers. And I
remember his alluding to this and saying mournfully to me
in his slow, careful voice, "The truth is, sir, Sir George likes
an *anaemic* garden".

At Hay Brow, the garden, as I have said, was lovely, but
the house was negligible, the exterior, even, being rather ugly,
but my grandmother, with her very individual taste and with
the various fine objects she possessed, had made it into a charming summer residence, so that it appeared to be but an annexe
of the garden, a series of tents pitched for hot weather, since
the rooms were lined with *mezeries*, printed designs in light
colours on a cool white cotton background, made in Genoa
about a hundred years before—and the scent of the garden
drifted in at the wide open windows or through the Venetian
shutters, to join the perfumes exhaled by huge bouquets of
flowers, roses and sweet peas, and by more exotic blossoms from
the hot-houses, their pots concealed in very Victorian china
bowls, china of brightest blue and pink, her two favourite colours.

Here, in this house and garden, the activities of the inhabitants were very different from those that prevailed at
Londesborough Lodge, three miles away. No two backgrounds

[1] From *England Reclaimed*.

could have been more dissimilar than my father's and my mother's. At Hay Brow, theatre and circus, actresses and clowns had no part, for Lady Sitwell's interests were of an intellectual, but more especially of a devout order. Her whole life had been spent in carrying out, as she saw them, the Christian principles. Religion and charity had engrossed her every thought. Her upbringing had been of the orthodox pious type of the period, but in the course of time evangelical fervour had come to tinge strongly her outlook. Yet to a certain degree she could enter into the views of others, and would certainly have rather that faith took any form than none.

In the days in 1872 in which my grandfather Londesborough was paying for the production of *Babil and Bijou*, my grandmother Sitwell enters in her diary:

'*Renishaw. Monday.* . . . Mr. Body urged me very strongly to do something to break up the profound lethargy and indifference which have fallen upon our people and service, and he prayed with me. We had a most interesting conversation, too, about the necessity of a '*crisis*' in our life, of a distinct turning toward God, of knowing and feeling that our sins *are* forgiven, that we *have* passed from darkness into light . . . and then he forgot himself and his hearer, and lost himself in the fire of eloquence with which he spoke of his Master's love. . . . A Service again at 7, much fuller, and more than 30 stayed for the after service at which Ramsay prayed, extemporary prayers, and Mr. Body spoke to the tearful ones, 'Brother, is it Peace?'— 'I hope so.'—'Oh, but that shouldn't be a matter-of-doubt, you know; *have* you come to Jesus? *Have* you passed from darkness into light?'

"*Wednesday*. Mr. and Mrs. Howard from Whiston came here yesterday, to meet Mr. Body, and today Lady Frederick Beauclerk and her son, and Mr. Hamilton Gray drove from Bolsover to join our early dinner—all went to the Service at the Church together afterwards—it is perhaps enough to give Mr. Estcourt's verdict on the sermon. 'It was magnificent: thank God for it.' He held a class for the candidates for confirmation afterwards, they said it was most touching, but I couldn't stay.

"*Thursday*. Extemporary prayer by Mr. Body. . . . He left us by the 10 train—the departure of which was watched by weeping maids from an upstairs window. . . ."

Such entries are continual.

As for the stage, my grandmother Sitwell abhorred it. Even Grand Opera was taboo. Many years before, as a young girl, after her engagement to Sir Reresby, and during the great religious tide that flowed in at the end of the Crimean War, she wrote in her journal: "*June 25th*, 1857. . . . Minnie and I went to the Opera with Fred and Arthur. The music was so delicious, I admire the new tenor, Giulini, very much, and Piccolomini sang like a great thrush, but I think—I think—this must be the last opera for me. I had a strong feeling that I ought not to be there, and there were many things that shocked and offended me. . . . And the ballet! How anyone can like it—or look at it, I cannot think!" . . . And she maintained this attitude: it hardly softened, except that, when entertaining for my father at Renishaw, at the time of his coming-of-age, she so far relaxed as to allow a theatrical entertainment of a kind. A cousin, who was there in 1881, has written to me to tell me of it: "More house-parties at Renishaw—grouped and spread over successive seasons—comprised a variety of nice and interesting people; Archbishop Tait and his daughters, the nice old rector of Eckington, Mr. Estcourt, his family, and many married daughters, Carmichael, Mary Cholmondeley, Dean Bromley (of Hobart Town), and, on one occasion, George MacDonald[1] and his whole family, who acted the *Pilgrim's Progress*. The scenery was most simple. Beulah, I think, was

---

[1] George MacDonald (1824-1905), poet and novelist and author of stories for children, came of a Jacobite family. His great-great-grandfather, a red-haired piper, lost his sight in the Battle of Culloden. The family moved to Huntly in Aberdeenshire, where George MacDonald was born. He was ordained in the Congregational ministry in 1850, but resigned in 1853, giving his time to literature. Later he became a lay member of the Church of England. He was a close friend of, among others, the Carlyles, William Morris, Dean Stanley and Matthew Arnold. Among his well-known books are *David Elginbrod*, *Alec Forbes*, *Robert Falconer*, *The Princess and the Goblin*, *Ranald Bannerman's Boyhood* and *At the Back of the North Wind*. The *D.N.B.* says that his wife, Louisa Powell, daughter of James Powell, "adapted for stage representation a series of scenes from the *Pilgrim's Progress* in which her husband and her children took part, and the experiment led the way for the later revival by others of old miracle plays".

just tall lilies beside a blue curtain. The cry from the 'Slough of Despond', '*I thought I should never get out*," was most realistic." This act must, indeed, have been a permanent one with the members of the MacDonald family. For some five years earlier, in 1877, I find an account of it in the memoirs of Augustus Hare,[1] that reservoir of information concerning the social history of the late nineteenth century. "On the 19th [of July] I went to Lady Ducie's, to see the MacDonald family act the *Pilgrim's Progress*. They go through the whole of the second part, George MacDonald, his wife, his twelve children and two adopted children. Christiana (the eldest daughter) was the only one who acted well. Nevertheless, the whole effect was touching, and the audience cried most sympathetically as Christiana embraced her children to go over the river."

The sounds of laughter at Hay Brow, then, were different from those at The Lodge. They were musical and subdued, though clear and modulated as peals of bells: no barrel-organs ground out their music from beyond the peaceful trees' horizon, but sometimes the voices of children singing hymns would rise up from across the pool and seem those of a celestial, though still evangelical, choir, or the happy, subdued hum of a missionary meeting would mingle with the drone of bees and bluebottles. The music, when not religious, was usually that of Chopin, Schumann or Tchaikovsky, nostalgic and lovely melodies, played by one of my grandmother's relatives. In the evenings, there would be reading aloud of poetry and philosophy and of books of political interest,—except on Sunday when only "good books" were permitted—, and descriptions from the columns of *The Times* of the exhumation of buried cities in Eastern Europe and Asia, and, of course, of progress of the enterprises of the Church among the Heathen. To give an example of the life there, let me extract a further passage from my Aunt Florence's journal:

"*Tuesday, 6th of August*. Mother and I got on well with Bismarck's Love Letters; he seems so simple, honest, lovable and God-fearing. We are making plans (Mother's idea) for inviting Bar-maids for quiet Sunday afternoons in this garden, where we could read to them, with perhaps a little sacred sing-

[1] *The Story of My Life.*

ing, and get to know and help them if we can.[1] ... Polly, to our happiness, has broken with the rowdy friends who were getting hold of her and making her restless. ... I saw Mr. Bunting at the Y.M.C.A. and Miss Allen at the Y.W.C.A. about girls at Marshall and Snelgrove's."

Lady Sitwell's appearance and personality, though they made a profound impression on all those that met her, are not easy to reproduce. As a girl she had been considered beautiful, and her features, in their aquiline mould, were symmetrical and distinguished. But radiance is a better word to match her quality, I think, than beauty, and a certain sad radiance still clung to her. The cast of her face was unusual and mysterious and sweet in its aspect, and she possessed a rare dignity of carriage and demeanour, and a grace of movement that I have never seen in another woman of her age, and which helped me to understand what I was told, that in her youth she had delighted in dancing and riding; pursuits that seemed now so far removed from her. As you could see in the decoration of her houses, she loved bright colours, though she now no longer wore them, but black in the day-time, and dark-hued green or brown or blue velvet in the evening. She liked to wear ornaments, brooches, necklaces and bracelets, and even when in mourning she would wear long heavy chains of onyx, jet or ivory. Though she observed mourning, like all the other conventions, with great strictness, after the appropriate period she had discarded her widow's cap and would never again wear it. ... She had been in mourning for her husband at the same time as two of her sisters for theirs, and one day, as Queen Victoria, also recently widowed, was passing through the windy, curved corridor of York Station on her way to her refuge in the Highlands, she caught sight of this little group in black on a platform, and, presumably interested by the theme of widowhood that they shared in common, enquired of her lady-in-waiting "Who are those handsome young widows?"

Her habitual expression of sweetness, sympathy and resignation—the first thing you would notice—masked, however, an

---

[1] Alas, of the following Sunday, we read, "Only two nice-looking Barmaids came, but they seemed to enjoy their quiet afternoon. One confided that she would like to leave her work."

iron will, and disguised with a semblance of calm the fires of
her temperament. She was never happy except in bestowing,
both of her energy and her possessions, yet she was, and must
be, the dominant influence in her house, and an absolute ruler.
She would tolerate no least evasion of propriety or respect,
either due to herself or to others. All the members of her household must feel themselves to be part of one concern, and must
think nothing of the trouble to which they were put. Her orders
on all points had to be strictly carried out, and her old servants
firmly supported her (except that Leckly allowed herself some
laxity in that she would go to church where and when she
wanted, and nothing could ever persuade Hill to stop re-gilding
the furniture—but these were time-honoured idiosyncrasies).
Otherwise there would be little effort to spare,—and all effort
must be given over to religious causes.

From this quiet spot was generated the power which gal-
vanised the good works of Scarborough and many other towns
and villages. Here were founded the charities for the relief of
those sins fostered by the love of pleasure, so evident in the
other side of my family: here, as I discovered in after years,
were thought out those various plans that resulted in the
removal of the inebriate from his drink and in the conversion
of sirens into Magdalene washerwomen. And whereas even
the most eminent member of the stage, Sir Henry Irving himself, would have been received at Hay Brow—if at all—with
suspicion, almost any curate could be sure of a welcome, and
treated to long and intimate hours of conversation. They
circled round my grandmother like flocks of crows, and, when
we visited her, we were obliged to listen to their cawings—
unless my mother came with us and dispersed them. The best
flowers would be reserved for their invariably sick mothers, the
best peaches and grapes and melons—at the growing of all of
which Ernest de Taeye excelled—for their invariably sick
friends. A continual manna descended upon them in generous
measure. This was the weak, or at least the soft, spot in her
ardent, compact, clever character. For them, she evinced a special
kind of esteem, which included, perhaps, in its components a
little of that kind of regard later exhibited by members of her sex
for film stars, Gary Cooper or, in his day, Rudolph Valentino.

As for her grandchildren, she would give us flowers also, but I believe children tired her, for she was growing old and had never been strong since she had injured her spine in a railway accident. In consequence she was obliged to rest a great deal now. She would show us, too, coloured plates in the fine old books which she collected, flower-books with illustrations of cactuses that coiled serrated green tentacles after the manner of squids, of orchids, lolling their tongues, and of pagoda-like blossoms, tier upon tier, from Mexico and China. Other volumes were devoted to birds, shells, volcanoes and the Wonders of the World. All were stimulating to the imagination. But of this, and the other traits and possessions which went with them, I shall have more to say when I write of her house in the south of England and of the personal and pleasant machinery of life with which she surrounded herself, for when I was a little older, I became more and more fond of her, and grew increasingly to appreciate the particular qualities of loyalty and intelligence, and of fascination, which she embodied.

In the various causes I have mentioned, in the various technical processes she and her friends invented for separating the vicious from their vice, she was wearing herself out, no less than her daughter—that mild and trustful character, a Fra Angelico saint in type, who seemed to have tumbled accidentally into this century from the days of the early Church or from the age in which prevailed the gothic seclusion of women, and to have remained somewhat dazed from the impact of the alien civilisation in which she now found herself. . . . But my Aunt Florence I have described as I remember her, in my preface to *Two Generations*; and indeed, in the second part of it, she has, with incomparable if unconscious skill, etched her own portrait for us. So, in order to distil again the atmosphere that surrounded her, I will only add a passage or two from a letter I have received from one who knew her well, and who had just been reading *Two Generations*:

"There was so much more in Florence than was generally realised. She had devoted friends who knew and loved her, and those to whom she was specially devoted (as appears in her journal), but she was often a 'hidden Saint', though always more interested in things eternal than in those temporal. . . .

Your grandmother, I remember, was once asked by a young man, diffident about his chances, to sound Florence as to whether she would consider marrying him. After for long vainly trying to approach the subject, your grandmother was obliged to reply that 'her dear daughter was so much taken up with heavenly things that she could not gain her attention'.

"I do not think that Florence consciously sacrificed herself, for she never wished for any career that would have separated her from her mother. But no mother and daughter could have differed more in character, your grandmother was so clever and decisive; whereas Florence did not always make much way with difficult people who did not understand her outlook. But she could rise well to an occasion when prepared, and I recollect, notably, a paper which she was asked to read on some spiritual subject at a York Conference, attended by great ladies and many clergy. She delivered it well, and was full of her enthusiasm, ending, in ringing tones, with 'Our *Living, Risen* Lord!' (her testimony), and I recall the awed silence that followed."

In the early days of which I am writing, though my aunt was always kind to us, and though my grandmother was devoted to Edith, I am inclined to think that she regarded me with some distrust. In my character, the fondness, for example, that I evinced for dancing and for the clichés of the barrel-organ, gay and tawdry, showed the most clearly defined imprint of the cloven hoof. She had been the mother of only one son, and had had four sisters but no brother, and, in consequence, unused to the young male, expected less self-will and more resignation in him than is usual. In spite, therefore, of her kindness and charm, it was then a greater pleasure to me to visit my more hedonistic relatives on the maternal side, for I was devoid, to an unusual extent, of the conventional religious sense (though, as will be told, I suffered precociously from a religious crisis, albeit of short duration, at the age of eight). Clergymen frightened and bored me. My other grandmother, too, loved the clergy, but more temperately; besides, my grandfather's attitude towards life cancelled this out. Therefore I preferred the parrots, the flesh-pots and the fun, even though it may have grown a trifle thin-sounding to the ears of some of my elders. I dreaded the mysterious charities for which sales-of-work were organised continually at Hay Brow, and the talk about "the dear Bishop": I positively disliked the "dear Bishop" himself. . . . Thus, when I visited my grandmother Sitwell, I often fortified myself first by going to see Mrs. de Taeye, a charming, rustic, Noah's Ark figure of kindness and common sense. And in her cottage, quilted with buds of rose and clematis, I was given endless home-made cakes, scones, buns and jam. Indeed Mrs. de Taeye was a rock in my defence, rigid in totally rejecting any imputation of selfishness to me, however plainly I was at fault

CHAPTER FOUR

Let There be Light!

MEANWHILE my father was watching, waiting for me to betray those symptoms of extravagance, weakness and self-indulgence which from my family history he so confidently —and not without considerable justification—expected. He blamed me for resembling members of my mother's family, while, rather unreasonably, he entered a judgement on a contrary plea against my sister; because he thought she resembled members of his own mother's family. He had always hoped that a daughter of his would have a straight, Grecian nose, and here she was at the age of eight or nine, already provided with an aquiline! Most provoking and inconsiderate.

As a child I was slow as my sister was quick of apprehension. And in each of us this was wrong. She should have been slow, being a girl—dedicated, as girls of her class then were, first to a life of Infanta-like seclusion and then to marriage. On the other hand my childish difficulty in pronouncing certain consonants was regarded as downright original sin.

The development of my character for which my father was looking was not the only trouble that existed between us. There was, for example, my misunderstanding of the nature of humour. This discordant theme continually recurred to perturb him and—to go forward in time again—I remember very well, when in London, at the age of eighteen or nineteen, being taken out for a walk by my father so that he could speak to me upon, as he said, "a serious subject". I had the usual "sinking feeling" which the thought of such a process entails: but eventually we sat down on a bench in St. James's Park and he told me what the trouble was. He was very much afraid, he said, that there must be something wrong with my sense of humour. He had often noticed that I laughed at things in which he could see no joke, while at other times when he said something extremely amusing, I apparently saw nothing funny in it.

Well, the same rankling trouble was at work even in this early period. We were in the middle of one of the great practical-joke epochs (it must have been about '97, when I was four years old). One morning I went with my father into the dining-room before luncheon. He was expecting as a guest at this forthcoming meal a supporter of his in politics, an alderman, mighty in stature, a very heavy man, and he now placed ready for him at the table a Chippendale chair, the seat of which collapsed when you sat down on it. As a matter of fact, over this particular incident my sense of humour at that time coincided entirely with my father's. I remember thinking it an extra-ordinarily funny joke. And so, after he had left the room, I changed this chair—with tremendous labour, for I was very small at that time—with his own, and then hid under the table to watch the effect. . . . My father sat down, rather slowly, waiting for the alderman's collapse, and then fell through his own chair with an expression of intense amazement and con-sternation, while my merry laughter rang out from under the table. He was not in the least amused, but got up, very red in the face, remarking at the same time, "I might have most seriously injured my back." My laughter soon changed to tears and it was some time before I was forgiven. All the same, I had meant no harm.

On the other hand, my father was always helpful and sympathetic about such things as nervous symptoms or health generally—though, with illnesses that might prove contagious, himself would go to any length to avoid possible infection. (Thus, for example, when subsequently at the age of eleven I was very seriously ill, in bed for four months, and the doctors did not quite know what was the matter with me, he never once came near me, never even to the door.) He would be extremely kind to me, however, about my fear of the dark, a fear which I suppose all children have, but which I suffered in an exagger-ated form. For this I daresay many things are responsible, including heredity and a sensitiveness to atmosphere. I forget at what precise age I was first made to sleep by myself, but it was a moment which I dreaded, and my father was most sympathetic. However, when that awful first night of estrange-ment did arrive, an incident occurred which I believe, though slight in itself, to have been responsible to some extent for part of my attitude towards life; that if you are afraid of a particular thing, that thing takes advantage of your fear to establish itself as the reality. It is an attitude which I tried to illustrate in *The Man Who Lost Himself*.[1] For my new bedroom I was given a big room—or it seemed big to me then—on the first floor of Belvoir House, facing the sea across various gardens. It was with great difficulty, and only after a relay of persons had looked in from the lighted passage, that I contrived on this first night to fall asleep at all. But no sooner had I just lost consciousness and the fears of dark had been after that fashion temporarily banished, than there came a tremendous gust of wind which blew the French window open, though it was summer, and upset various objects in the room. This finally disorganised my nervous system for the night. . . . I doubt if it had happened ever before—and it had happened, I realised, because I was frightened.

The dawn of neurasthenia, though it is an hereditary complaint, varies with each individual. It is born anew with him, yet is so personal to him that it is difficult for even the most sympathetic to comprehend its symptoms. No apology for neurasthenics is needed after that fine passage in which Proust describes what this army has achieved. Without them, achievement in the arts would be limited in the extreme. Every time that you open a book, remember that countless bad nights, composed of torturing and unnecessary fears and worries, have gone to its making, as well as the fire, the energy and the zest of its writing; all sorts of nights in the past, as well as while the book was being written. . . . And I recall here the first occasion of this kind for me. At Scarborough, when I was three or four, my mother always came to say good-night to me at seven o'clock, and I well remember one night when she was a quarter of an hour late, how I thought to myself, "Now I shall *never* get to sleep tonight: it is past the time," and how she noticed that I wanted to get rid of her and, being hurt, told my father, who spoke to me severely. . . . It was all too complicated and unworthy, too difficult for a child of that age to explain.

In such ways, even Davis could not help. Her character was too simple. Besides, she and my father disliked each other very thoroughly. She thought him "too clever for a gentleman",

[1] Duckworth & Co., 1929.

opinionated, abrupt and irritable: he thought her stupid and old-fashioned. Further, she had been in the service of my mother's family, and this seemed in itself reprehensible to him. Over one matter only, then, did employer and employed agree: over the food that a child should eat. It must be nourishing and, "to do the child good", be disliked by him. All the things for which children now clamour—and are often indeed obliged against their will to eat—oranges and sweets and fruit juices, were beyond the pale. Boiled mutton (fortunately without capers) and a stodgy eternity of rice pudding, stretching spotless beyond the horizon or, like the Church of England Heaven, a pale eternity of jelly, constituted our recognised diet, based on scientific knowledge. Glucose especially—now recognised as "a prime body-building food" —was the bogy of those days. "You must not eat a sweet. There may be glucose in it!" was the warning continually issued to all children of the time. . . . Fortunately my mother paid no attention to these rules, and my native cunning taught me to keep on good terms with the cook. (Indeed, while we had a French chef, I even contrived to learn a few words of French.) Whenever I managed to pass through the kitchen—which was frequently—I would nonchalantly seize a handful of candied cherries or sultanas, and eat them.

The darkness begins now to clear with more coherence. Birth and death entered my life about this time and together, and with them came the sense of mortality. . . . Mortality, a spectre, peered at me first through a conversation that I heard murmured between my nurse Davis and a female assistant in a toy-shop; who was dressed, after the manner of her calling in late-Victorian days, in very voluminous, tightly-waisted black clothes that smothered her body from foot to chin, while a fringe draped her naked forehead. For a long time they discussed something in undertones, as if it were a matter to which no reference could be made in public, and then, out of the words, I pieced together the fact of a dreadful operation on some unmentionable part of the unmentionable human body. An atmosphere of intolerable and muffling sadness envelops this incident for me in the memory; for it was only then that I realised that we were all condemned to death in a world of swathed dejection and faint voices. Not here were the dying tones of youth and beauty. Though brightness fell from the air, sure enough, it was not because

> Queens have died young and fair;
> Dust hath closed Helen's eye,

but because Helen had lived on from her flaming and legendary world into this humdrum life of prison routine, with execution for each of us at the end of it; Helen of Troy, faded or grown insignificant or swollen and over-emphatic, muffled in sadness and suffocating black clothes. . . . And soon after this initiation, my Aunt Lilian died. I did not know her very well, but I had been a page at her wedding the year before and could remember that ceremony and the excitement of it. And now the bitter weeping of my mother made me comprehend the existence of a world of sorrow beyond the world I knew. . . . All this Davis emphasised—for she possessed a naïvely morbid mind—by taking Edith and me every Sunday afternoon when in Scarborough for a walk in the municipal cemetery, to admire the white marble angels, with a touch of green mildew on their wings, and the damp-clotted, mouldering chrysanthemums that adorned the graves of which they smelt. . . . My father would have been furiously angry with her for leading us on these mournful expeditions under dark, grey-blue northern skies, with the wind howling round the sharp-edged headstones; but he never found out. And perhaps it was for the best, perhaps her instinct led her to anticipate the advice of a great foreign doctor and psychologist, whom I heard maintain in after years that the best possible cure for anyone with an undue fear of death was to think every day, for ten minutes or so, of his coffin and how he would lie in it.

Then birth came, a miraculous baby from the void—but for some reason this seemed to me no more strange than the truths of revealed religion as I was learning them. If one had to believe one, why not believe the other? . . . At the age of nearly five I became an elder son: for a great event in the family occurred with the birth of my brother Sacheverell, from his earliest years my chief friend and companion. I suppose that when he was a very small child I understood him better than did anyone else, I instinctively comprehended what he wanted to say, before others could: and on this foundation our friendship was soundly based. He was a particularly fascinating and genial child, as well as exceptionally good-looking, and—to anticipate—when he was three or four years of age, his love of life and of people was so intense that if Davis and I were not looking, he would often run up to strangers and say to them, "My Mummy and Daddy would be delighted if you would lunch with them tomorrow." The stranger would easily find out, if he was not already aware of, our identity, and the most amazing raggle-taggle gypsy crew would thus occasionally assemble to be entertained in response to his invitations. It made things difficult for my poor father, who was either candidate or member at the time, and on whose part it would therefore have been most impolitic to turn constituents away. This love of life, shown in his earliest days, this curiosity, was undoubtedly the root of my brother's subsequent search for knowledge, and perpetual eagerness to know the ways of humanity in every part of the world.

It can be imagined that some of the guests, thus hospitably gathered from highway and byway, were surprising in the extreme to my parents: and among them they included one or two of the untouchable class, known to us as "People At Whom You Must Not Look". This diverse regiment existed only, of course, at Scarborough—and not at Renishaw with its industrial and rural background: these were the eccentrics in behaviour and morals, blown hither on some wind of curiosity and misfortune, and here stranded, listless, unaffected by life outside the town. As the light grows stronger, it reveals this strange population against the background of a world, stippled and very pale in tone, with the glitter of the sea about it on the fronts and the roofs of the houses and in the sky itself. Even the ordinary people—the men in their bowlers, boaters, close-fitting caps and with their carefully trained or trailing moustaches, the women with their narrow-waisted bodies, like continents, their huge hats feathered and contaminated with milliners' flowers, decaying in purple and deep pink— walking, riding horses, riding bicycles, driving in varnished shells of wood, were strange enough, looked back upon; but how do justice to these other capering figures at the world's edge, on the faces of whom the light plays with the same trembling power of emphasis as a mirror flashed in the sun upon the features of an unsuspecting person by some small child? . . . There was, for example, Count de Burgh. A tradesman, retired and prosperous, who had bought a papal title, he always wore, over tightly laced stays, a frock-coat, and to the rim of his top-hat he had attached a row of curls, so that as he walked down the middle of the road—he generally seemed to be advancing from a broad cul-de-sac into the main street—and doffed his hat to his acquaintances, in a gesture reminiscent of the court of old France, his hair swept off with it. He seemed ever to be acknowledging the homage of the crowd, gravitating with certainty to the middle of every picture. Again, there was an old man, with a divided beard like that of Mr. Dunlop in the advertisement, or King Leopold II of the Belgians, who always wore a grey bowler and a grey frock-coat and who had an unhappy and too meaning way of staring at Edith's governess. It was alleged that on one occasion he had even followed her. Then there was a lady who dressed, in the day-time, in a ball gown of blue chiffon sprinkled with silver stars, a man who thought he was a cat and mewed, and a whole host of glandular children of one sort or another.

The same light that shows me these faces, wry and contorted, also illuminates for me the countenances of those I loved dearly, such as Miss Lloyd who, until her death in 1925, remained a great friend of mine. Her background was a little mysterious and we knew little of it except that she was related to Sir Charles Wyndham, the actor, who used to come and see her, and that she was partly of French extraction,—but her gifts were plain to us all. She was, for an old lady, exquisitely pretty, with small beautifully chiselled features and a round mass of long white curls spread all over her head, on which, when she went out shopping,—after the manner of a French-woman, with a basket on her arm—she put a sort of black poke-bonnet. Her fingers were the nimblest in the world; she painted flowers, did feather-work and embroidery, designed and baked china, embroidered and painted in a thousand different ways and as well and delicately as she cooked. I have never eaten chicken or cutlets that were so delicate and fragrant, or bread that was as delicious as the many different kinds she made. She lived in a tall red house full of the things she had created, and the window-boxes were always a-flutter with the feathers of birds, so that they seemed an extension of the room itself and of herself too, as they darted with their quick, neat movements and bright, woven wings. But though fond of all three of us, she constituted herself from the first especially my champion. And since—for she was intensely practical—my father valued her advice on many subjects, she was able, as I grew older, to exert, from my point of view, a very valuable influence on him—that is to say, to the extent to which he could be influenced, which was not very considerable. But she had, as well as this practical ability, a romantic side to her life. She did not see things in the tones in which others saw them and she was capable of exaggerating to their limit incidents which occurred, so that they possessed a grotesque and interesting distortion. All through my early life—and indeed, until I was thirty or more—she was an important figure, frequently staying with us at Renishaw, while when in Scarborough we would always go to tea with her and often to luncheon.

She used on many occasions when I was a small boy, to give me presents, things she made, and I remember my grandmother Sitwell warned me against selfishness in this respect, and that, in consequence, an ethical difficulty assailed me thus early, for I, too, used to give Miss Lloyd small presents, bought with my pocket-money, in return, as often as I could, and soon discovered that I preferred the pleasure of giving to that of receiving. Was it not, therefore, still more selfish on my part to give? And I remember my father, unintentionally, did not help me in the matter, for I heard him remarking, apropos of some member of the family, that it was "easy to be generous with other people's money"; an aphorism which caused me much reflection. . . . Nevertheless, I liked receiving as well as giving, and that brings me to my great-aunt, Lady Hanmer—Aunt Puss, my grandmother's sister; the most worldly member of an unworldly sept. I frequently used to go to see her with Miss Lloyd as my herald—for Miss Lloyd helped her in a thousand useful ways. Richly apparelled in layers of lace, satin and velvet,

Aunt Puss lived near the railway station, in an incongruous house, very ugly outside but full of lovely French furniture, and china and silks from Weston. She sat in an armchair, with a lace cap poised on the top of her head and with one eyebrow lacquered—for her hair was rather colourless—in its normal position and the other flicked artistically into the middle of her forehead, with the consequence that it looked as if it had been put there—so exquisitely had it been placed, as it were, upon the paper—by the hand of some great Chinese artist: and again, to paraphrase Pater, it seemed as if she had become what men in the course of a thousand years had grown to desire, for she was the prototype of the models whom Matisse and other French artists were, unknown both to herself and to me, at the time painting in Paris. Originally she had come to live near my grandmother, Lady Sitwell, and now that my grandmother had moved from Scarborough, and only came to her new house outside the town for a month or two in the year, she, too, was stranded on this desolate shore; but she did not dislike it, for webs of amusing scandal glistened in the perpetual sunshine of her room, being woven especially for her by the amateurs of the town. And among these enticing threads she spent much time. To myself and to my brother she was invariably kind and I was very fond of her, though she kept us at the full distance of the seventy years that separated our ages.

I went to see her every week when I was in Scarborough, and later took my brother with me, and four times a year she would give us a tip. The suspense for some weeks before each of these occasions was considerable, the atmosphere carefully worked up. Miss Lloyd would say to us, "I think your aunt has a present for you." Our visits to her would consequently become more frequent and anxious in tone, but the gift that had been prophesied would not materialise. When eventually it did, the procedure was always the same. The old lady would ring the bell. Alfred, her harlequin butler, would alight on the drawing-room rug—an Aubusson—for her commands, and then conduct us away into another room. After a few minutes she would ring once more. This time, it would be to summon us. Alfred would leave the room and she would bestow upon each of us a golden sovereign wrapped in a neat piece of tissue

ENTRANCE TO THE WILDERNESS AT RENISHAW

Plate XVII

NORTH FRONT, RENISHAW

Plate XVIII

SOUTH FRONT, RENISHAW

Plate XIX

NORTH FRONT, RENISHAW

Plate XX

THE BALL-ROOM WING, RENISHAW

Plate XXI

SOUTH FRONT, RENISHAW

Plate XXII

THE ARCH IN THE PARK AT RENISHAW

Plate XXIII

VIEW FROM THE NORTH FRONT OF RENISHAW

paper. We would then, as it were, kiss hands on relinquishing office, and be ushered out by Alfred, who would be waiting discreetly behind the door with a slight smile of congratulation, but not enough to give offence. He would make no allusion in words to our good fortune. . . . At her death in 1908 or '9, she left her property to my father, with appointment to Sacheverell and myself, and in her drawing-room, inside a cabinet, with ormolu mounts, and with a Dutch flower-piece for front (it faces me now as I write)—a cabinet made for her father in Paris, when he was with the English troops in their occupation of that city in 1814—were found fifteen hundred golden sovereigns done up in tissue paper in ones and twos and threes, ready to be presented to us in the course, as it were, of the next three hundred and fifty years: for we received them as I have said only four times a year, and my sister because of her sex was never given a sou. This rather differentiated her view of Lady Hanmer from that held by my brother and myself: since, for us, she had been at an early period, and continued to be, the great-aunt upon whom our liveliest interest was focussed.

I will not here, however, unleash on you the whole ancient pack of my great-aunts. Each of my grandparents possessed numerous sisters and, drawn up four-square, they would constitute a formidable though varied regiment of old women. Other single units of them shall make their appearance at the proper time, but to three of them I must introduce you now, as the light first touches their faces for me; two, because otherwise they will slip away into the darkness again before I can show them to you, and the third because she survived to become a beloved part of our grown-up life—though at the time of which I write none of them seemed so much to belong to every week, or at any rate to every quarter, as Aunt Puss, with her ceremonial maundy presentations.

These other aunts, then, were three of the sisters of my grandfather, Sir Reresby Sitwell. First came Aunt Mary, Lady Osborn; a very old lady with eyes that were still lucent and dark blue as the harebells of our native slopes, she was already tottering down the steep return to childhood. Thin, pale, transparent, with white hair and a trembling lip, one could almost watch her growing smaller, as she slipped down it. For

G

my benefit, and as though it were her duty to hand on some sacred flame, she would temporarily pull herself together, to question me, to see that I could say my shibboleths correctly, and that my manners, deportment and knowledge of the world were equal to my age—of four or five years—and station. (Of this I shall have more to tell in the next volume.) Then, after her examining of me was over, she would relax, and talk to me of her life as a child, eighty years before, in the Highlands; would speak of Kinrara, Birkhall and Balmoral—which houses her father had rented for consecutive periods from the time she had been my age until she had grown up—, but more particularly would she relate to me in her faint and quavering old voice, the details—as if they had occurred but yesterday—of the loss of a pet white kid that had escaped, only to perish on the mountains round Balmoral. . . . The adventures of this little animal used to bore me profoundly, but now that they reach me as her theme song across the years, they have come to possess a certain melancholy beauty.

Next there follows her sister, Aunt Georgie, Mrs. Campbell Swinton,[1] my father's favourite relative—though since he was always so undemonstrative, I doubt if she ever realised it—, a delightful and distinguished old lady, more authoritative than her sister. I think it was her love of the family, and of Renishaw, of which she had made innumerable sketches, that had particularly endeared her to him. And I, too, liked to listen to her stories of life in the house long ago, and much preferred her reminiscences of her sister Lucy's red deer there, which used to follow her like a dog, or of the escape of a wild mountain cat brought thither from Balmoral, to Aunt Mary's stories concerning the white kid.

Last, there comes Blanche Sitwell—even the run of her names as you speak them, Blanche Susan Rose, is typical and enchanting—, twenty years younger than the rest of her brothers and sisters, and the only one of them to remain unmarried. She belonged to the rarest of the many diverse types to be found in a family such as mine, by the very variety of its members so essentially English; and can be classified as a

[1] The author of the Reminiscences which form the first part of *Two Generations.*

Hunting Radical. . . . Others of her relations, it is true, had been fine horsewomen, but they, together with the males of the family, were all Tories, whereas she was an ardent Radical of the most advanced outlook. This generous attitude was, I believe, due to an adventure that befell her as a child, no less than to the warmth and kindliness of her nature. At the age of five, while in Italy with her parents in 1848, she had witnessed in a street in Milan, a fight between the followers of Garibaldi and the Austrian governmental troops. The redshirts were temporarily the victors, and one of them, seeing that she was an English child, and knowing that English sympathy lay with the rebels, stopped pursuing the foe, to tear off his red cockade, and pin it upon her dress. This youthful initiation was something she had never forgotten.

The contradictions in her character helped to make up the sum of her great attraction. Her beautiful manners and exceptional charm were opposed to her views and to her expression of them. In art and politics—though art did not so much appeal to her—her mind ranged freely, whereas she was conventional in manners, in her code and religious outlook. She expected good manners in all members of her family. A strong feminist, she was horrified at any lack of a chivalrous attitude in a man, and, while herself a pacifist who would rail against the causes of the war, if a war was in progress she expected all her male relatives to be serving in the forces. She was able to enter equally into the beliefs held by generals and poets, archbishops and anarchists. Among them all, among people of every age and every creed—or lack of it—, she found friends. In later years, from Lambeth, where she would stay with Archbishop Davidson and his wife, who was her first cousin, she would champion the undeserving, and even introduced on one occasion a well-known anarchist within the Palace precincts. She was very fond of the Davidsons and they of her; but this did not prevent her saying what she felt. Once we heard her, from her house in Egerton Gardens, telephoning to Lambeth. The chaplain tried to guard the Archbishop from her, but she insisted on speaking to him; on the subject of a condemned man, who was to be hanged, but with whom she sympathised. "Are you going to do anything about it?" she enquired. "It's your job!" The Archbishop must have said "No"; for she ended abruptly with "Go to hell, Randall," and rang off.

From our earliest years, we three children were fortunate in that this unusual, courageous and fascinating woman—who in later years reminded me so much of Aunt Alethea in Butler's *Way of All Flesh*—took an interest in us—a great interest, but not too much, for she was never fussy. We knew instinctively that she, too, was in league against authority, and saw through the shams. (She told me later that as a girl she had driven past the Guards Club in a hansom cab, and that her mother, when she heard of it, said that neither she nor her daughter would ever be able to lift up their heads again. It meant RUIN.) With my mother she was always on terms of cordial friendship, but she did not get on so well with her own nephew, my father; for he, though himself no less original in character, resented in her the opposing manifestations of this same quality. . . . As to her view of him, although a feminist and religious, she attributed what she considered his shortcomings, his formality and isolation, to having been "brought up by a pack of religious old women, and never carin' for huntin' ". About myself—though we were extremely fond of each other —her chief complaints were that I, too, did not hunt, nor persist in taking a cold bath every morning. I remember in this connection that when, many years later, I told my father that my Aunt Blanche attributed her good health at the age of eighty-seven to having had a cold bath every single morning of her life, he remarked morosely, "Not at all! It merely shows how strong she is: it would have killed *me* long ago!"

As we grew up, she was continually more interested in us, always giving me in particular her support and advice, until, in the end, although some sixty years my senior, she had become one of my most intimate friends. And while I write these words, I can still see her slight, active figure, as she used to run downstairs to greet me, her kind blue eyes, grey hair and sweet —for that adjective, sullied though it is by wrong use, remains the only word to describe it—smile, and I can still hear her charming voice and laughter. Though her counsel was so valuable to others, about herself she was supremely careless, never worrying, hardly bothering even, about her clothes or

what she looked like. She was, indeed, vague to a degree about
her appearance, and far from vain; though as a girl she must
have been pretty. About others, however, and their worries,
she fretted herself perpetually and minutely. . . . But now we
must leave her, for we shall meet her again in later years, when
her house—which she shared with another enchanting old lady,
Miss Anne Hutchinson—became a great place of resort for
their nephews and nieces.

I see two other figures, not such constant landmarks through
our childhood, but going back to very early days and then disappearing. These figures, contrasting so violently one with the
other, are nevertheless bound together; they belong precisely
to the same epoch, and their antithesis is so strong as almost to
present a likeness. One of them was Sir Henry Pennell, a
magnificent old soldier, brave and handsome in his old age,
gay, even when he suffered, and altogether charming, who had
earned great distinction in the Crimean War; the other was
"Old Charles", a deserter from the same conflict. These two
old men, so different in their styles and virtues, though contemporary, constituted to Edith and me an insoluble puzzle;
because, while my grandmother Sitwell and my mother, whose
points of view were often divergent from one another, both of
them encouraged our loving veneration for Sir Henry, Davis
never failed to solicit and to claim our sympathy and respect
for "Old Charles". Secretly my sympathies were—and still
are—with Old Charles. "Think of him *daring* to desert!"
Davis used to say with the light of wonder and simple love in
her eyes. . . . Certainly, these two contrary currents of opinion
worried us: yet, looking back, I think I understand them and
that between them can be discerned a very ancient rift, a
difference of mind due to status. In Davis's attitude can be
distinguished that common-sense view of war which prevailed
in England among the working classes from the time of the
Norman invasion until the end of the nineteenth century (an
outlook similar to that of the Chinese, which saw in soldiering a
low and disgraceful profession), the same which in medieval
times had made the villeins shake their sides with laughter as
they saw their ridiculous masters strutting off to the wars;
while in the opposing attitude of my grandmother and mother

could perhaps be seen the survival of that same fire that had caused the nobles to kill each other off for no reason, except an exaggerated sense of honour and loyalty, during such struggles as the Wars of the Roses.

Sir Henry I see always sitting, muffled up, in a garden under the faint sunshine of the first spring days, the sea showing distant, misty and fitful glints of blue. His heavy, rugged limbs seemed to be sinking with fatigue into the earth, cruelly sprinkled with the shrill, unheeding cups of the crocuses, insistent for attention: he was too old for the spring to do anything for him but tire him further. When he saw us, though, he would rouse himself, and throw round him the old fiery garment of his courage and gaiety, and tell us stories. . . . Old Charles was not nearly so attractive a character as Sir Henry. He appeared to be connected by analogy, as well as by profession, with milk. He delivered it, and everything about him was milky. Always faintly splashed with milk, in addition, his hair and beard were milky, and his face had the milky complexion of a baby's. If you pricked one of his veins, this opalescent liquid would most surely have run out of it. He was very badly paid for his work, it appeared, and, being a veteran deserter, as it were, could obtain no Poor Law Relief, because—or so Davis led us to believe—if he demanded it and gave his name (which incidentally he could not write, being only able to make a mark), the authorities would instantly recognise him and claim him for the Army. (I can hardly believe this now, unless a post in the War Office had been reserved for him; even then he must have been rising ninety.)

Davis, and my sister's governess of hierarchic name, Miss King-Church, both agreed that children ought to try to be charitable, so we were encouraged to put away for the old man sixpence a week out of the shilling each allowed us. . . . And here I must confess that my earliest charity was inspired by greed. Miss King-Church delivered a lecture to us which, rightly or wrongly, I understood to mean that each gesture of charity brought in a substantial and immediate return in cash from Heaven. Accordingly, I rushed with my pennies to Old Charles's help, and was therefore, albeit gratified, in no way surprised when, by chance, a day or two later, my grandmother

Sitwell presented me with five shillings. . . . As a result, I pegged away month after month, and was dreadfully disappointed to earn no further dividend from the higher powers. . . . These figures, old, so very old, fade into the mist, sink into the ground, though the light still grows.

At Renishaw I see many more people; of whom a few—a very few—still remain. Maynard Hollingworth, for example, the present agent at Renishaw, who first emerges in my memory when I was aged seven, and he came to the house to try to teach me how to take a large clock to pieces and put it together again: (for my father, I do not know under what inspiration, at the time believed this to be an essential part of a child's training): alas, my native lack of sympathy with the machine in all its forms triumphed over his every effort to instruct me. I was much more interested in talking to him about other matters, and in finding out what a delightful being, decisive, ingenious and unusually versed in the lore of animals, flowers and trees and yet with a rare comprehension of character in human beings—hence his long friendship with Henry—, was screened by his reserved manner and great height. Perhaps it is only because he seemed so tall to me then that I still see him after this fashion, for I am only an inch shorter myself—but I have never seen anyone who *looked* taller for his height.

These horological visits laid, at any rate, the foundations of a friendship by which I have been infinitely the gainer, for the little that I know of the country, of woods and flowers and trees and butterflies and birds and fish—apart from the elementary lessons of Davis—, was taught me by this best and most genial of teachers with his innate sympathy for all wild things; a man whose interests would make him the most perfect country squire and naturalist combined. It was he, for example, who would give me rural tidings; that he had seen a Camberwell Beauty the previous morning down by the old Sawmill at the edge of the lake, the first seen in the neighbourhood for a century, and how the local entomologist, a rather proud, airy and eccentric character, had chanced to come over the same afternoon to roam in the park for a few hours with his nets and bottles and cases and snaring tackle in general. Maynard Hollingworth said nothing about his morning's adventure to this trafficker in wings, but when he called, about five o'clock, to bid a somewhat *blasé* goodbye, adding that there was no point in his staying further as there was little of interest to see at present, asked:

"What would you say if I told you that I had seen a Camber-well Beauty this morning?"

Catching wildly at his nets, the snarer rushed from the room crying, "Where? Where? Where?"

It was Maynard Hollingworth, too, who told me of the pair of kingfishers of pure white plumage that nested beyond the lake on the dark, miasmic waters of the Rother; and he can give one countless bits of information unknown to others, that on a particular hazel bush grow oval nuts instead of round, that his father had told him this forty years before, and how, remembering it, when the bush began to sprout again after regular attempts to extirpate it by the farmer, he took a cutting for his own garden, and there, sure enough, it bore oval fruit; or that wild violets must grow in one secluded ravine in the woods, because, though he had looked for the plants and never yet found them, notwithstanding, every summer he has seen fritillary butterflies there, the larvae of which—true gourmets in the fashion of the Romans, eating nightingales' tongues—feed only on the leaves of violets. . . . Sometimes I fear that my lack of feeling for rural pursuits, hunting and fishing, and my constitutional ignorance of farming, must pain him; indeed his interests would have made of him a much better country squire than am I; but, on the other hand, as the years developed, we became the two greatest authorities on an abstruse subject, and one of moment to both of us: the character and conduct of my father, a subject of endless interest.

Alas, many others from those days have gone back into the darkness; the old bearded woodsmen, Topham and Kirton, for example. When at Renishaw I would pass them nearly every day, and even now, on Sundays, Kirton, with his bearded Elizabethan face, and sombre clothes and cap—so permanent a part of this landscape did he appear—still seems, in my mind's eye, to sit on the rugged knot at the base of an enormous old elm between the house and the stables, keeping watch to be sure that nothing comes to harm. . . . These I saw frequently, but I also catch sight occasionally of a face that I have seen only once, modelled by the light of that distant decade, the 'nineties: old Staniforth, for instance, one of the family of farmers who are our oldest tenants—having been, indeed, established in the district as long as we have, from at least the thirteenth century. When I was very young and he was very old, he came to tell me of how he remembered being present at the festivities that attended my grandfather's christening. The Bachelor Duke was the godfather, and came over from Chatsworth, there had been skating—it was hard, frosty weather—and a ball in the evening, and an ox roasted whole in the park. . . . I can still see the rather delicate face of the old man as he talked to me, and hear his quavering voice. . . .

There are too many characters for me to tell you of in detail, and some will introduce themselves later, but it is plain that Mark Kirby must enter here; an enchanting rural figure, a great friend of mine, and one who seemed to sum up in his short, sturdy person, his boots, gaiters and stout clothes of Bedford cord, and in his red, very red face, peppered all over with blue shot, lying protuberant just under the skin, the essence of the countryside. Haughty in manner with those—and their name was legion—whom he suspected to be poachers, and for whom he delighted to lay the most elaborate traps of dummy pheasants, made of straw and fastened to branches, so that in the moonlight they looked most realistic, he was known widely, from the situation of his cottage, as the Duke of Plumbley (Dook o' Ploomly), and his rule within the woods, of which he knew every inch, was vigorous and absolute. Accompanied by Clumber spaniels, night bitches of the local breed, he would roam hills and valleys throughout the hours of darkness, and thereby gained an infinite experience of their poetry, of which, in an unexpressive rustic manner, he seemed to be aware. . . . Always the centre of incidents, on one occasion, I remember, he caught a poacher who refused to answer him; the more Mark shouted at him, the more dazed and silent and sulky the man seemed to become—and it was not until an hour or so had passed that he realised that he had caught the rarest of all his poachers, a deaf mute.

To give you something of the quality of a world that has

vanished before our eyes, I append a letter I have found from Mark Kirby.

PLUMBLEY COTTAGE
[*Undated*]

P. Turnbull Esq.

DEAR SIR,

We are heartily sorry to hear of your resigning Sir George's agency, but it is sorrow mingled with joy to know that you will be able to enjoy your well-earned leisure.

I have always said I should give up my job when you resigned, as I know it is easier to work under a master that understands the whole business. But really I don't know what I should do without these woods, our people say I should soon be dead if I had to leave off going down there.

The foxes are very difficult this season. In the spring I reckon I lost over a hundred eggs and young chicken. On Friday, a brace of foxes came to the morning feed in Lady Bank. It was exactly 8 A.M. Later, I saw one run across with a fowl in its mouth. And there is lots of vermin. Here is a list of them I killed last season.

Hedgehogs	6
Rats	9
Jays	2
Hawks	2 (one was 2 ft. long)
Hunting Cats	7
Weasels	4
Stoats	2
Magpies	7

In all my experience, I have never known so much night-shooting as there is this winter. They paid me a first visit on the Wednesday before Christmas in the early morning, as you will know the moon was favourable. They came and had a shot at Lady Bank, at a dummy, as we could find no evidence of a live pheasant being shot at, not even a feather. They next sprung an alarm gun. I was in an opposite direction, and, though I was soon at Lady Bank, they had cleared off.

On Christmas Eve I got the assistance of P.C. Hartshorn, and on Christmas Day in the morning we had been laid in one place some time when I was seized with cramp. I then thought we would go to where I had some dummies fixed, a favourite place for birds roosting, and stay there until daylight, and on our way bang goes a shot at the very place we were going to fix at. I then did the silliest thing imaginable, I made a rush, but we were too far away, and Pan took the lead out of my hand. I know he is handsome, but he is very headstrong, will have his own way and will listen to no one, and I had great difficulty in keeping him back, for they would have shot him as dead as a nail, as it was impossible for us to get near them, as they were at the top of the wood. If only I had exercised a little patience, and let them have another shot, and found out which way they were working, we could still have got them. I did not know how to contain myself for a few hours. Although I could not eat any breakfast, I could have bitten my finger-ends off!

I intended sending you the game-book, but have stayed in the wood too long listening cocks up, and it is past time.—Yours faithfully, M. KIRKBY.

The light of hills and sea shows in these faces: and my first Dionysian or rhapsodic experience was, too, connected with light; light which has always meant so much to me, its quality even affecting my writing. I was about five years old, and had been involved in what seemed at the time irretrievable misfortune. It was a Saturday afternoon in June, the first real exquisite day of summer that year, and I was doing some of my first lessons; but so much did I long to be in the golden air outside that it became an obsession. From my high child's chair I could obtain a view of sea and sky and, lured by their temporary but seemingly ineffaceable gaiety, I resolved to make a dash for freedom. Accordingly, I hurled my copy of *Reading Without Tears* down upon the floor and ran out of the room, a screaming Swiss governess in pursuit after me. But I had obtained a good start and hid under the billiard table in a room in the furthest part of the house. Extricated with some difficulty, I was carried upstairs by my father, who had been summoned by the governess, and in the course of the journey kicked him very hard in the belly. Naturally he could not let that pass, and fearful scenes ensued. I felt disgraced and humiliated for ever. . . . My mother had been out at the time but, when she returned, may have divined the original source of the trouble, because she took the same exaggerated delight in fine days as I did, and felt the same depression over those that were black and foggy: —at any rate she rescued me, restored my self-respect, told Davis to give me tea and, though it was by now rather late for my usual promenade, for it was about six, sent me out alone with Davis.

We went a little further than usual, to the gardens on the north side; flat, level lawns, broken off above the sea (the gardens there had slid into the water about ten years before), which were usually lacking in charm. On the edge of sea and sky great, white, furry clouds, golden-tinged, wrestled and tumbled like Polar bears clumsily in the summer wind. But tonight, skilfully eluding Davis, I ran to the edge of the precipitous cliff and stood there looking straight in the face of the evening sun. The light bathed the whole world in its amber and golden rays, seeming to link up every object and every living thing, catching them in its warm diaphanous net, so that I felt myself at one with my surroundings, part of this same boundless immensity of sea and sky and, even, of the detailed precision of the landscape, part of the general creation, divided from it by no barriers made by man or devil. Below me and above me stretched the enormous merging of blue air and blue water with golden air and golden water, fathomless, and yet more and more fervently glowing every moment, the light revealing new vistas and avenues up into space or out towards the horizon, as though the illimitable future itself opened for me, and, as I watched, I lost myself. . . . All this must have endured only an instant, for presently—but time had ceased to exist—I heard Davis calling. The eye of the sun was lower now. The clouds began to take on a deeper and more rosy hue, and it was time for me to return home: but this strange peace, of which poetry is born, had for the first time descended on me and henceforth a new light quivered above the world and over the people in it.

Like Cellini[1] before me, I had seen the salamander; I had seen it, not in a fire within a house, but in the flames that lit the eye of the sun.

[1] The reader will remember a passage at the beginning of Benvenuto Cellini's Memoirs, where he describes a strange event in his father's house in the Via Chiara in Florence (see Cust's *The Life of Benvenuto Cellini*): "When I was about five years old, my father being in our small cellar, in the which they had been washing the clothes, and where there was still a good fire of oak boughs, Giovanni, with his viol in his arms, played and sang to himself beside that fire. It was very cold; and as he gazed into the fire, by chance he saw in the midst of the hottest flames a little animal like a lizard, which was sporting about amidst that most scorching blaze. Having immediately perceived what it was he caused my sister and me to be summoned, and, pointing it out to us children, he gave me a violent box on the ear, at which I began to cry most excessively. He comforting me kindly, spake to me thus, 'My dear little son, I did not give you that blow on account of anything wrong that you have done, but only that you may remember that this lizard which you saw in the fire is a salamander, a creature that has never been seen by anyone else of whom we have reliable information.' So he kissed me and gave me some coppers." . . . The salamander, an elemental being that inhabits the fire, is the symbol of all art.

CHAPTER FIVE

Entry of the Muses

MY first contact with the worlds of art and literature occurred a year or two after this early experience of Dionysian or creative emotion. My father, gifted though he was, spent his life apart, alone. Indelibly stained with gothic darkness and its accompanying colours, pure and soft in tone, his mind inhabited that ivory tower of the thirteenth century, complete with every convenience of the time—cross-bows, battlements, oubliettes and thumbscrews—that growing unhappiness had obliged him to construct for his protection against the exterior and contemporary world. Like an elephant, he carried his castle on his back, or, after the manner of a snail, could retire into it for dark hours and a hard winter.

More and more he came to frequent his solitary refuge, until just as Pirandello's Henry the Fourth finally declined to emerge from the imperial character part for which he had cast himself, so my father played almost continuously his lonely rôle. Occasionally, he would lower the drawbridge and make a sortie; but these forays became rarer and rarer. The ivory tower, within its magic circle and protected by the stout stone fortifications of a Harrison Ainsworth castle, grew more and more fantastic, and, with each passing year, he spent a longer time in it, until, gradually, he was able to produce within himself even the views obtainable from the loopholes of his fastness, and began to be unwilling to contemplate reality at all. In later life, indeed, he was able, as well, to leave upon a Tuscan villa-fortress the impress of his lifelong and very individual dream, until sometimes that great building seemed to float upon a little fleecy cloud, as in the vision of some saint, between the deep blue Italian sky, always unreal, and the baked Italian earth, so earthy, castles and peasant houses clamped to it with the golden chains of a million vines that every year renewed their fetters.

Even in these days of which I write, when he was a comparatively young man, he inclined to shun the company of living human beings, for they disturbed his ideas, forced him to adjust them with so much violence that slabs of ivory would fall from the tower, exposing its furniture to the light of the outside world. And this he disliked, becoming shy and paralysed under its vibrations. Only where business was concerned did he see, or wish to see, things as they were, with a sharply outlined reality, though in this, also, some slight medieval bias attached to his acumen, and manifested itself in his methods. But, though he felt no sense of anachronism in sitting in his thirteenth-century retreat, reading the latest scientific theories by electric light, at all other times he liked to be surrounded with archers, bowmen and servitors. (Henry, however, subtle and robust and fitting perfectly into the pattern of his time, was determined to be no henchman, but a servant, and continually drew up the blinds, as it were, with a bang. He had a passion for mechanical devices, trouser-presses, instruments for coring apples, special appliances, ingenious but complicated, for cleaning various objects—all these, besides revealing the enthusiasm of a sailor for all things neat and cleverly contrived, were in addition bought in order continually to bring my father up of a sudden against the epoch in which they were both living.) For the rest, if my father *must* meet the living, to him as insubstantial as were the dead to others, he preferred them to be in a trance-like condition of subservience and astonishment. And even my mother's friends treated him in a rather frightened way, for to them he bore that intimidating label, *clever*; a word pronounced as though in invisible inverted commas.

Thus, in spite of his respect for artists and men of learning —a quality he most certainly possessed—he was acquainted with very few, and although he intended to see a great deal of them in some ideal and nebulous future, and, indeed, boasted of getting on well with them in a visionary present, in fact he seldom met them, and always remained apart, though not without an effort to impose his will upon the two or three antiquarian soul-mates who from time to time crossed his path. Before, however, proceeding further I must illustrate his genuine reverence for these beings, together with his attitude of aloofness, even from those to whom his temperament most nearly related him, by two anecdotes picked at random out of time. When I was eleven years old, my health compelled my parents to take a villa at San Remo for the winter, and during that period Mr. Horace Round, the great authority on heraldry and genealogy, came for a few days' visit. In appearance he was hirsute and solid, in the manner of the late nineteenth-century Englishman. Just before he left, he suddenly asked "Are the young people interested in genealogies too?", and then, before there was time to answer him, slid with abandon down the whole length of the banisters. This unexpected behaviour on the part of one who was normally dignified, and by no means young, made us children laugh, and my father subsequently reproved us, saying "Don't laugh! These Great Men have their Little Idiosyncrasies."

The other incident took place some time in the insouciant twenties of this century. Our dear friend Arthur Waley was staying with us at Renishaw, and my father very much admired his translations of Chinese poetry. My father's manners are later in period than himself—about the time of Charles II, but with a touch, too, of the Meredithian baronet, Sir Willoughby Patterne or Sir Austin Feverel, clinging to them; or again they might belong to the eighteenth century, as seen through the pale amber spectacles of one of his favourite artists, once so famous and now so greatly neglected, Orchardson. But, formal, exquisite and elaborate though they are, they could scarcely be more beautiful than Arthur Waley's. Upon a Sunday morning, then, my father was walking round the lake which he had caused to be created, regretting that he had not moved the old river-bed further back, and thinking out possible fantasies in stone, torrents to fall through the hanging woods above, pavilions upon islands and decorative effects generally (a few years before, he had determined to have all the white cows in the park stencilled with a blue Chinese pattern, but the animals were so obdurate and perverse as in the end to oblige him to abandon the scheme). The lake is shaped like an hour-glass or a figure-of-eight, and a bridge spans its waist. On this bridge my father met Arthur Waley advancing towards him. Each took his hat off ceremoniously and said to the other, "How much I wish we were going in the same direction!" and passed on. Half an hour later they met again at the same place, having pursued their contrary courses as though they were planets whose goings and comings are immutably fixed by the sun, and repeated the salutation.

This aloofness, which hedged my father ever since I can remember him, possessed its own beauty and interest. Yet, how remote he was! For example, in those days of house-to-house canvassing, he had personally visited each dwelling in the borough of Scarborough several times, but he seldom remembered any single constituent when he met him. (He has frequently in later years passed me by in the street, looking at me without recognition.) My mother's friends he saw very seldom, even when they were his guests. He liked to have his luncheon alone, an hour earlier than the rest of the family, and he always had tea by himself in his study. Often at Scarborough, when I was a small boy returning from a winter's afternoon walk with Davis, just as we entered the hall, he would open the door of his room, which was on the ground floor, and call me in to talk to him. (He loved children until they were old enough to reason, express their views and show a will of their own; he loved their originality and the amusing, naïve things they said.) He would talk—always interestingly. But, looking back, I realise how little he told me of himself. My mother, for example, would, when I was with her, tell me of incidents from her childhood, and of her brother, her sisters, her mother, her adored father who could do no wrong in her eyes. She enabled me to enter into her childish life as she had lived it. But my father, I suppose because it had not been happy, never mentioned his childhood. His range was wide, and intentionally instructive. It touched inevitably at some point or other in history, geography or art, with, occasionally, the wonder of an elementary conjuring trick, with pennies disappearing from between the fingers, for amusement and to hold wandering attention. Even this, I have sometimes thought in later years, was really designed in order to prove that magic could not exist, and that everything that occurred possessed a material explanation. He would tell me not to be frightened of the dark (he was very sympathetic about it): there were no bogies in dark corners, no ogres or ghosts; they were only stupid and ignorant nurses' tales. Why, he had himself exposed that sort of thing once and for all, years ago.[1] . . . Then he would veer to medieval times, tell me a story he had read lately about a knight or a minstrel, or lift me up to look at a painting—a painting brought from Renishaw.

It was by George Morland, a picture of the Westminster Election, and represented Georgiana Duchess of Devonshire kissing the butcher, or about to kiss him, in an attempt to win his vote for Charles James Fox. On each side of the butcher's are the usual Morland sheep, the foreshortened face of a farmer's boy, the usual thatch and trees, and the rather horrifying concomitant detail, the meat hanging up in the open shop, the dingy, mangy collie running out of it with a sheep's head in his mouth, all this was painted with, for all its convention, an extreme realism, so that my father had chosen it out of the other pictures, very skilfully for his purpose. Its story was easy to explain, and it was precisely the painting to arouse a child's interest and hold his attention at an age when the greatest work of Titian or Raphael or Michelangelo would to him signify nothing. Thus it would ensure an early inclination towards noticing pictures, and looking at them. . . . From the time, therefore, when I was four or five, I remember *The Westminster Election* much more vividly than the lovely Copley group of *The Sitwell Children* or *The Fruit-Barrow* by Henry Walton: but, notwithstanding, it may be that the intense pleasure I have derived from seeing works of art all over the world, and the influence they have exercised upon my mind, are due, at any rate to some degree, to this ruse of my father's; for he was very anxious that, when I grew up, I should care for pictures— though, of course, only for the pictures himself admired. . . . At any rate it became a regular turn, a treat, and I was constantly worrying him to "show me the butcher's shop".

My first impression of a great artist—I do not mean a great painter—dates from the age of five, when Edith and I went to spend Christmas in London with my Londesborough grandparents, and without my father or mother. Looking back to that time, it seems to have been a season of primrose-yellow fogs and of snow, of brilliantly-lit shop windows, full of toys

[1] See Appendix A, p. 255.

and flowers and sweets, and from the distant darkness of the nights that followed I recall—so that our nursery must have looked out on the square—the occasional clip-clop-clop of the horses, their hoofs muffled by the snow. Very clearly, too, I see the carriages, (who, that has known it, can ever forget the peculiar smell, mingled of oats and beer and leather, which haunted every four-wheeler, and accorded so well with its speed, and the face and voice of the driver?). In my ears still vibrates the tinny whistling that went on desultorily through the night; another London sound that has vanished, a whistling all the more shrill and forlorn because the world of the 'nineties was so quiet. As it died upon the thick night air, it left behind it, you would have said, a trail of sadness, of disillusionment; while the very hopefulness of its original start, until the break came in its voice, was as though someone were seeking a a needle in the haystack of the enormous night. That sound, so typical of the city to which it belonged, was killed by the coming of the telephone—though it continued until forbidden at some period during the war of 1914-1918. And, accompanying it, I see the face of the crossing-sweeper under the gas-lamp as he limps to open the door.

His was a trade which had belonged to nineteenth-century art and literature, had inspired Dickens and Gavarni and many more. Other cities had possessed their own specialities—Paris, the cake-sellers and jugglers of the Champs Élysées; Rome, the women who sold flowers, and who wore white flowing head-cloths and wide, striped skirts with aprons; Naples, her blind men singing and clawing at guitars; Seville, the *aguadores*, with their hoarse cries; but of London, the crossing-sweeper's was the most typical of the semi-mendicant professions. He belonged as much to this, the metropolis of mud, as modes to Paris, sand to Timbuctoo or coal to Newcastle. His apotheosis, no doubt, had been during the 1840's, before London had been paved, when, for example, even Oxford Street more resembled a derelict canal on the outskirts of Venice than one of the chief thoroughfares in the richest modern city. Then, as soon as for a moment the mud was swept back, the immense tide rolled in again. The sweepers often gave it up in despair, and the two opposite sides of the street were for hours as remote from

each other, though the passers-by on one side could so clearly
see those on the other, as in the opposite alleys, divided by a
canal, of the Adriatic city, save that here there were no bridges.

The crossing-sweeper, in those days, was all-important;
but even then it was constantly remarked that no one had ever
seen him with a new broom, only such a stump as I remember
my crossing-sweeper carried. But this was no sign of poverty,
for fortunes had been not seldom amassed in the trade. The
same persons, men or women, would occupy the same pitch
year after year. They inherited it from their predecessors and
bequeathed it to their heirs. The work, or rather the hours of
work, varied with the locality. On the whole the crossing-
sweeper rose late, for experience had taught him that the entire
race of early-risers was unworthy to be served, apt to be costive,
poor and in a hurry. It was necessary for him, of course, to be
astir earlier in the City than in the districts devoted to fashionable life. Moreover, in the squares, contact was usually established between each family and the sweeper, who thus obtained
benefits, scraps from one house, and a regularly paid salary,
however small, at another. In the prime of this career, one or
two well-known characters were ambitious, and went in for
ornamental sweeping. In the 'forties there was one man who,
near the present Marble Arch entrance to Hyde Park, sculptured out of the dirt all sorts of designs, hearts and diamonds
and icicles and stars, and another, by St. Giles's Church, who
hedged his right-of-way with holly twigs, and after dark
decorated it with lighted candle-ends and small tallow lamps
until it glittered like a Neapolitan *presepio* at Christmas.[1]
When the crossing-sweeper, however, had finished his day's
work he "shut up shop", that is, swept the dirt, upon which
he had during his hours of duty imposed some kind of order,
back over the road again.

The crossing-sweeper I remember used to have a chat to
my grandfather every day, and be given a shilling: he knew
everybody's business, but the great days were already gone,
abolished, as a writer in the 'forties[2] had foretold, "by wood,

[1] See an article by Albert Smith in *Gavarni in London*. (David Bogue.
London, 1849.)
[2] *Ibid.*

asphalt and granite, gutta-percha and India-rubber". Nevertheless he was still an essential part of the life of London. Yet, he disappeared as swiftly and quietly as a ripple in the mud. It was only yesterday that I used the expression "crossing-sweeper" and, seeing a look of incomprehension on the face of the girl to whom I was talking, realised that both word and trade were now obsolete and void of meaning.

Even to a child, the London of my young days presented its peculiar qualities of fascination and excitement. The very squalor of its climate, the cold and darkness and fog, the greasy tracks in the roads, the streets patterned by feet, made the luxurious life, the entertainments, the dresses, the carriages, the lighted windows of the shops like baskets of flowers or sweets, or even like rockets offering their flowers and stars to you, all the more alluring, as if you found a great picture in some dusty auction-room or saw a diamond shine suddenly from a lump of mud. And above all, there was the size of London, vast and intricate, and seeming in those days of horse-drawn traffic, when to go from Mayfair to Regent's Park took half an hour, of a shape and lay-out that it was impossible for the mind to grasp. Sprawling over a whole county, it imparted that sense of the unnaturally gigantic, of unparalleled immensity, which those who wrote upon romantic taste during the eighteenth century had held to produce the esthetic emotions. In this city dwelt whole nations of the rich and poor, whole tribes of atrocious drunkards, and cripples gnarled like trees, as well as a thousand times as many dancing girls as ever postured on the terraces of palaces for Cambodian kings; in it were Chinese towns and Indian settlements, and Jews congregated round their synagogues. Yet it was the heart of England, beating to the tune, unmistakable in vigour and rhythm, of its blood. An understanding of the world-wide roots of this great city, passing deep under the surrounding water to the rich soil of the five continents, was enforced by a visit to the Zoological Gardens, whither beasts had been brought from every direction across the seas. My grandmother's love of birds, and especially of parrots and cockatoos—a trait, which, as will be seen in the next chapter, finally affected very directly the course of her life—inspired her to take us to the parrot-house. I have never forgotten first entering it from the darkness of that afternoon, how triumphantly and gaily the feathers flared in the cages, and how the shrieks and squawks and chatter were so intense as almost to offer another element, like water or fire, in which you could drown or scorch yourself.

The culmination of our visit, however, was the opening of the Drury Lane Pantomime on Boxing Day, to which our grandparents were escorting us in state. All through the afternoon which preceded the performance, Edith and I were made to rest in bed, in a darkened room; that kind of resting which during childhood makes those subjected to it so much more tired than would the perpetual running about which both their limbs and spirits crave. We were mad, drunk, drugged with excitement. Drury Lane on Boxing Day had been a subject of conversation between our nurse and her friends ever since we could remember. It had seemed an ideal, visionary and beyond attainment. . . . Yet now it could almost be touched, its air breathed in, and we threw our pillows wildly into the air, and even shouted, in our enthusiasm. Still time advanced. Outside the drawn blinds, the yellow murk was deepening into a thick and nearly palpable darkness and the whistles that sometimes pierced the silence sounded lonely and choking. (Perhaps the fog would be so bad that we should be unable to leave the house? . . . But we knew, we felt, that this could not happen.) . . . At last, the climax arrived; we climbed into the carriage, and after half an hour arrived at the immense portico, got out, were conducted to the stage-box, sat down on our chairs, our chins just resting on the dusty red plush of the curving ledge that hemmed us in. The curtain went up. Already our grandparents were watching us, with the strained and anxious attention which elderly people reserve for children, to see if they are enjoying themselves. . . . Alas, right at the beginning, just as the devil had appeared in a red enveloping cloud through a trap-door, the accumulated feelings, the long-drawn-out sense of expectation and, above all, the total exhaustion resulting from so protracted a period of resting, overwhelmed me and my nose began to bleed. . . . Hastily I was taken out, to the little room at the back of the box, and told to lie down, flat, upon the gilt sofa. . . . As I lay there, I heard Davis remarking that it might be a good thing in the long run, because it was said that a week or two before the Prince of Wales had only just been saved from apoplexy one night after dinner by his nose beginning to bleed. . . . Whether I, too, was saved from this fate by the involuntary following of so illustrious an example, I do not know; but I know this, that all the first part of this performance, to which I had so eagerly looked forward, was spent by me, lying there, with a rusty key down my back, a piece of melting ice upon my forehead, and, in addition, the whole time undergoing threats of being subjected to other ill-judged and empiric remedies.

Fortunately, I recovered early enough to see Dan Leno as the Beautiful Duchess, wearing a hooped dress and a large picture hat with a feather flowing from the brim, fall through the harp he was playing. I can still remember vividly that supreme representation of artistic abandon, and also, before it, his virtuoso plucking at the instrument, the strings of which were made of elastic. I even recall a fragment of Dan Leno's dialogue with Herbert Campbell. I believe it took place in the same pantomime, though I saw him subsequently more than once. At any rate on this occasion his appearance contrasted violently with that of his former rôle. Gone were the Gainsborough costume, the wig and the plumes. Instead of them, he wore a tattered white silk dressing-gown: and a little tail of hair, screwed up at the back of his head, together with a curl-paper or two, completed a masterpiece of slatternly *ensemble*. His face looked unmade-up and wrinkled. He was, temporarily, a pantomime Queen interviewing her cook in the morning. Herbert Campbell, Leno's large and wonderful foil, acted the part of the cook. The Queen was finding fault with the household accounts.

"Cook," she was saying, "the bills for the Palace are far too high. Look at them! Onions, onions, onions, always onions. I don't understand. Did we give a garden-party?"

"No, Your Majesty, you forget. Onions repeat."

Such jokes may not sound funny—though this still seems funny to me—, but Dan Leno's personality in effect raised everything he did or said on to a plane of its own, for he possessed a sense of comedy that transcended comedy and became tragic, just as his face, one of the most sad and individual masks that any actor ever presented to the public, went beyond laughter and placed him on a level with the most famous clowns who have ever lived. He must, I think, have been a master of make-up, as well as of facial expressions, and I long to have watched him, as later on several occasions I was privileged to see Chaliapin, in his dressing-room, engaged upon this branch of his art. Always one was aware, as the Russian giant sat in front of his mirror, with a huge arm raised, waiting to modify the shape of his nose, or to alter his hair and eyes and eyebrows and mouth, so as to turn himself into the pock-marked image of Don Basilio, or into the handsome, impressive tyrant, Boris or Ivan, or into a drunken monk or a tramp, that a great artist was at work moulding the most intractable of all materials, the human face. The individual essence is always the same, but transmuted into a new form. The true actor is seldom so happy, it may be imagined, as when he is thus preparing himself for his rôle, every night he varies his work of art a little, trying some new effect that will give life to his impersonation, shed light on the character he is creating. But there may, too, enter into this metamorphosis other than a merely conscious transference of personality. Alexandre Benois, in his recent delightful book of reminiscences,[1] tells us that Nijinsky only emerged from the lethargy that he always showed at rehearsals when he finally put on his costume—about which he was always very particular that it should be an exact realisation of the designer's sketch. Then "he gradually began to change into another being, the one he saw in the mirror. He became reincarnated and actually *entered* into his new existence. . . ." Looking back, this could perhaps also be said, in a different way, of Chaliapin. . . . But then the art of histrionic make-up is a subject that requires an entire book to itself, though Daumier, in a magnificent drawing, has rendered something of the strangeness and splendour of the spectacle, of seeing how a being, chameleon-like in his attributes, salamander-like in the fire of his blood, can alter before your very eyes, become unrecognisably raised above himself.

[1] *Reminiscences of the Russian Ballet.* (Putnam & Co., 1942.)

Chaliapin, great artist though he was—a greater actor than a singer—, nevertheless possessed the unparalleled instrument of his voice, personal and grandiose as his physique, to help him: he had the temperament, too, of one who had been spoilt by the fashionable worlds of all Europe and America, and this helped to give him confidence, for he knew that he could impose his will. Dan Leno, humble and unspoilt, was no less of a personality after his own fashion. His range was limited to certain parts, but within the bounds of these he showed true genius. And I like now to think that I comprehended at an early age a little, at any rate, of that peculiar gift which had won for him, when he was a boy, the astonished admiration of Charles Dickens, himself the chronicler of the celebrated Grimaldi, and an author for whose works I cherish feelings of such affection and reverence. . . . Yet Dickens's keen and swift judgement of him comes as no surprise, for to anyone who saw Dan Leno it must be plain that, although of Irish extraction, he, in the same manner as Dickens himself, though in a different medium, was essentially a poet of London,[1] one who could, beneath the brilliant shell of exaggeration that contained them, create characters who are real to us as the comic characters of the novelist. "He evolved," says one writer, "galleries full of quaint beings, male and female, grotesque, whimsical, bizarre beings, yet sufficiently human for us to see and understand the solid foundation on which the burlesque was built. . . ."[2] "I am not sure", writes Clement Scott, pondering on a lifelong experience of the stage, and imbued with a specialist knowledge of its history for the past two centuries, "that in certain gifts of expression, variety and,

[1] Dan Leno's real name was George Galvin (1860-1904). He was born in Somers Town, on part of the site of St. Pancras Station. His father and mother, itinerant music-hall artistes, performed professionally as Mr. and Mrs. Johnny Wilde. His father was Irish, and Dan Leno showed traces of this parentage in his voice. His first appearance was as "Little George, the Infant Wonder, Contortionist and Posturer", when four years old, in the Cosmotheca, off Edgware Road. He occasionally stayed in Ireland in his youth, and it was during a visit to Belfast in 1869—where he appeared as "The Great Little Leno, the Quintessence of Irish Comedians"—that he attracted the attention of Dickens, who happened to be in the audience (See E. V. L. in the *D.N.B. Supplement*, 1901-1911.)

[2] *Dan Leno*, by Jay Hickory Wood. (Methuen & Co., 1905.)

if I may so express it, tornado or instant comic force, Dan Leno ever had a rival."[1]

In addition to this most aptly termed quality of "tornado" —which, indeed, I was privileged to see at work that evening, when he fell through the harp—, Dan Leno manifested very strongly another most rare attribute, difficult to name. Everything pertaining to him was mysterious, because curiously affecting. . . . Two decades later, when I obtained permission to visit the old Bethlem Hospital in order to examine a fresco upon one of its walls by the hand of Richard Dadd— a little-known but interesting painter for over forty years incarcerated, as the result of having murdered his father, in 1843, in that enormous and concrete synonym for madness—, I saw there, too, in Bedlam, a sketch by poor Dan Leno,[2] who had for a time, at the end of his life, become an inmate. It was signed, if I remember rightly, "Lord George Montagu Scott,

---

[1] *Christmas Pantomime*, by A. E. Wilson. (George Allen & Unwin, 1934.)

[2] The delusion concerning the nobility of his birth was one of the symptoms of the insanity that afflicted Dan Leno, but the real account of his origin and upbringing, given in the note above, seems too detailed to admit of any doubt as to its accuracy. Miss Constance Collier, in her book, *Harlequinade* (John Lane, 1929), has an account of how she and her mother came home one night, to their flat near Seven Dials, to find Dan Leno, who was unknown to them in private life, waiting in their darkened sitting-room. It was past midnight, and he had been there since 10.30, for he wished to see Miss Collier in order to offer her a five-year contract to star with him in various tragedies of Shakespeare's, notably *Richard III* and *Hamlet*. Her whole account of the episode is remarkable, and in her description of Dan Leno himself she says that "his eyes were beautiful, like the eyes of a wounded animal or a great tragedian." However, I must confine myself here to quoting the following apposite passage. Directly she came in, she says, "I sensed something alien in his manner, and those tragic eyes, when I looked into them, were full of deep sorrow. There was no comedian here. Without any preliminaries he burst into his life story. Whether it was the true one or not I have no means of verifying, but this is how he told it to me. He said he was the son of a Scottish marquis, and that his mother had been a housemaid in his father's great mansion somewhere in the north. He was nine years old when he tramped up to London with her, and they walked all those miles in the bitter winter. He sang outside village public-houses for a few coppers to get their food, and they ate snow to quench their thirst as they tramped along the frozen roads! It took them nearly a month to get down from Scotland, walking all the way. He told me of his life of direst poverty in London, of his struggles until he began to be known and fame came to him at last. All the time he was holding my hand in the most painful grip. My arm was nearly paralysed. And then he told me the ambition of his life was to play Shakespeare."

otherwise known as Dan Leno". But, in spite of the hallucination of its signature, nevertheless even this water-colour,
executed while the brain of its maker was out of order, seemed
to possess some quality of its own, a feeling for space and for
stagecraft, that proclaimed it to be the work of a great actor
though not a great painter. It was conceived, for all its lack of
skill, in theatrical terms.

As I have said, everything connected with him was unusual
and moving, and I find the appearance of his ghost to the late
Stanley Lupino—which he describes in his excellent book of
memoirs[1]—most credible. He prefaces the story with the
avowal that, though he had no belief in spiritualism, he was
conscious of life being full of suggestive coincidences. Thus he
had always felt that Dan Leno, for whom from his earliest
years he had cherished a feeling of hero-worship, had exercised
a kind of influence upon his career. His own first appearance
on the boards had been when George Lupino, his father, had
carried him on the stage of Drury Lane as a property baby,
at the time of Dan Leno's acting there and of his greatest
renown. Later, when as small boys Stanley Lupino and his
brother Mark were living, so he tells us, in a garret in Kennington and unable to buy food or provide a fire, they discovered
that they could obtain fuel by collecting at night the wooden
blocks that were thrown aside upon the road during the
construction of the first cable tramway. Being thus employed
they sheltered for a time on the steps of the stage door of
Kennington Theatre. While they crouched there, shivering,
a hansom cab drove up and a little man jumped out. He paused
on seeing the two children, felt in his pocket, and said to them,
"Here, sonnies." It was half a crown, and before the two boys
had recovered from their surprise he had disappeared through
the stage door. But the driver told them who the stranger was,
and thereby inspired their devotion to him. Indeed, in after
years, Mark Lupino was buried, at his request, next to Dan
Leno.

When Dan Leno had long been dead, and Stanley Lupino
was, in his place, the star of Drury Lane, he was snowbound

[1] *From the Stocks to the Stars. An Unconventional Biography.* (Hutchinson
& Co., 1934.)

and obliged to spend a night in his dressing-room there, and, though he did not see any identifiable person, the manifestations were so vivid and alarming as to convince him that the room was haunted. . . . But some time later, a more singular incident occurred and, on this occasion, not on a snow-hushed night, but while all the lights of the theatre were blazing, and the noise of the crowd, waiting outside to enter, could very plainly be heard through the window. It was the hour of that rite, sacred to the stage, which I have attempted to describe, the hour of make-up, and the star was very busy, adding to and altering his mask, and his mind was occupied with this and nothing else. . . . Suddenly, just above his own face in the looking-glass, he saw another, also in make-up, regarding him with a smile. He noticed a line across the forehead where the wig had been removed. Lupino winked, and the newcomer winked back at him. . . . Then he saw who it was—there could be no mistake, it was Dan Leno! . . . At first he thought someone was playing a joke on him. He swung round, but the room was empty and quiet, and the usual sounds came in from the street. The only door in the room was still shut, as it had been. Nor could the phantom be explained by any accident of light or movement in the mirror. Lupino learned subsequently that this had been the favourite dressing-room of Dan Leno, and the last he had used.

In reading this story we must remember, too, how intense had been Dan Leno's sentiment for Drury Lane and his desire to appear on its boards; so intense that when his lifelong friend, Johnny Danvers, took him for the first time, when they were both young, to inspect the outside of it, he looked at it for a few moments in silence, and, after walking up the flight to the entrance, knelt suddenly upon the topmost step. Then getting up from his knees, he returned to his friend, and, seizing him by the arm, said quietly, "Johnny, I shall act there one day."[1] If any spirit, therefore, haunts the theatre in which, when embodied, his chief triumphs had occurred, it would assuredly be the ghost of Dan Leno. . . . And I, too, must try to conjure it up for you again, so that you may watch for an instant that slight, lonely figure—always indeed lonely,

[1] *Christmas Pantomime*, by A. E. Wilson.

because it was impossible, if he were on the boards, to look at anyone else, even Herbert Campbell, who served as a foil in the sense that the setting serves as a foil for a stone—posturing on the stage, seeming in every contour of face, every line of body, to glow with a special lustre in the glare of the footlights to which—and for which—he had been born. Every gesture, every turn of the hand, the dress, the wig, above all the make-up, the air of tremulous precision with which he sat down to the harp, the winsome, nervous flicker of those mournful eyes, the incised lines round the mouth, which so clearly spelt resignation before life's uncertainties—indeed almost a preparation for them,—the often melancholy accents of the voice, all went to build up a character that remains unforgettable. And then, on the top of all this detail, he brought to bear upon his audience the power of that irresistible comic force that has been noted, until the roof echoed as a great wind of laughter swept and swept again the heads stretching before him into the darkness as a wind passes over a cornfield. . . . So, though the figure has long been still, we leave him in that light, burning with his own flame.

Drury Lane on Boxing Night, then, presented me with my first glimpse of the stage. . . . The next of the arts to come my way—though I was not aware of it at the time—was music, and a year or two later, in the person of Rubio, the well-known 'cellist.

Looking back, it seems as though Rubio were always in my life, in the background, recurring with frequency at many points and from different directions, and though I never knew him with any intimacy, later I came to bear towards him a feeling of great affection and respect. In after years, when I so often met him at the house of Mrs. Gordon Woodhouse, that beautiful virtuoso of genius, in the modern world the only representative of ancient music who, by her inspired playing of clavichord and harpsichord, can make it come to life in the full glory of its precise yet involved fire, and thereby captivates the hearts of all musicians, so that, in her drawing-room, congregated to hear her play, you will find the scholarly massed with the original and audacious, with the leading composers and artists of Europe, I learnt to understand his character, and

how great an artist he was. I shall have much to say of Mrs.
Woodhouse later, so now I need only conjure up the image of
Rubio, sitting near by her at the harpsichord, with a face of
rapture, the light on it like the light on the face of a saint
painted by Ribera: yet, so far as she was concerned, he would
have been only content if she had been able to play Bach for
twelve hours without a break.

In the days of which I am writing, however, I saw him only
in London, where he came to teach, or try to teach, my sister
the 'cello, till the whole house echoed with wooden groans,
melodious certainly, but formless and inchoate as the singing
of the choirs of fallen angels; or at Blankney during the English
Saturnalia, when there were always a great many foreigners in
the house, friends and governesses and teachers of the various
generations. And so he must enter the book here, and not later.
At that time I never realised, as I have said, how great a
musician he was. And, indeed, how would it have been possible
for me to tell? since my Aunt Raincliffe, for all my uncle's love
of music, saw to it that Blankney was, most emphatically, no
house in which you were likely to encounter an artist. London
existed for parties—and very good after their own fashion they
were,—and the country as a place in which to kill things, foxes,
deer, hares, pheasants, snipe, partridges, woodcock, rabbits,
even rats—almost anything you saw except horses and dogs.
Horses were enthroned in a state which even Caligula never
dreamt of for his favourite, in the temple dedicated to them
near by, and dogs were allowed to run about the house itself
unmolested; sad, dank Aberdeens, white or peppered. Yet
music was so much in the blood of my mother's family that it
is only right that Rubio should enter here, and down the
perspective from her side. . . . How, again, could any child, not
possessed by music, recognise Rubio's quality?—to him it
would be preferable to look at Rubio, rather than hear him
play. Indeed, I thoroughly enjoyed watching him, under the
early light, arrive at the house in his dark clothes and vast
black felt hat, with his hair and beard, then of a raven blue-
blackness, and his glowing eyes, full of a foreign fire. He was,
in fact, the first representative I had seen, and a very fine one,
of the Latin races.

Agustín Rubio had been born in 1856 in the southern province of Elche, with its oasès of date-palms and flocks of camels. Before coming to England, he had toured the Continent with Patti and had played in many European capitals. He settled in London early in the 'nineties, about the time I was born, and lived there for nearly half a century. During this long period he was the friend, and acted as the guide, of every Spanish musician of importance who visited England and, especially, he was the intimate friend of Albéniz. Though a most remarkable musician, he was poor: he had never saved money, nor, indeed, would it have been possible for one of his unique temperament to do so. He lived in two dusty rooms in the Fulham Road, and gave away every halfpenny he earned directly it came to him. He no sooner saw the beggars, the wretched, the dispossessed, than he bestowed upon them anything he happened to be carrying on him. In every circle he had people who loved him, and when this fact, together with his own genius, is taken into consideration, it would seem almost impossible for such a man to go in want. Nevertheless, in later and, for his friends, sadder years, money had from time to time to be collected among them for him. At first, when the news was broken to him, he was furious at the smallness of the sum subscribed, which he regarded as in some way constituting a slight upon St. Peter, whom he held in reality to be respon-sible. But, later, he was pleased, and at once—and on every subsequent occasion when a similar sum reached him—proceeded to give it away, much of it to the indigent of the district, or to private persons in Spain, whom in any case he could not have seen for whole decades, and the rest to the charities in his native land. His only expenditure upon himself consisted of a fraction, shillings rather than pounds, which he retained in order to add still another to his collection of old masters, all of them bargains, but, in spite of the great names he attached to them, and in spite of his genuine feeling for painting, none of them what he aspired for them to be. The walls of his rooms were covered with these dark and sultry daubs. . . . He would spend nothing on himself, nothing on clothes for his massive frame, or on food.

To the very end of his life he remained as full of sparks as a magneto. He spoke—and, indeed, often *roared*—with a strong Spanish accent, and his vocabulary in English was no less personal than his appearance. The strangest hybrid words came in profuse and glorious procession from his mouth; words which bore to the ordinary counters of the English language exchanged in talk the same relation that dragons and hippo-griffs and unicorns, and the other inhabitants of the medieval bestiary, bore to the horses and dogs of every day. He was fond, too, of illustrating a musical remark vocally, humming, singing and roaring, with the prodigious power of the bellows within his broad chest. Everything about him was warm and generous, yet austere and grand. And, as he grew older, he became still more impressive in his looks; with his silver hair, sweeping over and round his head, his swarthy Spanish skin, his eyes, which contained in their white a suggestion of blue, and seemed all the more large and full of dark fire because of the spectacles he wore, with his long black beard that swept over the upper part of his waistcoat, and was striped, not flecked or streaked, with dazzling white, this splendid-looking old man in whom beat the heart, stern but generous, of a saint, came more and more to resemble a prophet, a Moses who was not a Jew but a chivalrous Iberian. Often, until the time of his death, I would see him walking in Chelsea, his huge eyes looking within him to solve the mysteries of God and of music. He saw no one who passed until you called him, when his face expressed so clearly, first the shock of, as it were, landing in the day of the week, and hour of the day, then pleasure as he thundered out a greeting.

He died in London in April 1940, having survived long enough at any rate to see the end of the Spanish Civil War, which had caused him, because of his love of his country and of his strong religious convictions, misery of the spirit. . . . A great musician, who knew and understood him, wrote to me about him in some such words as these—I have not the letter by me—: "He was the most musical person I ever met, and many great artists owe him more than they could ever express: for his was the rare and unselfish gift of imparting this genius to others. He never cared, as long as the performance was beau-tiful, who made it so. He was a genius, a genius on a large scale but in a very special sense, very complicated in his musical emotions, and he possessed an amazing gift for combining the utmost beauty of phrasing with the strictest time, so that a whole world of liberty existed within these rigid and prescribed bounds; the same liberty, with the same passion prisoned in it, which is to be found in early English verse. . . . Only one person in a thousand could appreciate him in this way: thank God, I was one. "

Looking back at those gatherings, long ago, at Blankney, I often wonder how Rubio fared: he can scarcely have enjoyed the killings with which the days were full, or, at any rate, they must have become a little tedious. But it is easy to understand how the un-ordinary behaviour of his host stirred a response in him. He was present when my uncle—who was a man who cared for food—was called away from a most delicious dinner in order to race off with his engine to attend a fire. Rubio would often, more than thirty years later, recur to this incident with pleasure and wonder, describing as he put it, "the glorious behaviour of Lord Raincliffe", and how he had returned with his face dirty and his hair singed. "No Espanish nobleman would do that", he would remark reflectively at the end.

If Rubio represented for me the birth of music, my earliest recollection of an author, and of the impression such a being is apt to create, goes back to the same year, when I was seven.

Renishaw was full of guests, mostly relations of my mother's; poor relations who spent a shadow-like existence silhouetted, at discreet intervals, upon the walls of great house after great house. They were said—and proudly they bore their label—to be "such fun"; though, somehow, one never gathered precisely how or why. ("Do you know Tita? She's such fun.") . . . Nor did my Sitwell and Hely-Hutchinson relations ever seem to enter into this ambiguous, esoteric category: serious-minded, their every thought tinged with religion, no one attempted, or dared, to say it of them. Though they prided themselves upon the possession of a sense of humour, they would have been the first, I think, to resent being dismissed as "such fun". No, these relatives of whom I am talking were in the main distant female cousins of my mother's or "connections", spinsters for the most part, though they included a few married couples. But the worst of it was that this fun-brigade stood divided against itself, mutual back-biting was rampant, although it must be admitted that sufficient *esprit de corps* prevailed to prevent a general break-up. No member of it would insinuate about another anything so definite as to make it unlikely that that person would again be invited to the house; such an action would have constituted a breach of the unwritten rules. Notwithstanding, when several ministers of fun were gathered together at the same time, an unmistakable acerbity would before long begin to make itself felt. Tempers were short, owing to pressure of work. In this resembling the members of a second-rate provincial touring company, they would stop at station after station along the line, to fulfil, as it were, a week's engagement. As soon as it was finished, they must pack again and be off. . . . Then there would be a wedding or a memorial service, and they would all be obliged, at great expense, to troop back to London. But they *had* to be there, or someone might be offended. Besides, they must be seen, could not afford to drop out. It provided, too, an occasion for them to meet, concoct their future plans and see that these would not conflict in any way. It was hard work, harder every year now. Fun, oh, such fun, but they had little of their time to spare, and none for the children of the house. If they could think of nothing to say, they just laughed, which kept things going, and compared with saying things to make the others laugh as treading water does with swimming. It kept them afloat, and just maintained their reputation for gaiety and humour.

At such moments the children regarded them with a horrid, round-eyed wonder. Indeed, they hated the children in every house at which they stopped, and the children returned the feeling. But though the young were so great a trial, experience had taught these relatives that it was usually necessary to mask their animus, because the mothers never really seemed to *like* a show of it and one pleasant place of resort had already disappeared from circulation owing to a piece of over-enthusiastic and too hastily improvised mischief-making. In so far as the members of my own family were concerned, they had already detected the existence in Edith of some germ of poetry, which had made them single her out as an object for spite, pretending

H

to be pity, and had soon found that the game was safe. I was an "elder son", so, quite apart from the fact that my parents would have resented criticism of me, it was wiser to pet and to take trouble; you never knew; this treatment might pay a bonus later on. They did not, I apprehend, care much for my father either. He had the reputation of being "clever", and if you were "clever" that somehow or other cancelled out "fun". Of course they did not see him a great deal in the day, hardly ever until dinner, but the ice-coated politeness with which he enveloped them made them feel, often, that they were being strangled or had fallen unaware into plaster of Paris. And, in any case, instinct told them that they would have got more out of it if only he had not been there—and, indeed, would have been there more often themselves. And the place was very convenient —situated on two main railway lines—the food was good, and they were really treated with some consideration. . . . Even here, however, it was hard work. (Such fun, oh, such fun: the tread-mill again.)

We returned their dislike heartily enough, but, if compelled to see much of them at any particular time—beyond all things, I resented their being brought up to say good-night to me— I could always find relief for my feelings by going down to the pantry the next morning, where I enjoyed a talk about these visitors with Henry, whose vivid tongue and acute judgement of people were a continual, if inhospitable, source of pleasure. . . . Generally, I would find him polishing a piece of silver with great vigour, and to the same rhythm as the tune he was singing. The August sun was pouring in at the windows, which looked on to the yard, where an enormous lemon-coloured St. Bernard dog—one of the last uncrossed with Great Dane, for these massive creatures had been bred here for over a century, at some time during which period a great storm had wiped out the pure strain in their native Alps—sat, as if it were posing for a portrait by Landseer, at the mouth of his kennel. Opposite, a passage led to the office, so that there was a continual bustle of farmers, come to ask for a new barn, of woodmen and gardeners and estate workers, and of eccentric characters, too, who had just walked up here through the park in order to waste the agent's time. In front, at right angles, the chef, in his high white hat and white clothes, could be seen against a background of iron spits through one of the three tall windows of the great kitchen, three storeys high. He seemed to be directing operations with vigour and vivacity. Henry, in the morning, usually chose hymns for his singing, rolling the pious and familiar words round his tongue with an inconjecturable unction and rendering the notes in his well-known bellow, deep and melodious. Or, again, he might be singing a favourite song—"The Pope, he is a happy man". This poem I take to have been a free variation of Thackeray's "Commanders of The Faithful" and was concerned with a comparison between the sensual indulgences affected by the Pope and the Sultan of Turkey, for, whereas the Holy Father was allowed as much wine as he liked, but no wives, the Caliph was permitted as many wives as he liked, but no wine. After he had finished his song, which he had given with the utmost formality, as though in front of an audience, he would stop, and catching sight, through the window, of the chef and his underlings preparing food, would remark, "Miss Vasalt looks hungrier than ever this year, Master Osbert. All you've got to do now, if you want her to come and stay, is to hang a bit of bacon outside on a hook. She'll smell it, wherever she is, and walk straight in and begin laughing at once—unless she catches sight of Sir George ('*No, no, no!*')—fit to bust 'erself, poor lady."

Fortunately, in those worlds apart of child and adult, except upon a picnic or outing of some sort, we saw little of the fun contingent. One such occasion presented itself, however, when an old elm, at the near end of the avenue, was cut down. We were all of us, fifteen or sixteen persons it may be, taken out to see the giant fall, for this is a process that most of humanity loves to witness. And it proved, indeed, an interesting spectacle, because, as it fell, a cloud of bats, hundred upon hundred of them, flew out into the, to them, impenetrable daylight, and wildly sped and spun and circled, squeaking in their voices that are so high-pitched as to be felt rather than heard. With shrieks of terror, as though they had just witnessed the landing of Mr. H. G. Wells's contemporary Martians, the women of the party, clasping their piled-up masses of hair tightly with their hands, so as to protect it—for a myth persisted that bats loved to become involved in those nests of crowning glory—, fled towards the house. It was an extraordinary scene, such as I now see might have inspired the brush of Nicholas Poussin, the flight, the stricken faces, the gestures of despair, the eyes round and welling with terror. (Incidentally, some much more attractive inhabitants of the tree, a family of white owls, also thus forcibly ejected from their ancient home, flapped through the air, though no one seemed to suspect them of wishing to nest within these flowing locks, whether golden or raven; and indeed that same afternoon they turned my mother's beautiful prize pigeons out of the dovecot on the lawn, and remained therein established for many years.)

Even at so early an age, I found this rhythmic flight of women towards the house impressive: I scarcely expected to witness again soon such a classic scene of anguish. But I was wrong, for a few days later Miss de Rodes, the heiress of the beautiful Elizabethan house of Barlborough, brought over to tea at Renishaw the members of her house-party. When, arriving on the lawn, she introduced one of them as "Mr. Augustus Hare, the writer", her words created obvious panic. There ensued, metaphorically, the same tragic rush of women, away, off stage, holding their hair and, this time, crying, "He may put *me* in a book!" . . . It was then brought home to me for the first—but alas! not the last—time, the universal horror in which the writer is held in England, in elegant circles no less than among the common men. The lurking, inexpressible, awful fear haunted each of their hearts, like that which, were it sentient enough, would haunt the mind of a butterfly about to be netted, anaesthetised, killed and pinned out upon a square of cardboard. The prejudice was immense. Each man—though my father's attitude, of course, was exceptional, for he was interested—and each woman felt sure of being herself the quarry. Perhaps, also, beneath the horror, sprang up a certain feeling of self-importance, in the same way that it had been, in a sense, self-flattery in each woman to have been so convinced that the bats wished particularly to snuggle in *her* hair. . . . But then, writers, in addition, were *clever*. Even bats were not *that*! Again, the victims recoiled.

Later, I used to wonder whether they had expected to find

themselves pressed, as are wild flowers by sentimental old maids, between the pages of *Walks in Florence* or *Walks in Rome*, but now I realise that Hare's *The Story of My Life* had just recently appeared, in which many names of persons, and accounts of them, occurred, and this they must have known, or sensed. But I still consider it to have been on their part an unjustifiable panic. I can conceive of no writer *wishing* to "put them in a book". . . . Yet I suppose at the very moment I am being guilty of it.

This, then, was my first glimpse of a writer. My initial contact with a painter, on the other hand, began during the following spring, when with the rest of the family I sat for a portrait group to John Sargent. And, though I did not then realise that art was to be the paramount interest of my life, I intend, in order to complete this first volume, to write something about the picture, how the artist painted it, and about himself as well as his sitters. The minute circumstances attending and leading up to the painting of a conversation-piece of this kind are not without an interest even today, and will possess still more when the rendering of such groups is finally an extinct art. And though I prefer broader effects, the describing of all this, the domestic and intimate detail of it, resembling to some degree the task which the Dutch seventeenth-century artists set themselves, is itself not without a certain fascination for a writer. But, beyond this, I want also to reverse the previous process and, instead, as hitherto, of noting only how the growing strength of the light had revealed to me two stylised landscapes, filled with people, either posturing for the regard of the outside world, or quiescent, content with the world within themselves, I will try to revive for the reader the look of the figures before the painter in the hard north light, like that of a permanent arctic dawn, of a studio near the river, to see how that light showed *us* to *him*, as either we posed there—in that big room, bristling with canvases and containing the smell of paint which binds all studios, whether the working-places of good or bad artists, into a kingdom of their own, hedging their occupants off from the rest of mankind—uneasily balancing, modelled for him by the cold fingers of a wintry day, or fidgeted, waiting our turn, in the dark background behind him. Although at the time occupied with some particular physical aspect of one of the persons before him, or of something connected with it, of how the scarlet dress of my pale young sister—with her hair of shallow gold that was almost a polar green—blazed out against the lying avenues of the tapestry, that led from nowhere to nowhere, of how the glistening white of my mother's dress must flicker like a spectral flame against the figures of the tapestry, frozen in gesture, rigid in imagery, or of how he was, in general, to balance into a tolerable whole the various patterns which people and things imposed upon his facile and poignant brush, how, for example, to reconcile the warm and breathing yet correct beauty of my mother with the woven figure of the woman at her side, in a classical robe, with her cold face reflected in the mirror she was holding before her, and with one foot poised above a basket full of enamelled masks; although, as I say, occupied with all this, he would nevertheless often peer round at us with his prominent eyes, saying a word or two to amuse or pacify or keep us quiet until the moment when we were due to mount the scaffold before him.

CHAPTER SIX
The Sargent Group

FIRST of all, since I possess a horror of hedging over matters wherein art is concerned, let me a little elaborate my views of Sargent's paintings: a body of work all the more necessary for us to explore at this moment because it constitutes an approach to the age which we are about to enter. These portraits are the guardians of the Edwardian shrine, comparable to the figures of the Four Marshals, those grotesque and stylised generals, with their swords and shields, their purple faces and bulging, glaring eyes, who customarily guard the entrance to temples of the Buddhist faith in China. . . . I do not—as, for example, did my father—consider Sargent a great portrait painter, in the sense that Velasquez and Goya and Manet were great portrait painters, but neither, on the other hand, am I content summarily to dismiss his name, in the manner of those who were led by the late Mr. Roger Fry.

Fry's enthusiasm for pure painting, and its progress, induced in him a rather contemptuous attitude towards survivors from other epochs: but, just as types of animal and vegetable life elsewhere extinct remain living, to be seen and touched, to this very day, in parts of the world remote from contact with other continents, so portrait painters lingered on in England. But a spoon- or duck-billed platypus is none the worse a platypus because it has long perished from all other parts of the wide globe excepting Australia alone; nor, for that matter, is it a better, and the fact of its withdrawal from the rest of the earth must not be understood in any sense to make it rank as an innovator. . . . To the aim of continuing to paint likenesses in a particular style, Sargent added his own smartness of eye, and many a touch from the Spanish and French Impressionist masters. And here the Ruskin-fed ignorance of the English public came to his aid, and helped to build him a reputation for brilliance: the mass of art patrons in this country, who had remained steadfast in their ignorance of Manet and Degas and Renoir—and even of Goya—, although these painters had been famous on the Continent for a quarter of a century, mistook a reflection of this technique—now itself discarded in the lands of its origin, or, rather, actually antiquated by the complete transformation in the aims of painting that had occurred during that period—for genuine and personal invention. Nevertheless, and in spite of his lamentable frescoes in the Boston Library, it must be allowed that Sargent was a painter who lived for his painting, and that, albeit not of the first, or even second, order, not of the quality of the two other celebrated portrait painters that America has given us, not as sound in workmanship or as true in colour as his fellow citizen, John Singleton Copley, nor as inspired a poet of his period as the great Whistler, yet he can be compared in value, though not, of course, in the method of his painting, to such other fashionable portraitists of their epochs as Sir Thomas Lawrence or Winterhalter; painters who will always be of more interest to writers and social historians than to their fellow artists.

In order to make a living in England during the late-Victorian and the Edwardian ages, every portrait painter had, to a certain extent, to become a faker of old masters, because the clients who could afford to patronise him demanded, "Give me the sort of Gainsborough that my grandfather had,"—or, more usually, that somebody else's grandfather had, and which the grandson had sold—"but not so old-fashioned!": that was the clamant cry. Sargent, by supplying old masters, to which was added the skin-thin glint of the French Impressionists, novel to the English public, precisely met this demand. His portraits are usually good period-pieces, *de luxe*, and bearing the same relation to the portraits of Gainsborough or Sir Joshua, that the Ritz Hotels in the ruined capitals of Europe present to the Place Stanislas in Nancy. But they will always retain their own charm; a charm often founded in the repulsiveness of their subjects. For to light upon a fashionable painter who knows how to paint at all is a rarity, and Sargent knew how to make—or, rather, fake—his obvious effects better, even, than did Winterhalter.

Moreover, Sargent matched the Edwardian Age to a nicety; he was entirely occupied with outward and superficial effects. Money, one would hazard, bore for this painter the identical Edwardian sanctity that it possessed for the City magnates,

sporting peers and old-clothes and furniture dealers whose
likenesses and those of their wives he was obliged to perpetuate.
Yet the fact that he was so plainly more interested in the
appurtenances of the sitters and in the appointments of their
rooms than in their faces, from which he sought refuge in the
tilted top-hats, with their sombre but water-light reflections,
the cravats and fur coats of the men, or in the tiaras, flashing,
stiff but uneasy, above the heads of the women, or in the
brocades and velvets they were wearing, in no way detracted
from his popularity with them. To the whole age which he
interpreted, these values were true values, and so could not
be resented: sables, ermine, jewels, bath-salts, rich food, covered
every lapse or defect. Sargent remains the painter of Pêche
Melba, the artist who exalted this dish to the rank of an ideal.

Notwithstanding, this occupation with the exterior of life
presented, too, another aspect: his still-lives, his water-colours
of Spain and Italy, are better than his portraits. His swift,
camera-like eye could net very quickly the particular quality of
surface and texture at which it was looking, the shadow and
glitter, unified and become one, of vines and colonnades and
silks and sails and pearls and water. Again, his charcoal drawings
of men and women are often beautiful, nearly always characteristic, and, even when meretricious, are to be preferred to the
cautious pencil drawings of those artists aptly characterised
by Mr. Augustus John, in his recent autobiography, as miraculously "able to turn wine into water". At least Sargent converted
the wine into *wine*, though often it became of an inferior, if
heady, quality; as it might be, an American Burgundy.

The events and opinions that, in our particular case, led up
to the execution of the Sargent group, offer a field of minute
observation and present a microcosm of the development of
English esthetic opinion; so I propose to examine them in detail.
My father and mother were married in November 1886.
Early in January of the year following, they arrived in Scarborough. My Aunt Florence notes in her journal, "George
and Ida made their first appearance after their wedding. They
were received with 600 torches. The scene was quite lively.
The carriage was drawn by the life-boat crew, and all the town

turned out to see the procession." Two records in gouache of
their entry into the borough seem to have constituted his first
experiment as a patron. But in the course of the years following
he gave considerable thought to the question of having my
mother and himself painted—partly, no doubt, because so
many family groups and portraits hung at Renishaw. In his
conduct of the matter, and in the reflections he makes on it,
he displayed the usual idiosyncrasies of his character. He
refused to accept the wedding present of the accustomed
elephantine silver inkstand which the tenantry of that time
seemed always eager to offer on any suitable, or unsuitable,
occasion. Instead, he employed Frank Miles, the fashionable
portraitist in pencil of the 'eighties, to come to Renishaw and
draw a series of heads of my mother and himself—preparatory,
it may be, to a painting. But he changed his mind, paid for the
drawings himself and, instead, as a present from the tenants,
commissioned an artist called Heywood Hardy to paint my
mother driving in a chaise through Forge Valley, the celebrated
woods near Scarborough which belonged to her father. In
reference to these transactions a letter from my father to his
agent at the time says, "I must absolutely decline to accept the
silver inkstand. Silver in these days is bad in design and still
worth a burglar's while to take away. Instead, I am asking
Heywood Hardy to paint a picture of Lady Ida which the tenants
will both like and understand."

The drawings by Frank Miles, done when my father was
twenty-six and my mother eighteen, are rather charming in
their slight way.[1] The cause of Heywood Hardy's[2] being finally

[1] Much prettier, and truer, likenesses of my mother are, however, to be
found in Du Maurier's illustrations to his novel *Peter Ibbetson*. He greatly
admired her looks, and she figures in them, wearing a small fur cap on her
head, as the Duchess of Towers.

[2] Concerning Heywood Hardy, I know nothing except this one picture,
but I wrote to an old friend of mine who, I felt sure, would be cognisant of
his work and identity. In his reply, written on 5th September, 1941, he says:
". . . About sixty years ago I first knew of him as a painter through Robert
Hilton, the then Westminster Abbey *basso-cantante*. Hardy was doing a
picture of a Viking father who was just in time to save his young son from a
wolf. He could not find his ideal, but going to the Abbey, he saw Hilton,
and implored him to sit for the picture, *The Slain Enemy*. '*Safe in his father's
arms*.'
"He was versatile. Perhaps his chief work is the altarpiece for the Haslar
Naval Hospital Chapel. He died—aged ninety—in February 1933."

employed for the painting, however, was, I understand, that in the interval Frank Miles had gone mad. The first symptoms of his approaching insanity, indeed, manifested themselves during his stay at Renishaw. One afternoon, while being driven over to see Welbeck, he looked at the gangs of black-faced miners walking with their wooden tread along the road, and suddenly enquired, "Why are there so many sweeps here?" . . . It may, perhaps, have been his conduct during this visit which induced my father to adopt towards artists his very individual attitude, compounded of patronage, irritation, always "knowing better", admonishment and qualified applause.

The extracts that follow are all taken from letters, otherwise mostly concerned with estate matters, that passed between my father and his agent, and former tutor, Peveril Turnbull. It must be explained that both Mr. and Mrs. Turnbull were cultivated and intelligent, and friends of such people as Walter Crane and D. S. MacColl, both of whom wielded in their own spheres considerable influence.

On 14th September 1887 my father writes: "Will you approach Alma-Tadema, if you know his address, and ask him if he would be willing to paint a portrait of a young lady, and what would be the price of such a portrait without hands? . . . I am not sure whether to go to him or Richmond."

Fortunately Turnbull must have failed to recommend Alma-Tadema; but it must be admitted, in defence of my father's judgement, that my mother possessed the 1880 Greco-Italian ideal-of-womanhood appearance which Tadema delighted to depict amid marble baths and cypresses. At that moment, too, he was considered a great artist by many others, as well as by those belonging to the fashionable world. . . . Indeed, Roger Fry—finally, after their deaths, the herald of Cézanne and Van Gogh—(I have always more sympathy, though his courage wavered, with St. Peter than with St. Paul)—began, during their lifetimes, as a fervent admirer and disciple of Alma-Tadema's genius, and his own early paintings were so much influenced by him as to be indistinguishable save in their lesser competence. The peculiar specification concerning the hands was in no way bound up with some complex about the Venus de Milo—such caprices were not, in any case, then tracked to these odd causes—but was inspired by my father's comprehension that Tadema could never paint them successfully.

So, Richmond[1] the younger was chosen. I do not regard this as a happier choice; nor, in the end, it is evident, did my father. . . . On 4th February 1888 he writes again to Turnbull, from 41 Clarges Street, Piccadilly: "I am here for a week in order that Richmond may begin his portrait of my wife. He wishes to paint her in an amber dress of a loose and rather æsthetic character and totally unlike in every particular to the style and feeling of those she wears. I fear that much of the character of the sitter must be lost when arranged in a fancy dress of someone else's choosing."

Three weeks later, he adds the following details: "Richmond gave up of his own accord his dress after it had been made and looked hideous. Now, he has begun a portrait of Ida in one of his lolling-back positions. I have told him I dislike it, I wonder if he will kick? If so, I think of going to young Herkomer, do you think highly of him?"

Richmond, however, did not kick, and the eventual portrait of my mother that resulted, not sitting in "one of his lolling-back positions", but uncomfortably upright, dressed in a turquoise-blue coat and playing a zither—an instrument she had never seen in her life until she sat to Richmond,—is very hideous and insignificant, although a pretty likeness. My father, on receiving it, was anxious to cut out the head, frame it as a small oval picture, and burn the rest. Nevertheless, and for all its lack of merit, it has, today, a certain period charm.

A lull of nearly a decade ensued on the painting front, excepting for one letter which my father wrote to Turnbull, in the very middle of the 'nineties. Dated the House of Commons, 21st March 1895, it runs: "I see that the Scarborough Con-

---

[1] Sir William Blake Richmond (1842-1921) was the second son of George Richmond, the charming portraitist, whose profession, but not whose gifts, he seems to have inherited. Sir William is now chiefly remembered for the bombastic scheme of decoration he carried out, at considerable expense to himself, in St. Paul's Cathedral. For this scheme he chose to use mosaic, of the rules of which he remained, obviously, in complete ignorance until the end. . . . By a stroke of irony, this painter was named after William Blake, for his father, as a boy of sixteen, had met that great genius, and had fallen under his spell. Indeed, after Blake's death, it was he who had been chosen to close the dead man's eyes.

servative Testimonial on my marriage now amounts with interest to £198. What shall I do with it? If I had spent it on silver plate as proposed, the plate would probably have been worth about fifty pounds now. I do not care to be painted except in a big family group. I might get large silver mirrors for the drawing room, or a fine escritoire or sideboard by Lethaby or Blomfield, or a picture by a good artist of my small boy, but I still incline to a china dessert service with circular caricatures by Harry Furniss. One can use china as ornament when not on the table, and political caricatures by Furniss would reproduce also for fireplace tiles, illustrations to a book, and one might make a book-plate. This idea also seems more original and in keeping with the circumstances."

After that, the decade continues peacefully along its esthetic course, although during that time my father's ideas crystallised considerably. The great exhibition of English Art at Burlington House had taken place, to which my father had lent the Copley group of the Sitwell Children. He had spent many hours at it, comparing the merits of the various famous portrait painters of the eighteenth century. And at about this time, or perhaps a year or two later, he wrote me a charming letter, which I found and mislaid again only the other day; a letter wherein he gravely and politely discusses with me, although I was only six or seven, the various excellencies and faults of such masters as Gainsborough, Sir Joshua and Romney. . . . But of all the pictures he had seen, it was the family groups that he had most enjoyed, for these appealed particularly to the ancestor-and-descendant theme which so largely dominated his conception of the family; "A delightful thing for one's descendants to have!" Besides, in 1898, he sat, in evening dress with white waistcoat and tie, to Tonks for his portrait, though I find no reference to it in his correspondence. Tonks stayed at Renishaw for some time, and I remember dimly that he stared for several hours a day, as it seemed, at the Copley group, and, more clearly, his appearance, so lank, damp and forlorn, as he came back to the house one afternoon, when the punt he had been sailing on the lake had capsized. A sudden squall had swung the sail right over, and he had been immersed. I have never seen a figure that looked more wet, almost as though clothed in water weeds. The visit, I think, was not a success, and he never repeated it. There must have been a clash of temperaments. But all I know is that when, after the last war, I came to be friendly with Tonks, my father always referred to this austere artist, with his passion for connoisseurship and tradition, as "that Bolshevik", and that Tonks, for his part, told me, without making any comment, that when he had been beginning his morning's work at Renishaw, my father had looked across at him and said, "Don't paint the hair today: it's not quite in its usual form." . . . Be that as it may, he was not satisfied with Tonks's portrait and realised now, finally, that it was a family group that he would like to commission.

On the 29th of April 1899, from Belvoir House, Scarborough, he writes once more to Turnbull, a long letter, for the most part concerned with balance-sheets. To his surprise, he says, he finds that he is slightly better off than he had feared. He adds: "I feel now equal to paying for a large portrait group, and wish you would ask your artist friend MacColl whom he recommends. I also wish to buy two pieces of land behind Morewood the butcher's shop. . . . What is to be done about buying a billiard-table?"

A few weeks later, he reminds Turnbull to ask MacColl his advice and outlines vaguely the sort of picture he requires: "I want a picture that will mezzotint well and someone who can paint figures in landscape or *genre* figures. I could pay a good price to a good artist, but if it is better to employ a young and little-known painter, the thing is more of an experiment and the price should be in accordance."

In his reply, Turnbull must have informed my father that MacColl had recommended for the task Jacques Émile Blanche, that charming man and brilliant talker who, during his career, had been the owner of so many good, and the painter of so many bad, pictures. (He was very generous, as they say, "with his own". Before the war, hardly a gallery in Europe existed in which did not hang several portraits by Blanche, the gift of the artist.) But it is plain that in reality my father, though he still asked for suggestions, no longer needed them. He had made up his mind. . . . Accordingly on the 14th of June he wrote to Turnbull—from Scarborough again—the following long letter, this time devoted entirely to the question of the group, and of the esthetic principles underlying it, and making no mention of butcher's shop or billiard-table:

MY DEAR PEVERIL,

So much obliged for MacColl's advice. Is it possible anywhere to get a photograph of Blanche's portrait groups, or a landscape of the painter Thornton and his family? I should much like to get one if possible.

I believe I have settled with Sargent for next year, but "there's many a slip". Sargent is very much the kind of painter MacColl recommends. He will only paint in his own studio in London, won't hear of a motive for the group or an outdoor picture, and will please himself. It is evident therefore that I cannot get what I want, namely a portrait group that will give information and tell its own story, and will hang and mezzotint as a pair to the Copley. At the same time Sargent *is* a great artist, and I shall get the best this age can offer, if all goes well. What I am afraid of is that Sargent has not studied the principles which have to be considered in dealing with portrait groups, an art by itself, and that he will presently realise that five figures can't be grouped without a motive, and will "chuck" the picture before it is half finished. Sargent and the modern school seem actually proud of not being able to paint what they can't see. But what a misfortune that is, for that is where the highest art comes in. Sir Joshua and the old English painters were always doing it, and how much one would have preferred even a second-rate painter of that age who could give one a conventional landscape without too vivid greens and blues.

I showed MacColl Richmond's portrait and told him the story, which I dare say he doesn't remember very well. The difficulty there was that Richmond won't allow one to see his canvas from the day he commences it to the day he finishes it. When one did see it one was appalled at the length of leg. . . . I have had a good deal to do with artists and always get on well with them.—Yours very truly,
GEORGE R. SITWELL.

This letter is full of that minute concern with detail which always distinguished my father's dealings. Its air is peculiarly and individually authoritative, and denotes, too, that he has no intention of depriving any artist of the benefit of his own experience and of his advice. In the last short sentence alone, which a little suggests an heroic theme blown upon a cracked bugle, there is to be detected, perhaps, an under-tone suggesting, in spite of the assertive ring of it, that even the writer of the letter himself is unconvinced of the truth of his boast. . . . At the same time, apart from this, and apart, also, from the wealthy patron's eternally love-sick attitude for the latter half of the eighteenth century (but *before* the French Revolution) which it so typically manifests, a basis of esthetic good sense lies under what he says.

Several things had occurred in the preceding year to make my father alter the direction of his gaze, diverted now from Herkomer and Blanche towards Sargent. For a year and more he had been fascinated by Sargent's approach to his sitters, one so novel in England, and, besides, he had been introduced to the painter himself (as well as to his work) by George Swinton, my father's first cousin and a son of Mrs. Swinton, whom the reader met for a moment in a previous chapter.[1] George Swinton possessed a love and knowledge of the arts and was one of the first patrons—if not *the* first—of both Orpen and Sargent. His wife, Elsie Swinton, whose great portrait by Sickert is so justly celebrated, became in after years—and, I am glad to say, remains—an intimate friend of mine, and of my sister's, though to achieve this, we had, all three of us, first to fight our way out of cousinhood into friendship. She was perhaps the most gifted of all English singers of her time, an artist of a remarkable kind. Her childhood had been spent in Russia, and it seemed as if something of the genius of that country, of its generosity and fire, had entered into her spirit as well as into her magnificent appearance. The incomparable warmth of her voice cast a strange spell that served to keep even a fashionable audience quiet, and soon made the songs of the great Russian composers, which she had originally introduced to English audiences, both popular and modish. Moreover her beauty, as she sang, a beauty of an unusual and moving kind, inspired many celebrated artists to execute drawings and pictures of her. When I think of her— as a person, I mean, not as a singer—as she was then, there returns to me her interest in all that concerned her friends, her quick taking of a point and eager questions, but, above all, her gaiety. Her whole person glowed with it. She seemed always to be laughing, lovely, full-throated laughter, with nothing affected, and nothing ugly or irritating, as so often there is, in its sound. As a singer, however, not the least remarkable thing in her career was her decision to leave the concert platform in

[1] See footnote on p. 178.

the plenitude of her powers and with her vitality undiminished. Her sense of the theatre, so evident in her singing, made her determine to avoid the inevitable anti-climax of a declining voice, a gesture of sacrifice to her art which is, indeed, all too rare among singers.

It was through the Swintons, then, that Sargent came to Renishaw to make the acquaintance of his sitters and to see the Copley group, with which his picture was to tally, for it was to be of the same size, the figures in it of the same proportion, and, in so far as he could be induced to make it, of a similar feeling. (It remains, I believe, the only group he ever painted of that particular size, and with that particular proportion.) Rather unexpectedly, the Copley immediately excited Sargent's admiration, and his first words, on seeing it, were, "I can never equal that". George and Elsie Swinton accompanied Sargent at the beginning of his stay, but I can remember little of him from this visit, except that he spent a considerable time fixing a cyclometer upon Elsie's bicycle. I can, however, still see very clearly in my mind's eye George Swinton and my father walking up and down the lawns together, talking, but not listening, and pointing their sticks in different directions. This was the first time I had been privileged to see them together. They resembled each other considerably in appearance and manner, though George Swinton was taller (my father is six-foot-one), presenting a Byzantine counterpart to my father's Gothic; and their interests were akin. As the years progressed, this racing over the lawns, with their usual air of dignity combined with disapproval, their somewhat similar walk, their identical bearing and gestures, and the mutual but impersonal criticism by each of them of the remarks the other made, became one of the favourite "turns" of the Renishaw summer. "I should put the vista there, if I were you." "No—no—no!" . . . "But the eye should always be carried towards the horizon." "Such a mistake!" (with an air of finality) "they never do that in Italy."

I recollect, too, another incident of the visit. Sargent one morning, in the Upper Drawing-Room, executed a water-colour of my mother, Sacheverell and myself which was said to be astonishing in its virtuosity and swift, breath-taking resemblance, and then gave it to her. When they went down to luncheon, my mother left it, for safety, between the pages of one of the weekly social papers of the epoch, *Tatler* or *Sketch* or *Onlooker*, and then forgot all about it. By the time she remembered its existence again, a few days later, a new journal had arrived to replace the old, and one of the housemaids, in the fatal process of "tidying up the room", had taken the old to use for lighting the fires. (To match this story, I may say that in subsequent years my brother bought in Paris a very beautiful silver-point of Modigliani's—among the most beautiful of all his drawings. On arriving to join me at Biarritz, he showed it me, and forgot to put it away. In consequence, the valet of the hotel, while packing for him a few days later, tore it up and wrapped some shoes in it. My brother only discovered his loss when unpacking.)

Neither my father nor George Swinton seemed as a rule inclined to take the other's advice, though each possessed a respect for the other's judgement. Consequently I am surprised that my father, in the matter of the Sargent, should have allowed himself to be so plainly influenced by his cousin. . . . However, things were now set in train. Sargent agreed to paint a picture of the dimensions and kind desired, for fifteen hundred pounds: a charge by no means excessive, for, though not yet at the height of his vogue, which reached its climax in about 1910 when his prices ranged from two to three thousand pounds for a single portrait, he was already receiving large sums for his work.

Tremendous scenes of bustle and activity now began at Renishaw. "We have got the tapestry, picture and sideboard packed up, and the place put right again", the sub-agent reports to Turnbull, in a letter of the 20th February 1900: for, since it was intended, as I have said, that the group should be a conversation-piece of a certain size, with its own appropriate furniture and accessories, and since Sargent refused to paint except in his own studio, my father, when he set off for London during this first winter of the Boer War, took with him the Copley picture—so that Sargent should have it before his eyes while he painted—besides the other extensions of his own and the family personality that follow: a vast and dark panel of Brussels tapestry, measuring thirty by twenty feet, signed by

Louis de Vos (the least exotic, though not the least sumptuous of the five Louis XIV pieces I have mentioned as having been purchased by Sir Sitwell Sitwell), and representing the Triumph of Justice, a figure—for once un-blindfold—posed on a column, holding in her right hand a sword and in her left the scales, against a Versailles-like vista of clipped trees and of water, while other personifications of virtue, with their particular attributes, loll in classical attitudes in the foreground; a so-called commode, designed by Robert Adam, and executed by Chippendale and Haig, with ormolu mountings by Matthew Boulton—a large and exquisite piece of furniture, made for the marriage of Francis Hurt Sitwell in 1776, perhaps the finest example, certainly one of the two finest, of English furniture,[1] which reached the highest point of design and the highest pitch of execution in the decade from 1770 to 1780; a silver racing cup[2] won by an ancestor at the Chesterfield races in 1747; and, last but not least, my mother, my sister, my brother and myself, as well as the toys with which we children were to play and the black pug which was to be beside us; Yum, a sleek Chinese dog of changeable, oriental temper whom—because this is a convention for children, a liking for dogs being almost obligatory upon them—I was expected to fondle, in spite of his snuffling manners and snapping ways. . . . Even if London were not being bombed nightly at the time of writing, this would seem a heavy and curious cargo to transport today there; but ideas were, indeed, larger in Victorian and Edwardian times, and, though my father was so careful, and usually subjected every small item of expenditure to the most minute scrutiny and criticism, on a grand scale he could often be generous, and on occasions such as this remained undaunted.

We settled then, for the first few months of 1900, in 25 Chesham Place, a house which was almost opposite the Russian Embassy and belonged to Mrs. Moreton Frewen, a sister of Lady Randolph Churchill. (Only a few days ago I saw a ragged gap in the line of painted-plaster houses precisely where it used to stand.) It was "done-up" in the height of the fashion of the

[1] The piece of furniture was then supposed to be French, and is referred to, in the letters that follow, as "the French Chiffonier".
[2] This is the bowl in which, in the group, my mother is arranging the flowers.

moment, for interior decoration had only just started as a mode and on its present professional basis, and Lady Randolph had been almost the first person to interest herself in it and may perhaps have had a hand in these colour schemes. Before 1900, the esthetes alone had shown an interest in the rooms in which they beautifully existed; ordinary rich people had been content to live in the houses in which they lived, with their possessions, ugly or beautiful, about them. They accepted that which fate had decreed, unless a fire, or new circumstances of one kind or another, imposed fresh surroundings upon them. They had not hitherto felt a conscious need for self-dramatisation—but, with the turn of the late 'nineties into 1900, their confidence had all of a sudden wilted. Thus I believe that the rage for interior decoration can be related to the enormous social changes that were only hidden from them by the still shadowy outline of the new century.

In the house that we had taken, mauve, I remember, was the colour on which each scheme was founded. Indeed, mauve was the acme of fashion in all branches of decoration, whether for ceilings or wall-papers, and for coverings, of a woman herself no less than of her furniture. And so I remember an aunt, who wore very striking and modish dresses, appearing in a gown of mauve striped with turquoise blue, and a year or so later the rage for it had spread to other strata, and every toque, bolero and feather-boa was tinctured with this pale, aniline reflection of royal Tyrian. Henceforth, mauve and the Boer War were to be inextricably associated in my mind. Nevertheless, the house was to be memorable to me still more because it contained the first electric fan I had ever seen and, since I was young and the idea that electricity could move things, as well as illuminate them, was novel to me, I never wearied of turning it on and off to the violent peril of my fingers. The machine stood on a mahogany pedestal in a corner of the dining-room that was peculiarly draughty by nature as well as by this artifice, and I fear that before I had tired of this new toy, my mother and her friends had, during the bitter early months of that year, paid for my pleasure with many a cold, many a stabbing rheumatic pain.

One other feature of the house is perhaps worthy of remark.

Its owner's boudoir, in which we children were obliged to do our daily lessons, was lined with photographs of Winston Churchill at all ages up to the one he had at present reached, interspersed with, for some reason or other, large photographic groups of the Lesseps family. But the future Prime Minister dominated them. There gazed at us from the walls photographs of him in long clothes and short, in frocks and infant knickerbockers, in sailor suits, as a small schoolboy, as a Harrovian, as a young officer. Wherever we looked, that face, already so well known, followed us with intent gaze, determined and dramatic. It was impossible to work while those eyes followed us, and my sister was obliged several times to screen them with newspapers and exercise-books.

My father, meanwhile, was very busy. Sargent was to begin his picture in a few days' time—on 1st March—, and the tapestry, the furniture, the Copley and the silver bowl had all to be deposited and unpacked—under my father's personal supervision, of course—in the studio. He had, further, to arrange for the re-insurance of all the objects that he had placed there. And, during the whole time, too, he was jotting down in his note-book pieces of advice and various technical hints that he thought might be useful to the artist. . . . Then, after the furniture and objects had been safely installed in Tite Street, there was the arrangement of them to be pondered. The bowl—for instance: where ought it to be put? The matter required careful consideration. . . . Eventually it was placed on an Empire table, belonging to Sargent, who was a collector of furniture, and showed great taste and knowledge. This table is to be seen in other of his portraits, and it, together with the Aubusson carpet, and the pieces of china which stand on the commode, are the only things in the picture which did not come from Renishaw.

The china depicted has a history. . . . When everything had been set out in readiness to be painted, my father had, at the last moment, realised that he had intended, but forgotten, to bring several pieces of china, which were to be placed on the mirror-top of the commode ("to give scale", I recall his saying). Where, he wondered, and how else could he obtain similar ornaments, for it would take too long now to have them conveyed from Renishaw, and, moreover, he could not be there to

superintend himself the process of wrapping them up and sending them away, without which he would never have consented
to allow them to leave the house. . . . What, then, was to be
done? . . . At last an idea came to him. . . . Even when a small
boy he had been interested in objects of art and antiquity
(already, at the age of fourteen, he had taught himself, by
spending much of his holidays among old documents in the
lumber-rooms at Renishaw, to read black-letter English), and
when he found the opportunity, often visited antique shops.
Thus it had happened that, in the intervals of an hour or two
caused by having to change trains at Hull for Scarborough, he
would visit a shop devoted to the sale of watches, and of old
furniture and china, belonging to a very intelligent Jew from
Holland. Most of the furniture in it, too, came from that
country, and there was much Delft ware, and many Dutch tiles,
for Hull is very close to the Netherlands, and their influence
has always been most pronounced, both upon the city and the
houses of the surrounding country. The shopkeeper was
amused, I suppose, at the serious tastes displayed by so young
a boy, and they became friends. . . . By now the Jew had
become a millionaire, and had recently been knighted, Sir
Joseph Duveen (the father of Lord Duveen[1]). My father

[1] Since the following anecdote often appears in the Press, I had better
recount it myself, correctly. In later years, and especially in 1926, when I
visited New York, I used to see a certain amount of Lord—then Sir Joseph—
Duveen, and several times went to his house there. The following summer I
met him at the opening day of some exhibition in the Leicester Galleries,
and he rushed up to me, and said, "O my dear Mr. *Lytton Strachey*, I am so
glad to see you again."

Lytton and I were not much alike, for I was tall, fair, clean-shaven and
certainly by no means thin, whereas he was bone-thin and angular, as well
as tall, and bearded, with something of the reflective air of a pelican. In fact,
no two people could have resembled each other less. Consequently, I
telegraphed to him: "Delighted to inform you that I have this morning been
mistaken for you by Sir Joseph Duveen Osbert". Lytton telegraphed back:
"One can only say again how perfectly duveen Lytton".

Sir Joseph, with his expert amiability, which resembled that of a clownish
tumbler on the music-hall stage, heard of these telegrams and subsequently
always referred to them at some moment of any luncheon or dinner party
at which he and I happened both to be present, appealing to me to "tell the
story about Strachey". Being a remarkably astute man in most directions, I
think that, in this, different from most people, he enjoyed having the stupid
side of his character emphasised; it constituted a disguise for his cleverness,
a kind of fancy dress. . . . After the story had been related, he used to add,
"*Of course* I knew Osbert Sitwell. I love his books. He's written about *my*

approached him and he most kindly lent him, from his shop in Bond Street, the valuable and beautiful Chelsea figures which were to be seen standing on the commode in the Sargent group.

The sittings began on 1st March, as planned, and I remember the day because we heard in the morning that Ladysmith had been relieved. . . . Every second day for five or six weeks we posed to the famous portrait painter in his studio, and no picture, I am sure, can ever have given the artist more trouble, for my father held strong views concerning the relationship of the patron to the painter, who ought, he inwardly maintained, to occupy the same position as a bone to a dog—or, as for that, of a mouse to a cat—, being created and placed before him to be worried, gnawed and teased. That my father believed this painter to be a great artist at his greatest in no wise relieved him of his duty as patron, which was to offer an opinion upon every matter, whether of taste, of feeling or of technique, with an air of absolute and final authority, and to distract him by starting a new theory every instant, and then swiftly abandoning it or, alternatively, by suddenly behaving as though it were Sargent's theory and not his own at all, and by consequently opposing it with startling vigour just as the artist had agreed to accept it. At moments that became steadily more frequent as the picture progressed, he played a very strong hand and became positively dictatorial.

In some ways a man of gentle temperament, despite his full-blooded, energetic, resolute appearance, Sargent exhibited under this treatment a remarkable mildness and self-control. Notwithstanding, albeit difficult to provoke, there were enacted from time to time considerable scenes, though, even then, the sudden outbursts of the artist, his rushing bull-like at the canvas and shouting, were in reality the expression more of tremendous physical vitality than of rage. And, in any case, my

country." At first this statement rather surprised me, until I comprehended that by it he meant Scarborough and the district round, which are said to figure in my novel *Before the Bombardment*.

It is an ironical reflection that while Lord Duveen's magnificent gifts to the nation stand as a memorial to his name, much of the money that paid for them was earned by the sale to the United States of the flower of the English eighteenth-century and early nineteenth-century English paintings. We have the galleries now, but no pictures to hang in them. He was the greatest salesman of his time.

father himself enjoyed these exhibitions very much, for, according to his code, a show of temperament was expected of every
artist—who ought, indeed, to be goaded daily by the patron
until he gave it, that being part of the contract, as it were, existing between them, and a guarantee that the work would be of
the highest quality. . . . On one occasion, then, a really big scene
took place, but my father triumphed, and obliged Sargent to
paint out completely a table with some silver upon it, the most
skilful and typical still-life—so George Swinton, who had seen
it, told me in after years—that he had ever executed. There,
somewhere under the dark surface of the present picture, that
pyrotechnical display lies interred. But Sargent had been loth
to lose it and had not scrupled to state plainly his own views on
the painter-patron relationship. . . . I remember, too, another
incident. My father, who, as I have said, only admired in a
female small du-Maurier-like features, pointed out to the
painter that my sister's nose deviated slightly from the per-
pendicular, and hoped that he would emphasise this flaw. This
request much incensed Sargent, obviously a very kind and considerate man; and he showed plainly that he regarded this as
no way in which to speak of her personal aspect in front of a
very shy and supersensitive child of eleven. Perhaps, too, he
may already have divined in her face and physique the germ of
a remarkable and distinguished appearance which was later to
appeal particularly to painters. At any rate, he made her nose
straight in his canvas and my father's nose crooked, and absolutely refused to alter either of them, whatever my father
might say.

Even this difference of opinion, however, and the expressions of a turbulent and rebellious kind which accompanied it,
seem in no way to have spoilt my father's pleasure in the picture. Thus, on 19th March, we find him writing to Turnbull a
short account of the progress of the group, and a description
of it: "Sargent's picture is going on famously and will I think
be finished in a fortnight. We are all very much pleased with it.
Lady Ida is standing in a white and silver evening-dress
arranging flowers in that old silver bowl on a little first Empire
table. Osbert and the baby are on the floor to her left, giving
the black pug a biscuit. I am standing to her right in dark grey

and with brown riding-boots with one hand on Edith's shoulder —she is in scarlet. The tapestry and old French chiffonier make a most satisfactory background. We have put Lady Ida in a black 'shadow' hat, something like that in Copley's picture, with white feathers and red ribbons. . . ."

Certainly the artist had shown forbearance, had even been indulgent. He had permitted my father to have a considerable say in the action of the picture, and had, further, allowed him to choose the clothes, curiously and significantly unrelated to each other, in which the figures were painted: my sister, then still a child, in her scarlet dress, my father in his riding kit (he rode very seldom), my mother in her hat and evening gown, myself in a sailor suit, with white duck trousers, while Sacheverell wore a silk dress suitable to his age—perhaps the only sitter who did. . . . My father's brown riding-boots, at least, stood for something; they were, I am sure, an assertion of independence in a world that had grown drab. (He often told me later that the first appearance of brown boots for men—no man then wore shoes in the day-time—, as opposed to the black boots that had been current ever since anyone could remember, had seemed a very great release from the convention of sombre hues that had for so long prevailed for members of his sex.) Edith's red dress was calculated to set off his grey clothes; while the silver embroidery on my mother's gown was no doubt thrown in as a sop to Sargent; the rendering of it would keep him quiet and prevent him from interfering with his patron's picture, for he would enjoy painting it, and it would give him an opportunity of indulging in the particular, "clever", texture-technique in which he specialised.

The dress worn by my mother, though perhaps oddly chosen, was certainly very pretty in its way and had been made—this offers a singular footnote to the epoch—by the then celebrated dressmaker, Madame Clapham, who worked in Hull (another link between the Sargent group and that city). From the present distance in time it would seem improbable that any fashionable woman should go especially to Hull for her clothes; but so it was. . . . The mode had originated with the daughters of Mrs. Arthur Wilson and Mrs. Charles Wilson—afterwards Lady Nunburnholme—who, coming from that district, had startled

London a few years before with their good looks and their dashing clothes, and had soon made the reputation of the local dressmaker whom they were said to patronise. I remember, though I cannot be certain of the year, accompanying my mother and her cousin, Lady Westmorland, by train from Scarborough to Hull, and then being taken to see Madame Clapham, who was fitting them for the dresses they had ordered for a Court Ball. Lady Westmorland, a famous beauty, bought some of her clothes, it is true, in Paris, but as yet very few women—apart from the American contingent who thereby gained an unfair advantage over the rest—obtained them there. And though within a few years every woman who could afford to do so was following the American example, at present Hull was the rage.

To return once more from Hull to Tite Street, I recollect very well the look of the studio. At one end stood the large group, just painted, of the three Wyndham sisters; Lady Elcho (later Lady Wemyss), Mrs. Adeane and Mrs. Tennant (subsequently Lady Glenconner). It took up a great deal of space, and, as I gazed at this enormous canvas, and at the three lovely women depicted on it, they seemed strangers, belonging to the world of paint, and not of human relationship. I little thought how much pleasure I should one day derive from the society of two of them, Lady Glenconner[1] and Lady Wemyss, or that two of their sons would enter so largely into my life—although, alas, for so short a period: because Ivo Charteris, Lady Wemyss's youngest son, and Wyndham Tennant, Lady Glenconner's eldest, became, for the brief season of their grown-up existence that preceded their being killed in action during the First World War, my two dearest friends. But, indeed, I have loved and admired many members of this family and have often wondered at the strange vitality of the Wyndham blood, which seems to bestow, as a birthright, beauty upon its women, and wit and talent upon its men. I am very grateful, too, to Lady Wemyss and Lady Glenconner, since it was in their houses that I first learned that the ordinary, quiet life of a family—something which we had never experienced in our own homes—could be absorbing and delightful. . . . Richard Wyndham the

[1] Later, Viscountess Grey of Fallodon.

painter, their nephew, again was to be in the years following
the war one of my brother's and my own greatest friends. And
with his friendship, the Sargent group of his three aunts returned, as it were, into my life, for in 1926 it travelled on the
same boat as Dick and myself to the States. It was the year of
the Great Boom, and in the spring he sold it for twenty thousand pounds to the Metropolitan Museum; thereby temporarily
making ridiculous the murmurs of Fry and his followers, who,
beating their chests in the squares and terraces of London,
West Central, and making Bloomsbury lamentations and
ululations, had for many years past declaimed against the
patrons of Sargent, and warned them, crying, "You pay three
thousand pounds today for a Sargent portrait. When he dies,
it will be worthless: whereas, had you employed dear——, he
would make your fortune. . . ."

The Wyndham group, for all that, and for the interest it
created, was no more than a pleasant and competent record of
three lovely women. It even lacks the period interest that
attaches to most of the painter's work, and in reality the sum
given for it proves the folly of fashion more than it exposes the
falsity of the opinions of the prophets of the true faith. . . .
Yet ridiculous as was this price, it does not compare in absurdity
with the six thousand guineas which his small water-colour
rendering of a Velasquez Infanta had fetched the year before.
This occurred during the disposal of the pictures and drawings
taken from his studio after his death, and offered for sale by
Messrs. Christie at their auction rooms on the 24th and 27th of
of July 1925. The whole sale realised the vast total of £175,260.
Thus the touching devotion of the rich, so faithful, even though
he so frequently insulted them, followed him even across the
threshold of the shadowy kingdom. They loved him, I think,
because, with all his merits, he showed them to be rich: looking
at his portraits, they understood at last *how* rich they really
were. . . . But all this was far in the future, as I sat there, with
my head screwed round at the uncomfortable angle at which
Sargent wished it to be held for the portrait, and gazed at the
picture of the sisters, envying them in my heart, for I knew
that their likenesses were finished and they could now enjoy
themselves once more, move freely, away from the cramping

range of the artist's transfixing eye. They could, in fact—for children always interpret the enjoyment of everybody after the pattern of their own—, run about and shout as much as they liked.

A child of seven is granted very good chances of observation, for he is old enough to notice a considerable amount and, so long as he behaves himself, grown-up people are usually un-selfconscious, thinking that he is too young to understand their characters. Thus, if he is much with them, he can for the most part watch them being their natural selves, without any attempt at disguise, except, occasionally and only with certain individuals, for a special show of friendliness and condescension. I was privileged in this manner to watch at his work this tall, taurine figure, with his large, rather shapeless but forceful torso and strong arms, his head, small for the body supporting it, and his flushed face with its little beard, and prominent, bulging blue eyes. He was always dressed in a conventional blue-serge suit, for in those times fashionable portrait painters never indulged in the overalls or semi-fancy dress which they would adopt today, and no doubt the tight, starched white collar was responsible for the rather plethoric appearance of his face as he painted, for work of an esthetic and intellectual order is as difficult as manual labour in such constricting fetters. . . . I can still see him now, if I shut my eyes, as, when something he had done displeased him, he would lower his head and, as it were, charge the canvas with a brush in his hand to blot out what the minute before he had so rapidly created, bellowing, at the same time, in his deep voice, the words, "It's pea-green, pea-green, pea-green—it's all pea-green!"

I think Sargent must have liked children—or perhaps he only found them a pleasant change from the usual, more sophisticated occupants of his studio, public monuments of men, proconsuls and generals, grave and portentous mouths through whom spake spirits, the infinite army of the banal dead, or fashionable beauties, with psyches that resembled air-balloons, inflated, light and highly coloured. Certainly he was very patient, would go to almost any trouble, consistent with being allowed to paint, to amuse us. When the first fascination of watching him at work, a conjurer drawing effects out of the void, had worn off, we became restless—especially

Sacheverell who was only two years old. After a quarter of an
hour, it would be impossible for either Davis or me any longer
to restrain his childish impatience, or to cajole him into posing:
but Sargent could always contrive to hold his attention for a
few extra minutes, either by indulging in a peculiar and
elaborate whistling he had cultivated, like that of a French
siffleur upon the music-hall stage, or by incessantly intoning
a limerick, which ran:

> There was a Young Lady of Spain
> Who often was sick in a train,
> Not once and again,
> But again and again,
> And again and again and again.

With an air of rapt amazement and delight, Sacheverell would
listen to this recitation, rooted throughout the performance of
it to the right spot. . . . Even this, however, did not serve to
keep him quiet indefinitely, and, being so young, his fidgeting
was such that eventually a doll had to be made, of exactly his
size and colouring, so that it could pose for him. Sargent would
then paint him for so long as the restless child would allow,
and, when his continuing to sit any longer became out of the
question, this miniature waxen-faced lay figure, with the same
fair curls and the same clothes, would take his place.

   Although my brother and I were always pleased when the
time came to leave the studio, we both of us liked Sargent, and
appreciated his kindness, of which we saw many indications.
But I was told of an instance of it which, though belonging to
a later date, should be recorded here. Sargent had an especial
affection for Spain, Spaniards, Spanish painting and music.
It will therefore be no surprise to the reader that he was a
friend of Rubio's, whom I have previously described. Indeed,
that extraordinary old musician seemed to sum up in his person
much of the contradictory, chivalrous, exuberant, austere,
religious character of his land. It will be remembered, too, that
Rubio liked to spend the few shillings he kept for himself on
buying pictures. His rooms in Fulham Road were covered with
them, and all of them boasted great names; the saints and
virgins he attributed mostly to Greco, Murillo and Ribera, the
portraits to Velasquez and Goya. None of them, of course, were

genuine. His friends used to tease him affectionately about these works of art, but it would only infuriate him; and never prevented him from acquiring more.

One day, however, he added a hypothetical Sargent which he had found—blatantly spurious—, to his collection. He was immensely pleased with this atrocious landscape, in water-colour; lacking in brilliance of any sort. His friends laughed at him more than ever, and more openly, about it. They pointed out that the artist in question always signed his water-colours. . . . A week or so later, Sargent arrived to see him upon an afternoon when he was being chaffed about it again, and Rubio had grown very angry. As Sargent entered the room, Rubio waved the landscape at the artist and roared out, with his Spanish lisp,

"This is by you, *by you*, isn't it?"

Sargent at once comprehended what had happened and sprang gallantly to the rescue of his old friend.

"Of course it is!" he said.

"Then sign it for me now, here!" Rubio demanded triumphantly, pointing at a corner of it.

This was something for which even the kindness of Sargent had not been prepared, but, in spite of the pride of craft which he undoubtedly possessed, he did as he was asked. . . . No painter of renown could have made a greater sacrifice, no man could have done more for friendship's sake.

As for us children, we saw how kind he was in several ways: he always tried to avoid implicating us in any trouble, when trouble arose because we had been "difficult". He championed us, and especially my sister, who could not do very much that was right. So the platform on which we were painted was not so unpleasant as it might have been. Indeed I, for one, enjoyed watching him paint. He bore the reputation of being an extremely rapid worker, and it may be that, in his capacity of illusionist—for, at his best, he was that rather than an impressionist—, he was more interesting for a child to observe than many a greater artist. . . . But the pleasure of it endured for a few minutes only at a time; then we longed, naturally enough, to go out, even to move, for sitting still for more than a second or two constitutes the chief terror of childhood. And, looking back, we seem to have sat for the picture so very often

and for so long, in spite of his quickness of eye and hand. We
went to the studio always in the same groups or solitary units,
at the same repetitive hours; Sachie and I, always together,
for example, with Davis shepherding us, but without the rest
of the family. Our nurse would take great care to see that we
were smartly dressed—for to sit to a painter was, in her eyes,
merely a more expensive form of sitting to a photographer, you
must wear your best clothes and most disarming smile—and
that we reached the studio punctually; which, in practice,
meant about half an hour before the sitting began.

We would wait in a darkened corner, watching Sargent as
he stood there, with one eye shut, regarding his models for
several minutes from a very considerable distance, and then
bore down upon the canvas, which was much nearer to them
than to him. We would look, too, at the people he was painting,
my father, with a certain air of distinguished isolation, and
"with one hand on Edith's shoulder", rather in the manner of
a stage magician producing a rabbit out of a hat, Edith in her
scarlet dress, with her lank, golden-green hair frizzed out
unbecomingly for the occasion (for my father said that "all
hair should be inclined to curl, and so soften the lines of the
face"), and her pale face very intent, as though waiting,
listening for some sound she could scarcely catch as yet, some
sound in the future, the particular rhythm that had she known
it, it had been left to her, alone of those who speak our English
tongue, to seize from it, adding thereby a new and lovely
melody to the innumerable glories of English poetry; my
mother (who had usually brought with her a friend now sitting
with us, watching), with one long gloved hand, the fingers
pointed and bent back upon the table, with the other about to
make an ineffectual attempt to cope with a few crimson *anemone
fulgens* in the silver bowl; and I would wonder, too, at the silver
bowl itself, and the Chelsea figures and the silver embroidery.
Could they be *so like*, when the lights in them were just twists
and blobs of paint; so like, when you wished them to be like,
so unlike, so flat and simple, at other moments? . . . Then my
sister or my mother would step down from the platform, and
it would be our turn. . . . Soon Sargent would begin reciting
again, until finally came the hour of release. As the evenings

grew longer and finer, my mother would sometimes come back to fetch us in an open carriage, so that we could have some air. We would usually cross the Suspension Bridge that spanned the enormous river, and drive in Battersea Park, through idyllic groves of young trees, now fringed with the shrillest of golden and transparent leaves, until the light changed, as though a slide had passed over it, from that of golden afternoon in early spring, through the blazing and splendid smoky drama of a London sunset, when a thousand fleeces catch fire and smoulder in the sky above, down to the cool and tender dim green light that follows it. Then we would return to the mauve, brightly-lit interior of Chesham Place. The footman would open the door, and I would quickly dash through it into the dining-room, to turn on the electric fan before anyone could stop me.

Altogether, I liked London. In these months I did not experience the attacks of croup that I should certainly have had to endure in Scarborough; for croup is a kind of nervous frenzy brought on by boredom, that complaint of the spirit from which it is never admitted that children can suffer. The atmosphere of this city was exciting—though this, indeed, made the length of the sittings seem more dreary—and there was—oh, so occasionally!—a theatre to visit, and the Zoological Gardens, living continuation of Noah's Ark, were open to us on Sundays. But, besides, there existed the fascinating pleasure-round of every day: one could always go to Hamley's, to look at the latest and most enchanting tricks and toys; brightly lit shops that put to flight the yellow fogs outside. Or I could tease Davis till she took me to Harrods' Stores—"Anything for Peace!"—and, once there, while she was not looking, make a dash for the escalator; (the earliest, I believe, in London, not so much a moving staircase as a moving inclined-plane). Even out walking, treats were plentiful. We might meet a battalion of one of the regiments of the Brigade of Guards, with its red coats and enormous bearskins, lighting the grey streets like fires, as they passed with drums and fifes, or even occasionally accompanied by the regimental band. Or we might see persons or personages at whom we were actually *encouraged* to stare, in order that we might never forget having seen them, and how they looked.

Thus, one cold spring morning, when grey clouds clustered round the sky as grey feathers round a sea-bird, Edith and I were walking with Davis along the Mall—then an unpretentious street, and not a processional road modelled by elephantine Edwardian taste upon the Sieges-Allee in Berlin. Suddenly a clatter and scraping of hoofs told us that a body of Life Guards was approaching, and behind them, in an open carriage, sat a small figure, in black, with a black bonnet, bowing with a regular swaying motion to right and left, as the people thinly lining the road cheered her. She liked the air, and her face was rather red with exposure to it. . . . This was the sovereign who, at the age of seventeen, had mounted a shaken and a shaky throne and now, after a reign of sixty and more years, was about to leave it, transmuted into rock by the magic of the common virtues she exhibited, to her heirs. This was the presiding deity of a golden age, blessed and tranquil in spite of its manifold endeavour; this, the young girl who had re-mained, until the time she had become an old woman, the personification of a way of life, and who, by some combination of evolutional advantage and of instinct, had invented a new kind of sovereignty, so that the frontiers of it now stretched as the very portals of the world; this, the little old woman who, by virtue of her dignity, had magnified her image, so that in every town in Great Britain statues of a crowned giantess holding a ball and sceptre were even now being erected; this, the old lady, the straight glance of whose clear blue eye, protuberant and searching, made the bravest and the cleverest men con-fused, if they were not anxious to tell the truth. . . . "The course of the Boer War must be worrying the Queen," I heard my father say subsequently at luncheon; but she showed no sign, even at her great age, of strain or emotion and, still bowing, had driven through the gates up to the old front of Buckingham Palace, with its chocolate-brown façade by Blore, and a skyline, crowded as the roof of a roundabout, with stucco shields and lions and trophies and a great effigy of Britannia; a façade that was part of London architecture, and lacked the sterilised rigidity of the present Portland stone front. . . . As she drove in to the courtyard, my sister and Davis were talking of how, once before, they had seen the Queen. My parents had spent

I

a winter at Cannes when my sister was three, and one morning this plump small child had been walking with her nurse along the pavement of a straight dusty road lined with palm trees. They had been the two figures in all its deserted length, when they noticed from the distance a carriage rolling toward them down this straight perspective of painted villas with green Venetian shutters, and cobbles, and green palms, high up, and waving gently in the sun. As the horses neared them, Davis called out "Miss Edith! The Queen!", and my sister had accordingly stopped in her walk and had dropped a low but uncertain curtsey, which Queen Victoria had most ceremoniously returned with a bow.

At last, the picture was finished; at last the moment came when we no longer had to go to Sargent's studio—except, as the reader will see, on one more, and a different, occasion. The end came with a flourish and a gesture, for the painter had secretly caused the frame of the Copley to be copied for his pendant to it, and now presented this facsimile as a surprise to my father. . . . He, who did not usually like to receive gifts, was on this occasion enchanted. Then came the question of exhibition. The picture had been finished too late to be sent in to the Royal Academy of 1900, and so, as my father wished various members of the family who were living in London, or happened to be staying there, to see it, he asked Sargent's permission to allow them to come to the studio one afternoon in early April. . . . Accordingly they were invited, in order to give their opinion of the picture and Sargent the benefit of their informed advice; at least that is what they imagined was expected of them, though in reality my father only wanted to be congratulated on his taste and on having obtained so fine a bargain. But this, again, was not at all what the opposition— led by my grandmother Londesborough—intended: (the members of my mother's family, so much less interested in works of art than those of my father's, had nevertheless turned up in much greater force). On the contrary, she and her followers immensely enjoyed the sensation of allowing themselves to be amazed. Serge Lifar tells us[1] that in Paris, when

[1] *Diaghilev*, by Serge Lifar. (Putnam & Co., 1940.)

Diaghilev felt dull or was bored, he would always send for Jean Cocteau and say to him imploringly "Étonne-moi, Jean!" To the Russian impresario, therefore, the process of being astonished was evidently pleasurable as well as stimulating, but not so with this gathering of my relatives. To be astonished, was, to them, to be shocked; nay, *scandalised*. They may, secretly, have revelled in the emotion, but they pretended to be aghast. My grandmother, and her unmarried sister, Lady Geraldine Somerset—a fascinating and, indeed, cultivated old lady, possessed of infinite character, who lived inside what appeared to be a series of tents composed of fading photographs, pitched in Upper Brook Street, and who had to be shouted at, for she was very deaf and carried an elaborate ear-trumpet, flounced and pleated like an early lampshade,—concentrated on the picture, and pecked away at its faults after the manner of two powerful birds. "Why riding things and an evening-dress?", "Why an evening-dress and a hat?", "Why, if you wear a hat, have a hat with a transparent brim?", they demanded of each other rhetorically, expecting no answer. "Why?", "Why, d'you suppose?" (This last was a favourite phrase of theirs.) "And why not go to an *ordinary* painter?" ("Why, do you suppose?"), "Why go to an American?" (Everything, they thought, was becoming American nowadays; George had even taken a house belonging to an American.) "Yes, why go to an American?" ("Why, do you suppose?") . . . "Why, do you suppose?", the eager and attentive chorus of younger relatives took up the theme from them, and made it swell to a grand, imposing culmination, "Why, do you suppose?"

This memorable spring afternoon was the last occasion on which I saw Sargent in his studio. Indeed, I never met him again until I was nineteen or twenty, when I dined in his company one night at Elsie Swinton's. (When I mentioned this to my father, afterwards, he said anxiously, "I *hope* you didn't talk—these great men don't like it.") . . . It was also the last occasion on which I saw my grandmother arrayed in her ordinary clothes. Henceforth she wore widow's weeds, for, a fortnight later, on 19th April, my grandfather died. Already in the winter he had been unwell, had been advised to seek a more genial climate—and had, in fact, done so. But he had been brought home too early in the year and the weather had turned cold and had lowered his resistance. But the actual cause of his death was strange, or at any rate seemed so at that time, and I will relate it.

I saw him again, a day or two after the private view in the studio, for he was attached to me, and I was the last person to go out with him. One afternoon he fetched me for a drive. Himself was driving the vehicle—whatever it may have been; we sat very high up, I remember, with a groom at the back. Owing to the unpopularity on the Continent of the Boer War, an unknown man had just made an attempt on the life of the Prince of Wales[1] as he had been passing through Belgium on his way to visit Denmark, and my grandfather first called at Marlborough House, so that he could write his name in the book there. Then he took me in the growing dusk, through the streets of Pimlico, where the stalls, tended by costers, were lit by flares that flowed in the wind like ostrich plumes, to the door of a big yellow warehouse in which were sold parrots, cockatoos and love-birds. . . . The next day he fell ill, and died a few days later—it was said of pneumonia, but my father told me subsequently that this illness had been very rare, a form of pneumonia that could only be caught from parrots infected with it: (the disease in fact which, when, in after years, it grew more common, was known as psittacosis). And he added that it had struck him as singular under these circumstances that the delirium of the dying man had consisted in a reversion to the time, many years previously, when he had visited Central and South America in his yacht, so that, as if influenced by the source of the germs he had contracted, he was perpetually travelling again on the wide rivers through the otherwise impenetrable forests, the branches of their trees constituting gardens of orchids and other aerophytes bright-dyed as the humming-birds that quivered among them, or lying at rest upon the vivid, halcyon waters of the great land-locked harbours of those tropical lands; vivid dreams similar to those that the parrot itself, the first victim, may have suffered, were it capable of such feats of hypnotised hallucination based on memory.

My mother was devoted to her father, and his illness and

[1] 4th of April 1900.

death throws in retrospect a long dark shadow before it, even tingeing with sable the months preceding it. My sister and my brother and myself were sent down to stay with my grandmother Sitwell in her large honey-coloured house in Surrey, set among commons and leafy lanes. . . . Later, my mother, and a friend or two to offer profane and comforting company in this secluded religious community, came down to join us. Sometimes, we would hear the grown-up people talking anxiously of business and family affairs. . . . Where, they asked, *where* would my grandmother Londesborough live? And they would go and look for houses for her. My grandfather had left no personalty: Francis, they said, would be "badly off" now he had succeeded: he would only have forty thousand a year at first to spend, though eventually sixty. Taxes were so high. . . . They looked worried.

My grandmother Sitwell and my Aunt Florence took no part in these discussions. The older woman lay on a sofa in the Indian Room with a fur rug over her knees, with a Siberian sleigh dog on each side of her, and bowls of mauve and brick-red violets on the table near at hand. A smile, subtle and resigned, caused by the contemplation of the approaching Heavenly Kingdom, played round the edges of her weary mouth. Burmese cabinets showed their grotesque limbs in various corners, and the tablecloths, spotted like a peacock's tail, winked their mirror eyes in the light from the window behind her, but in spite of these exotic and heathen furnishings, her heart was most Christian. Schooled to sorrow, nearly forty years had passed since she had lost her husband. Personal loss, she realised, was more hard for the worldly than for the spiritual-minded, but though she entered fully into the sorrows of others, she could not, for all her practical ability, allow their material cares to bother her. She was beginning to feel old now, and the burden of her charities, and of the endless correspondence she kept up with relations and friends, all written in her beautiful early-Victorian hand, with its long *s*'s, was becoming too much of a strain for her. . . . Sometimes, I apprehend, though herself had for so long had one foot in the next world, she may have wished that Florence did not belong to it so completely, and had been able to be more of an earthly prop. . . . But poor Florence struggled to help her, and was even learning shorthand and typewriting, so that she could take down her mother's letters: though her vagueness, her preoccupation with abstract and religious ideas, prevented her from making the progress she would have liked. Indeed at this very moment, my grandmother could hear the discordant click and tiny screams of the machine from my aunt's room, as she practised, and in the smoking-room—for smoking was only allowed in a single room of the house, and was confined to the male sex, so that my mother had to go out on to the Common to smoke a cigarette—the men found concentration difficult. . . . But now the noise stopped, for it was time for my aunt to begin making up her journal, which, as usual, was "sadly behind", and for this she reverted to pen and ink.

"On Sunday Bessie gave an earnest address to the children on part of Our Lord's Life, and in the afternoon we walked to Shalford Church, and had a very solemn and touching 'Hymn in Time of War' sung on our knees; then to our tiny school for the Gypsies which Mother has had arranged in the little wood. They take such an earnest interest in the simple lessons on the New Testament at the end, and now several of them can say a few words of prayer themselves after the lesson. Coralina, aged about fifteen, is, it seems, beginning a true Christian life. Their name is Symes, and they live in a van two miles away.

"Better news of Claude, only a bullet through his helmet: he was not touched.

"Little deaf old Miss Webber came over to tea yesterday, odd in appearance, perhaps from her deafness. Now that I have got to know her, I like her. We talked about the most interesting of all subjects. In the morning I visited invalids in the District. Interviewed a possible Matron for Mother's Home. In the evening, finished reading aloud our pretty book, *Off the Highway*. . . . The children are with us owing to their grandfather Lord Londesborough's death. Yesterday, two-year-old little Sachie asked Mother where 'Grandpapa Sitwell' was, and when she said away, he questioned her, 'Gone puff-puff?' and then 'Gone ship?', but receiving no satisfactory replies, ceased his little questions."

Meanwhile my father's mind, absorbed as ever by so many

affairs, was still following, among other tracks, the pictorial. Sargent had not, for all my father's admiration for him, converted him to Impressionism.

In a long, cross letter to Turnbull, dated 26th May 1900, concerned mainly with coal leases and having in it such sentences as "Wardell's coal report is to my belief the first I have seen, and is not what I want", "I have long felt I have not sufficient information or control about my mineral affairs. I should have copies of all letters, so that I can interfere whenever I think interference necessary", and much more of the same sort, we are, at the end, rewarded with a fitful gleam of esthetic illumination:

I am sending the quarry leases, and should also thank you very much for the Sieveking book *In Praise of Gardens*. . . . I have been finishing Lecky's Map of Life and Stevenson's Velasquez. The latter is an excellent statement of the "impressionist" case, but has left me more prejudiced against impressionism than I was before. They seem to make truth of visual impression their one aim, and to turn up their noses at the highest qualities of a painter—imagination and a sense of beauty. No doubt the scientific problems of painting want working out, but the greatest art is to paint what one does not see.—Yours very sincerely, GEORGE R. SITWELL.

So that is—or was—that!

For the next year he confines himself to giving Turnbull advice of other kinds, breaking new ground in more than one direction, of which the following letter is an instance:

BELVOIR HOUSE, SCARBOROUGH
10 January 1901

MY DEAR PEVERIL,

When I was at Oxford I suffered much at one time from rheumatism . . . I completely got rid of it more by thought and ingenuity than by doctors' advice.

You should wear a flannel shirt and pyjamas at night and fasten sheets of coarse cotton wool by safety pins to the shirt over the shoulder joints. In the daytime until you have beaten the rheumatism, you should wear similar sheets of cotton wool attached to your vest. . . . You should have the shoulders and muscles well rubbed with a rheumatic embrocation in the morning, before dinner, and at night, and it would be well if you bought a small galvanic battery, and had a little galvanism before the rubbing. You should use a generous diet and drink wine. . . . If you do this, you will get rid of the whole thing, cotton wool included, and never have it again. . . . Put ashes on the top of your bedroom fire. . . . It is at night that rheumatism gets its grip, owing to the insufficiency of night clothing. The cotton wool is an artificial skin which no cold can strike through and gives nature protection while she puts the muscles right underneath.

For a time my grandmother Londesborough's attention had been diverted by her sorrow from the matter of the picture, but forgetfulness was not her way. The following year she again concentrated on the singularity of it, why in evening dress, and why choose an American—even if he was "clever" as George said—to paint it? She did not herself go to Burlington House to see it in the Academy, but she read accounts of it in all the papers, and discussed them with her relations when they came to see her. The press wrote about it at considerable length. *Punch* had the usual sort of *Punch* joke about it—"The Sitwell family—why, they're all standing up!"—and published a caricature drawing of it. And one weekly journal, *Illustrated London News* or *Sphere*, gave an entire page to photographs of the Copley and Sargent groups, one above the other, so that they could be compared. The letterpress beneath purports to explain the intention of the artist, and has, to my ear, a curiously familiar ring, excusatory, yet authoritative and full of suave assumption: "Mr. Sargent's picture furnishes another proof of the versatility of the artist's talent. Such portrait groups are most difficult to handle, and when one remembers that this picture has been painted as a pendant to the eighteenth-century group, by which it is largely governed, and that the scale of the figures is one half that which the artist usually favours, one may well be surprised at his success. The picture tells its own story. Lady Ida Sitwell . . . has dressed early for dinner and has been out in the garden. The flowers which she is arranging in a silver bowl are not sufficient to fill it, and she hesitates for a moment, doubtful whether to leave them as they are or to go for more. Sir George (who formerly represented Scarborough and has contested the borough seven times) in a dark grey suit and buff riding-boots has returned lately from riding; he looks on, with one hand on his daughter's shoulder. The two little boys Francis Osbert Sacheverell (born 1892) and Sacheverell (born 1897) are happy with their toys upon the floor. . . . One or two critics have complained that the children and the heads of the two principal figures are disproportionately small. The explanation, of course, is that both Sir George and Lady Ida come of a tall race and are much above the common height."

There are several reasons why I see a certain hand, or a reflection of it, at work in this old newspaper cutting. First of all, it presents my father's view that an explanation is necessary for a picture. Then, in the unfolding of that view, there is a very individual and subtle misapprehension of psychology, amounting almost, indeed, to defiance of fact. My mother, for example, was helpless as an Infanta, could not even fasten her own shoe-laces. She belonged to an age when to be helpless in this particular sort of way constituted, in a woman of that generation and upbringing, the mark, as in the Orient, of a certain breeding. And, although it is also true that she would still less have walked in the garden before dinner, especially with a smart hat on the top of a low evening-dress, for in those matters she was very conventionally-minded, never would she have deigned to pick or arrange flowers. Somebody else would have had to do it for her. . . . Then a rather Chinese disapproval of daughters, a waste of time and money, is manifest, too: (it will be noticed that, alone of those in the group, Edith's name is not mentioned; she is just "his daughter"). Finally comes the bland assurance of "the . . . little boys are happy with their toys, upon the floor", where anyone else would have written "are playing on the floor", and then, the clue, gracious and explanatory, concerning the size of his head. . . . No, in all this I see most surely the suppuration of the wounds inflicted a year before by my grandmother, and her obedient and well-trained chorus, in Sargent's studio: "Why, do you suppose . . .?"

The picture still hangs—I wonder for how long?—in the house in which I write these words. A few people occasionally look at it as they pass, and one or two enquire "Is that a Sargent?" My mother is indeed exquisite in it; though Sargent was inclined to see in every woman he painted the reflection—which himself projected—of Mrs. Charles Hunter, of whom he made so many portraits. Upon all his female sitters he liked to bestow a little of her massive, embalmed and enamelled beauty; whereas my mother's looks—which sometimes recalled a form in one of Michelangelo's frescoes, by the attitude which came naturally to her, and by the turn of her head and body— resided in her line, in her beautifully shaped features, and small head set so elegantly upon her graceful neck and tall figure, and in her carriage, which was, perhaps, in part the result of her having as a child been taught "dancing and deportment" by the great Taglioni.[1]

On the whole, then, the picture is impressive; the tapestry, clothes and furniture are rendered with a brilliance that is undeniable, the people themselves with a kind of uncomprehending scintillation, which, because the element of caricature, always present in the work of this portraitist, has its emphasis in the wrong place, yet lets in the light all the more clearly. The tapestry of the background is mysterious as one of the wind-blown arrases, covered with arabesques, in the stories of Edgar Allan Poe. The figure of Justice, with sword and scales, hovers, just out of sight, above the heads of my father and mother, and the wooden stiffness of the figures, which is the fault of the picture, is also its merit, imparting to it a sense of expectation. They are frozen in this cataleptic immobility only for an instant in time, and will presently thaw to life. A feeling of tension broods in the stillness and darkness.

In the year that intervened between the painting and the exhibition of the picture, much had happened. An age had come to an end.

From the mauve pavilions of Chesham Place, lined with photographs of the young aristocrat-demagogue-imperialist, to which we returned in May, I saw the celebrations of the Relief of Mafeking; caught the sound of them, more than saw them. This was my first experience of crowds; they trampled and

---

[1] "March 8 (1877).—Luncheon at charming old Mrs. Thellusson's, where I met Madame Taglioni, the famous *danseuse*. She is now an old lady with pretty, refined features, perfect grace of movement, and a most attractive manner. She has begun in her old age to give lessons again for the benefit of her family, though she is, at the same time, presenting her princess grand-daughter—the Princess Margaret Trubetskoi, a simple, natural girl. Madame Taglioni spoke of her dancing as '*un don de Dieu*', just as she would of music or any other art. We asked her if she would like to be young again. 'Oh, yes, indeed,' she said, 'how I *should* dance!' She said her father, a balletmaster, made her practise nine hours a day; 'however great a talent you may have, you never can bring it to perfection without that amount of practice'."
—Augustus Hare, *The Story of My Life*, vol. iv.

shouted and roared in the streets and open spaces; the air resounded with the cries of dishevelled mobs wild with joy. The heart of the herd beat loudly enough for one to detect its rhythm everywhere. This was the culmination of the Jubilees, and the end to which the multitude of jostling and good-natured subjects had been led. A tribe of strangers, I gathered, called Pro-Boers—an odd name to come by—dwelt among our own people. They had been stoned, it seemed, and serve them right! I noticed exultation in the tones of those who told one another of it; kind, ordinary, friendly people with a sudden note of dull, brutish enjoyment in their voices. . . . But the idea of stoning only made me think of St. Stephen: and I knew, indeed had been taught, that such treatment of someone who disagreed with you was wrong. My heart did not beat with the heart of the herd: for the first time I realised this, and the painful roads to which it might lead me. Herdsmen I admired, even when their opinions were wrong; sheepdogs seemed the wisest of animals, but the herd found no abode in my heart, even though I might love each member of it separately.

At Scarborough the following January, a tolling of bells at seven in the evening announced the death of the old Queen . . . "What *shall* we do now?" I heard people say in perplexity; for the loss was something in which no man, born and brought up in that long reign, could altogether believe. . . . The people mourned sincerely: but perhaps a few inwardly rejoiced at the overthrowing of the prim barriers of the Victorian conventions. Now it would be possible to live in the shell of these, in the space hollowed out behind them, as a wasp lives in a peach.

The ageing heir to the throne had at last inherited it. Within a few years it was boasted that nothing remained of the Victorian Age! . . . Yet this was not true, though those who made may have believed the statement, for henceforth it lived in the bones of English men and women, who could no more be deprived of it, with all its faults and virtues, than of the Elizabethan era, to which it provided so remarkable and strait-laced a sequel. But the Rich Man's Banquet, which was to last for a decade, had now begun: the feast, it was recognised, went to the greediest. And Sargent was to be the recorder of it in paint, as Veronese had been of the Age of Opulence in Venice. But

Beauty, today, was not everything—indeed, anything. The Venetians had lavished their fortunes upon the building of palaces and gardens, upon brocades and jewels in lovely settings, upon masques and entertainments of an exquisite loveliness: the Edwardians squandered their accumulated riches at the shrine of the strange new goddess Comfort; they spent them on the gilding of pathetic but vulgar dreams from South Africa and the Ghetto, on the installation of bathrooms, electric light, and radiators. (When the wife, noted for her malapropisms, of an American millionaire of the time, whose daughter had just married an English peer, remarked of her husband's generosity to the bride, "Where another father would have placed a diamond pendant, Mr. X. installed an electric elevator," she knew of what she was talking.) As Sir Epicure Mammon promised himself in Ben Jonson's *Alchemist*, "mists . . . of perfume were uapor'd 'boute the roome" and there were "baths, like pits to fall into". Cigars had never been more fragrant. Jewels, again, were sought after, for they retained their value; the settings were either ugly or invisible, but never had the stones been larger. South Africa supplied diamonds of an unparalleled materialism, lacking in the icy blue fires of those that came from Brazil; but they were diamonds none the less. And those who sold them joined the rout to Park Lane, whither Greeks, Armenians, Indians, Americans of the North and South, Syrians, Egyptians, Jews from every part of the five continents, poured in, with faces clouded grey or green or black, and ingratiating smiles, to offer feasts to the unembarrassed native chieftains, who in return declared their hosts to be "good sorts". The banquets might not be so sumptuous as those of Rome or Venice, but never had the food been richer or the mouths hungrier. It had been a long wait, both for those who gave and those who received.

They had waited, among other things, for Sargent to record them, and he snatched many of them from Time's effacement; the aristocrat with his top-hat and riding-whip, his handsome ram's head and air of dowdy elegance, the fashionable beauties who were beautiful, but in so unstylised and *fade* a manner that it was almost impossible to formulate them upon canvas, and the fashionable beauties who were ugly and so, much easier to paint. But all the women in his pictures are richly clothed and all have the same harpies' hands, grasping and ineffectual, with long grey-green talons, and hold, or allow to dangle, the same arm's-length white kid gloves. Then there are the generals, the statesmen and the viceroys, and a ponderous and pondering author or two, with domed forehead and business man's jaw, looking out of presentation portraits in expensive frames, and, milling round all these, the sly hordes from the Orient. One old oriental splutters shrewdly above his cigar, screwing up an eye from the smoke, and looks across at the pictures of wife and daughters, the deep colour of their faces glowing like the Rose of Sharon from the canvas.

Everything seemed still to be fixed and immutable. The wainscoting was very thick. . . . Soon we were back at Renishaw, in a life that somehow one knew had the patine of time upon it. The very nursery atmosphere itself was impregnated with that of other epochs; one of the blankets on my bed bore the date 1801 on it, the rooms were full of plain oak chairs of the time of Charles I, and long, long ago a hand that was now dust had scratched a phrase in French, with a date, upon one of the window-panes. Outside, in the passage, stood the large old rocking-horse upon which a former generation of children had been painted in 1836. It had lost one ear, so that it was more difficult to climb on to, but its rocking was as satisfactory as ever.

The world today was kind, and comfortable, it seemed: and padded, well padded, yet Renishaw, though luxurious in an old-fashioned way, was bare. You could see its shape. The bones were there, and you could feel them. And we were, as I have said, the last generation to be brought up by candlelight. At night the house was immense, and the rooms were caverns.

That year the autumn came early, and the afternoons had an unusual length. The leaves of the tall trees in the avenue that stood like masts above the garden assumed a peculiar air of glossy well-being that hid their approaching dissolution, and the flowers glittered in the autumn light. We would walk quickly through the gardens, and then run in the baking heat down the steep hill—so steep that it was impossible to stop running, and the momentum swept one inexorably down—to the lake. On that mirror, which reflected feathery golden clouds and cloudy golden clumps of trees, Edith and I would be rowed slowly in the blue, flat-bottomed boat by Martha, the nursery-maid, trailing our wrists in the water, so that over the beating pulses would flow a cool, slow tide. Or the girl would stop rowing, and we would drift listlessly toward the large yellow cups of the lilies, and their patches of green leaves, like stains upon the surface of the water. Once among them, and it was difficult to disentangle the oars. Meanwhile Davis would be sitting, nursing our small brother, near the boathouse, while the tea was being prepared for ourselves, and for the party, who were coming down to join us.

It seemed hotter upon the water than on the bank. It was September now, early September, the sepia and gold cylinders of the bulrushes were splitting open to show their lining of buff cotton, and the water-birds seemed heavy-winged, as though the thought of migration weighed them down already. On the shore was a faint odour of decomposition, and on the water mists began to rise, cloaking the end of every perspective, or causing, as it were, false quantities in the metre of the surrounding landscape, by suddenly obliterating one familiar feature. Or, again, in places, the evening being so calm, the mist lay like layers of disintegrating water, one above the other. . . . Davis called out, saying that it was getting chilly, we must wait for my mother no longer. There must be a mistake. . . . Martha could pack up and the boy could come down and bring the hamper back.

So we climbed the hill; this time we went up the straight path by the side of the kitchen gardens. As we passed them, we could see, through a window in the brick wall, the peaches, with skins of rosy and green-white velvet ripening within their tents of glass. Up here there was no mist, the sun glowed on the hill-top with a deeper and more burnished gold. And now, as we topped the steep path and neared the gardens, we could hear voices and laughter, and the sound of mallets and croquet balls. . . . They had forgotten all about us.

APPENDIX A

The Capture of a Spirit

From the *Evening Standard* for Monday, 12th January 1880

WE have several times had the misfortune to call down upon ourselves the ire of the Spiritualist journals by directing attention to various *exposés* of the tricks of persons professing to have communication with the unseen world. We were told, with much righteous indignation, that Spiritualism was not accountable for the scandalous proceedings of impostors who assumed to belong to the glorious body merely for the purpose of swindling the unwary by travestying the marvellous manifestations of the true Spiritualists. These marvellous phenomena were to be studied in the temple, where the gifted and favoured ones gathered to practise their cult and to drink in words of wisdom from the spirits of those who had gone before. There was evidently some justice in this appeal, and among others Sir George R. Sitwell and Carl Von Buch, F.C.S., resolved to go to the fountain-head at the chief temple of the visible world, namely, the British National Association of Spiritualists, to examine into the phenomena in question, for here they were assured the *séances* were the most genuine in England, and were conducted under strict test conditions. On the first visit they tied the medium with great care, and no manifestations followed. Upon the second visit, on Jan. 2, they again tied the medium, but this time under the direction of the chairman of the meeting, an official connected with the institution. On this occasion either the tying was less complete, or the spirits were more accommodating, for the "spirit", which was, they were told, that of Marie, a dead child twelve years of age, came upon the scene. Certain appearances, notably the fact that the spirit wore stays, excited some suspicion in the minds of the visitors, and the next time they presented themselves at the door of the temple of Spiritualism they were accompanied by Mr. J. C. Fell, M.I.M.E., the editor of a scientific journal, and his wife. The spirit "Marie" again appeared, and this time the suspicions of Sir G. R. Sitwell and his friend being excited by the sound of undressing behind the curtain where the medium sat, the "spirit" was seized by one of the visitors, while the others, pulling aside the curtain, displayed the medium's empty chair, with her discarded dress, stockings and boots. The meeting then broke up in confusion and adjourned to a room downstairs, where all present—excepting the officials, one of whom took refuge in abuse—entirely agreed with Sir G. Sitwell and his friends, as to the grossness of the imposture, and thanked them for exposing it. The importance of this conclusive *exposé* consists in the fact that here no mere self-dubbed professor has been shown up, but it has proved that at the British National Association of Spiritualists a gross and monstrous fraud has been practised. This is the heaviest blow which has yet been dealt to the ridiculous system of imposture known as Spiritualism.

From the *Daily Telegraph* for Tuesday, 13th January 1880

Spiritualism, as an imposture, is the more shameful because it trades on grief. From small beginnings and an obscure propaganda it now impudently assumes the dignity of a religion. "Professors" live by it, indulging themselves in idleness and luxury at the expense of public credulity. There are at the West-end of London private houses where every sort of Spiritualist trickery goes on from day to day, and where dupes in a good rank of life are eased of their cash in return for interviews with supposititious ghosts. The audacious quacks who make believe to recall the dead, not content with a personal connection of well-to-do simpletons, preach spiritualism as an evangel, describing the details of an after-life in Heaven, and affecting an intimacy with the unknowable which should excite contemptuous laughter but for its background of mischief. The victims of the spiritualist craze are more to be pitied than the slaves of opium. For while the one may leave to the sufferer intermittent flashes of reason, the other clouds the mind completely and perpetually with a curtain of fallacies hung upon the most daring of all modern forms of imposture. Exposure cannot silence nor disgrace suppress the professional spiritualist. Driven with contumely from one place he settles in another, still further to unhinge weak minds and in many instances to sow the seeds of insanity. . . .

Forsaking generalities for the firm ground of fact, we have to deal with a remarkable exposure of pretended spiritualism, which, were it not for the natural credulity of mankind, should strike a fatal blow at this insidious superstition. Sir George R. Sitwell and Herr Carl Von Buch, F.C.S., have written a letter in which they detail their experience of the results of experiments into so-called spiritualism. Being anxious to put its pretensions to the proof, they sought the advice of a person "eminent" in the art, craft, creed or whatever it be, and by him were recommended to attend certain meetings at an influential institution, at which, they were assured, the *séances* were the most genuine in England, and held under strict test conditions. On the occasion of their first visit no manifestations took place, probably because the enquirers themselves tied the medium. At the next *séance* which they attended, the chairman of the company assembled, himself an officer of the institution, directed the tying process, and this time a "spirit" did appear, in the form of a pretended ghost of a female child, aged twelve years, and answering to the name of "Marie". Looking intently at the messenger, assuming to come from beyond the boundaries of another world, the enquirers spied what seemed to be a corset beneath the diaphanous robes of ghosthood, and, doubting whether spirits wore stays, they redoubled their attentions, and ultimately came to the conclusion that, judged by voice and manner, "Marie" was no other than the professional medium herself. Influenced by a true scientific spirit, these gentlemen were not content with the result of a single experiment, but made a third visit of enquiry, this time accompanied by Mr. John C. Fell, engineer, and his wife. Once more "Marie" appeared. These four independent and credible witnesses heard audible sounds of undressing behind a curtain, and were shocked at the levity of "Marie's" behaviour and conversation. It is certainly not surprising that suspicion, already on the alert, should be confirmed by a display of volatility so inconsistent with the assumed character of the "appearance". Determined to make a still closer acquaintance with the vivacious and apparently youthful ghost, one of the four darted forward and laid hold of "Marie" by the wrist. According to the argument by analogy, the possession of a wrist postulates the attachment of a material body, and proves to demonstration that "Marie" is a common cheat. When one of the party had laid hold of the "spirit" another drew aside the curtains and discovered the medium's chair empty, and with the knot of the rope slipped, while, to make assurance doubly sure, the stockings, boots and other discarded garments of the medium lay about in ungraceful confusion. According to the report of Sir George Sitwell and Herr Carl Von Buch, the objects named were handed round among the strangers and friends present to make certain of their identity. It is almost needless to add that an official connected with the show hastened to put the company in total darkness, or that the persons belonging to the institution took refuge in recrimination and abuse. Sir George Sitwell, Herr Von Buch and Mr. Fell put their case fairly and temperately before the public when they say that, leaving general conclusions on spiritualism to others, they claim to have proved that in a society recommended to them as the first of its kind in England the medium has been publicly detected in the fraud of personation. When certain other famous mediums, whose names are familiar to the public, at different times found London no longer suited to the object which they had in view, the Metropolis knew them no more; and should "Marie" find Bloomsbury untenable, that ingenious but disingenuous materialised wraith, like the "uncouth swain" in *Lycidas*, may probably flit "tomorrow to fresh woods and pastures new".

If it were possible to credit the ex-parte announcements of professional spiritualists, it might be worth while to establish regular communications—a sort of ghostly postal system—between the material and the immaterial worlds, and, were such an innovation desirable, persons fitted, by pretension, for the office of postman in space would doubtless be forthcoming. Indeed, the exceptional cleverness of advertisers seeking patrons from among the readers of spiritualist prints can only be realised by the study of that form of literature. . . .

The mischief arising from pretended communications with the spirit world cannot well be over-estimated: and if, for the sake of argument, it were allowed that some so-called spiritualists really and honestly believe themselves to be possessed of the powers which they assume, they should be among the first to encourage prosecutions such as we have indicated.

APPENDIX B

From *The Lives of the Norths.* . . .

By The Hon. Roger North

(The Right Hon. Francis North, Baron Guilford, etc., 1637–85).
Edited by Augustus Jessopp, D.D. Publishers: George Bell
& Sons, York Street, Covent Garden, London, 1890

[195] ONE year his lordship, concluding at Bristol, made a visit at Badminton to the Duke of Beaufort, and staid about a week. For the Duke was descended from a North of his lordship's family, viz. one of the Lord Edward North's daughters,[1] whom a lineal ancestor of his grace married. So besides conformity of principle, with respect to the public, they were, by this relation, qualified for mutual respect and honour. I mention this entertainment as a handle of showing a princely way of living, which that noble duke used, above any other, except crowned heads, that I have had notice of in Europe; and, in some respects, greater than most of them, to whom he might have been an example. He had above £2000 per annum in his hands, which he managed by stewards, bailiffs, and servants; and, of that, a great part of the country, which was his own lying round about him, was part, and the husbandmen, etc. were of his family;[2] and provided for in his large expanded house. He bred all his horses, which came to the husbandry first colts, and from thence, as they were fit, were taken into his equipage; and, as by age or accident they grew unfit for that service, they were returned to the place from whence they came and there expired; except what, for plenty or unfitness, were sold or disposed of. He had about two hundred persons in his family, all provided for; and in his capital house, nine original tables covered every day: and, for the accommodation of so many, a large hall was built, with a sort of alcove at one end, for distinction; but yet the whole lay in the view of him that was chief, who had power to do what was proper for keeping order amongst them; and it was his charge to see it done. The tables were properly assigned; as, for example, the chief steward with the gentlemen and pages; the master of the horse with the coachmen and liveries; an under steward with the bailiffs and some husbandmen; the clerk of the kitchen with the bakers, brewers, etc. all together; and other more inferior people, under these, in places apart. The women had their dining-room also, and were distributed in like manner. My lady's chief woman with the gentlewomen; the housekeeper with the maids and some others. The method of governing this great family was admirable and easy, and such as might have been a pattern for any

---

[1] William, 3rd Earl of Worcester, married Christian, 3rd daughter of Edward, 1st Lord North. From them, in the fourth generation, was descended Henry, 1st Duke of Beaufort. Sir Francis North, the Lord Keeper, was descended in the fifth generation from Edward Lord North.

[2] "Family"—in the sense of "household".

management whatever. For if the duke or duchess (who concerned herself much more than he did; for every day of her life in the morning she took her tour and visited every office about the house, and so was her own superintendent) observed anything amiss or suspicious, as a servant riding out or the like, nothing was said to that servant; but his immediate superior, or one of a higher order, was sent for who was to inquire and answer if leave had been given or not; if not, such servant was straight turned away. No fault of order was passed by; for it may be concluded there are enough of them that pass undiscovered. All the provisions of the family came from foreign parts as merchandise. Soap and candle were made in the house; so likewise the malt was ground there; and all the drink, that came to the duke's table, was of malt sun-dried upon the leads of his house. Those are large, and the lanthorn is in the centre of an asterisk of glades, cut through the wood of all the country round, four or five in a quarter, almost *apert de vieu*. Divers of the gentlemen cut their trees and hedges to humour his vistos; and some planted their hills in his lines, for compliment, at their own charge. All the trees, planted in his parks and about, were fenced with a dry wall of stone, taken out where the tree was set. And with all this menagery and provision, no one, that comes and goes for visits, or affairs with the duke (who was Lord Lieutenant of four or five counties, and Lord President of Wales) that could observe any thing more to do there, than in any other nobleman's house. So little of vain ostentation was to be seen there. At the entrance, where coaches ordinarily came in, the duke built a neat dwelling-house, but pompous stables, which would accommodate forty horses, as well as the best stables he had. This was called the inn, and was contrived for the ease of the suitors, as I may call them; for instead of half a crown to his servants at taking horse, sixpence there, for form, served the turn; and no servant of his came near a gentleman's horse; but they were brought by their own servants, except such as lodged, whose equipages were in his own stables.

[196] As for the duke and duchess, and their friends, there was no time of the day without diversion. Breakfast in her gallery that opened into the gardens; then, perhaps, a deer was to be killed, or the gardens, and parks with the several sorts of deer, to be visited; and if it required mounting, horses of the duke's were brought for all the company. And so, in the afternoon, when the ladies were disposed to air, and the gentlemen with them, coaches and six came to hold them all. At half an hour after eleven the bell rang to prayers, so at six in the evening; and, through a gallery, the best company went into an aisle in the church (so near was it), and the duke and duchess could see if all the family were there. The ordinary pastime of the ladies was in a gallery on the other side, where she had divers gentlewomen commonly at work upon embroidery and fringe-making; for all the beds of state were made and finished in the house. The meats were very neat, and not gross; no servants in livery attended, but those called gentlemen only; and in the several kinds, even down

to the small beer, nothing could be more choice than the table was. It was an oblong, and not an oval; and the duchess, with two daughters only, sat at the upper end. If the gentlemen chose a glass of wine, the civil offers were made either to go down into the vaults, which were very large and sumptuous, or servants at a sign given, attended with salvers, etc., and many a brisk round went about; but no sitting at a table with tobacco and healths, as the too common use is. And this way of entertaining continued a week, while we were there, with incomparable variety; for the duke had always some new project of building, walling, or planting, which he would show, and ask his friends their advice about; and nothing was forced, or strained, but easy and familiar, as if it was, and really so I thought it to be, the common course and way of living in that family. . . .

The children of the family were bred with a philosophical care. No inferior servants were permitted to entertain them, lest some mean sentiments or foolish notions and fables should steal into them; and nothing was so strongly impressed upon them as a sense of honour. Witness the Lord Arthur, who, being about five years old, was very angry with the judge for hanging men. The judge told him that, if they were not hanged, they would kill and steal. "No," said the little boy, "you should make them promise upon their honour, they will not do so, and then they will not." (It were well if this institutionary care of parents were always correspondent in the manners of all the children; for it is not often found to prove so.)

APPENDIX C

Babil and Bijou

"SELDOM, of late years," wrote the dramatic critic of *The Times* in an extraordinarily long notice of *Babil and Bijou*, "has the play-going public been in such a state of excitement as on Thursday evening, when Covent Garden Theatre was opened for the winter season under the lesseeship and management of Mr. Dion Boucicault.[1] Although the one piece of the evening began at the unfashionable hour of 7, not only was every seat occupied (save some that had been previously secured), but there was a heavy demand for good standing-room long before the ascent of the curtain. The general impression prevailed that a novel experiment was about to be tried: that an entertainment of a kind altogether without precedent was to be given, and a general buzz of curiosity pervaded the vast assembly till the performance began: nor during the whole evening did the excitement

[1] Dion Boucicault was born in Dublin in or near the year 1820, and was an actor and dramatist of such remarkable versatility and personal charm, and one who enjoyed so prodigious a contemporary prestige, that it is difficult to do justice to his quality in a footnote. His guardian in youth was Dionysius Lardner, says the writer in the *D.N.B.*—from whom are taken these details of his career—and he showed an almost parental interest in the child. At first Boucicault worked in London under the name of Lee Morton.

flag. At the end of every act persons might be seen eagerly meeting each other in the lobbies to compare notes, and to declare how far expectations had been answered."

The reason for this excitement was the attempt to supplant the native Burlesque—an entertainment that though inherently and indigenously English was beginning to look as if it were wearing a little thin—by the *Féerie*, an importation from Paris, where this form of spectacle had been popular for two decades and more. It was no doubt in order to emphasise this foreign flavour which the producers wished to impart to the entertainment that Hervé[1] had been called in to compose the music, as the programme states, for "the 1st, 2nd, 3rd and 4th Tableaux". If this were the case, it was

He enjoyed many triumphs; the first being the production of his drama *London Assurance*, when he was twenty-one years of age. This piece remains, says the *D.N.B.*, "one of the best of acting plays of its period". . . . After that for many years came a flood of dramas, most of them being skilful adaptations of plays already in existence. Among the most popular were such creations as *The Colleen Bawn* and *Arrah-na-Pogue*, the first of which ran for three hundred and sixty nights, while the second constituted the great success of his life, being translated into several languages. In 1872, says the *D.N.B.*, he produced *Babil and Bijou*, "which may claim to have been the most scandalously costly spectacle ever put on the English stage". (The final sentence pronounced is: his "brilliant literary and histrionic qualities were not supported by any very rigorous moral code. He was for a time a strong advocate of Irish Home Rule.")

In many of his plays himself appeared, as did his wife, Miss Agnes Robertson, whom he had married in New York in 1853. He quarrelled with her in 1876, and spent the last fourteen years of his life in the United States, where he attempted to repudiate her and his children. For financial success and popularity in England and America, he can only be compared, contemporarily, to Noel Coward, but it is clear that he was agreeable personally, an interesting character and a most delightful talker. Clement Scott, writing of him in *The Drama of To-day and Yesterday*, says: "I knew Dion Boucicault in the *Colleen Bawn* days at the Adelphi, when he had a magnificent mansion and grounds at Old Brompton, now known, I think, as Coleherne Court. I knew him in the days of the *Shaughraun* at the same theatre, and I met him constantly at the tables of Edmund Yates, J. C. M. Bellew, and Shirley Brooks, and I was also a frequent guest at his own table, when he lived, as he ever did, money or no money, credit or no credit, *en prince*, at his flat on the first floor in Regent Street, at the corner of Mortimer Street. . . . Dion was a *bon viveur*, a gourmand, and a gourmet, and certainly one of the most brilliant conversationalists it has ever been my happy fortune to meet. To hear him describe the plot of a play, his small Irish eyes sparkling, and the words all well chosen, pouring out like a torrent and cataract, was to see it acted before your eyes in every detail, and his general information on every conceivable subject was quite remarkable. . . . How, with little or no education, he knew what he did know, was to me absolutely mysterious."

[1] Florimond Rongé, or Hervé, as he called himself, was born at Houdain, Pas de Calais, in 1826. He became an excellent composer of the light music of the Second Empire, and a runner-up, as it were, to Offenbach. His best known works were *Mam'zelle Nitouche*, *Le Petit Faust*, *L'Œil Crevé* and *Chilpéric*. When his Parisian audiences vanished with the outbreak of the Franco-Prussian War, he came to London. He died in 1892.

a pity that Mr. Planché[1] had been retained to write the "Lyrical Part"; for no one, in spite of his name, could have been more essentially English and, since he had been writing the librettos for burlesques ever since 1818, his working for this piece destroyed any element of novelty that might otherwise have been introduced into it. Nevertheless, a critic announced the next day that ". . . it must be remembered that this fairy drama is like nothing that has been seen on the stage before, and is as superior in mounting and magnificence to the fairy pieces of Paris as it is triumphantly in advance of the silly pointless and witless entertainments called burlesques." . . . But the English public, apart from the more lively of its members whom one would expect to find at a first-night, were by no means prone to xenomania. Thus, even the critic of the *Daily Telegraph*, praising in general, yet prefers the English side of it:

"The music is all most carefully selected by M. de Rivière," he writes, "who ably presides over an admirable band, and, though many voices will be raised in praise of M. Hervé's clever assistance, we doubt not that the musical honours will be ultimately awarded to Mr. Frederic Clay, whose songs are more in keeping with the graceful character of the undertaking, and who has presented us with some most welcome melody. The admirably arranged quartette, 'Wanda, sweet spirit of the water, hear!' and the choristers' chorus on Spring, are the musical gems of the opera, and are re-demanded with enthusiasm each evening."

Though the word *Burlesque* still retains a meaning for us, *Féerie* signifies nothing. We must, therefore, consult *The Times* again. It had long been the custom in Paris, the writer states, for one or two theatres to produce annually a grand *"féerie"*, "comprising within itself every form of splendour and grotesque oddity that the pencil of the scene-painter, the ingenuity of the machinist, and the skill of the ballet-master can achieve. Nominally, the *'féerie'*, as its name implies, is founded on some fairy tale, but this is almost forgotten in the course of the four or five hours required for the complete performance of the work, and the audience are satisfied to see a series of gorgeous *tableaux* succeed each other, without enquiring too closely into the dramatic links by which these are connected. As the *'féerie'* is accepted as a spectacle only, the laxity with which it is constructed is not without advantages. It may be desirable to enhance the attraction of the entertainment by the introduction of some new dancer, some extraordinary acrobat or some popular vocalist, and where there is little or no fable to interrupt, this, of course, can be effected without interruption to the fable."

New productions of this kind were infrequent in Paris in any one year, for, if a piece were successful, it was revived continually, being cut and re-touched and re-decorated on each occasion. During the

[1] James Robinson Planché, Somerset Herald and dramatist, was born in London in 1796. His father, Jacques Planché, was a watchmaker of Huguenot descent. He was the author of innumerable books, besides librettos, and a scholarly authority on armour and antiquities generally. (See *D.N.B.*)

Second Empire, in which epoch the *Féerie* chiefly flourished, notable successes had been *La Biche au Bois*, *La Chatte Blanche* and *Les Pilules du Diable*. The last *Féerie* brought out in Paris had been *Le Roi Carotte*, by Victorien Sardou, from which it was suspected that Boucicault had now borrowed some hints. A translation of this was in fact running concurrently at the Alhambra, but it was not presented with the skill and magnificence of the Parisian stage; whereas at Covent Garden *Babil and Bijou* possessed this quality of lavishness. Indeed one critic says that there were those who would assert that such entertainments "turned the stage into a large up-holstery and millinery establishment, or a shop for the display of glittering armour", but that the same accusations had been levelled against Charles Kean.

For an explanation, then, of the sort of entertainment this was, we will turn again to the columns of *The Times*. "The personage who ostensibly connects his (Mr. Boucicault's) five acts, or to speak more correctly, his eighteen *tableaux*, is Bijou (Miss Annie Sinclair), daughter of the Fairy Queen, Melusine (Miss Murray), and a shepherd-boy, named Launcelot, whom the august lady married in human form. Though the marriage was secret, it was discovered by the subjects of Fairyland, who, considering that their Queen had been guilty of a mésalliance, rose in rebellion against her at the instigation of Pragma (Mrs. Billington), an elfin Princess, and drove her into exile with her new-born infant. She, however, took with her the regalia, and, on the death of her husband, confided her sceptre to Mistigris (Mrs. Howard Paul), the Spirit of the Earth, her robes to Azurin (Miss Alice Phillips), the Spirit of the Air, and her crown to Wanda (Miss Edith Bruce), the Spirit of the Waters. With her capture by the elves, who are now ruled by Pragma's son, Skepsis (Mr. J. B. Howe), the 'prologue' of the piece commences. The child has been protected by the spirit of her father, but the mother is imprisoned in a huge ruby.

" 'Rosewood Forest', in which these incidents occur, is situate near the city of Zanzoozee (Sans-souci), capital of the principality of Lutitia—that is to say, of an imaginary France, costumed after the fashion of Louis XIV. The Monarch of this realm is Prince Pharselis (Mr. Maas), who leads a life of elegant merry-making with his courtiers, and encourages the worship of Auri-Comus (Mr. Lionel Brough),[1] a living idol, who represents wealth and pleasure, and is

---

[1] As previously stated, he acted as stage-manager.

Lionel Brough (1836–1909) had a long and distinguished career. He was the youngest of the four children of Barnabas Brough, a brewer and wine merchant, who, falling on bad times, wrote plays later in life under the pseudonym of Barnabas de Burgh. Lionel's three brothers, William, Robert Barnabas and John Cargill, all attained some distinction as writers.

He first appeared under Madame Vestris and Charles Mathews in 1854, but it was nearly twenty years before he became celebrated. He played all sorts of parts from Tony Lumpkin to Trinculo, but his pre-eminence was in burlesque and opera-bouffe. The *D.N.B.* says: ". . . he had little capacity for interpreting character, and obtained his effects chiefly by simple drollery".

widely different from Typo-Compus (Mr. Wainwright), the idol of the populace. Although everybody in the country is prosperous, there is a revolt, and the rabble enter the Palace, insisting that Auri-Comus shall be destroyed, and that the Prince shall marry Hydra (Mrs. Billington), the daughter of Typo-Compus. To the great disappointment of the rebels, he solves the difficulty of the position by quietly abdicating, and takes himself off with Auri-Comus. The people amuse themselves, however, with destroying the Palace, and raising Hydra to the throne, who begins her reign by imprisoning her own father.

"From the bustle of the revolution we are carried to a hut in the forest, inhabited by Melusine's daughter, Bijou, who has been brought up by Olaf (Mr. Elliott), an old goat-herd, and lives as a peasant. Here she is visited by the fugitive Prince, who woos her honourably under the name of Babil: but her quiet happiness is much disturbed when the Gnome, Skepsis, who has discovered her retreat, raises from the ground the captive Melusine, and she hears from the lips of her mother that she is half fairy, half mortal, and that in her present condition her love will cause the death of her devoted Babil. She is, however, recommended to seek the lost regalia, since if these are recovered she can release Melusine, abdicate in his favour, and thus become a mortal for the sake of the Prince. To aid her in her search Melusine, before she is again consigned to her prison, infuses her spirit into a nest of love-birds, in which are found a number of silver eggs. A voice from the earth tells Bijou to touch one of these, and her compliance with the request is immediately followed by the appearance of Mistigris, who tells her that every egg she breaks will ensure the accomplishment of a wish: and she begins to use her power by magically producing a feast in honour of her betrothal to Babil.

"The rest of the piece is occupied with the quest of the regalia by Bijou, Babil and Auri-Comus on the one side, and by Skepsis and Pragma on the other. The bottom of the sea is the first place visited, and Bijou and her friends, though nearly captured by King Octopus (Mr. Wainwright), whom a revolution has raised to the throne, contrive to escape in a diving-bell with the diadem of Fairyland in their possession. In the Land of Flowers they regain the sceptre, and in the silver City of Atlantis, situated in the moon, they obtain the robes. In this city, which is governed by the Amazon Princess Fortinbrasse,[1] ladies are considered the stronger sex, and from them proposals of marriage are expected. Under these circumstances, a difference arises in consequence of the undisguised predilection of the Princess for Babil, but all is made happy at last, and Bijou, having restored her mother to the fairy throne, returns to Lutitia and becomes the wife of Babil, who, as Prince Pharselis, once more wears the crown of his ancestors.

[1] Miss Helen Barry, who "attracted much attention by her magnificent appearance". Clement Scott in a footnote to *The Life and Reminiscences of E. L. Blanchard*. (Hutchinson & Co., 1891.)

"The story, which we have compressed to a degree that can hardly be suspected by those who are unacquainted with the piece, is told at length in a little book which is circulated about the house, and which everyone should purchase who desires to know the meaning of the spectacle on the stage. Many persons, however, without such enlightenment, will be perfectly satisfied with the train of magnificence that passes before their eyes. The decorations, painted by Messrs. Hann, Johnson and Hicks, are not only beautiful pictures, but specimens of stage contrivance of the most elaborate kind. The costumes, designed by Mr. Alfred Thompson, reveal the most exquisite taste, and present every variety, both of splendour and of grotesque invention. The ballet, which occupies nearly the whole of the fourth act, is a real ballet, such as has not been seen since Mr. Lumley's reign at Her Majesty's Theatre, and Mdlle. Henriette Dor [*sic*], the principal danseuse, is an artist who would have taken a high position in the days when the worship of Terpsichore was much more fashionable than it is now.

". . . Among the *tableaux* which will chiefly impress themselves on the memory we may mention an exhibition of the different types of man and man's attire from the present time to the 'good old days of Adam and Eve', a procession in which the Darwinian ape is brought into contact with Lord Dundreary being excessively elaborate and amusing. . . .

"Judged by the standard which one would apply to the *féeries* of the Parisian stage, *Babil and Bijou* may be pronounced as nearly perfect as possible. The question whether it is a good play is as irrelevant as the question whether a steamboat is a good windmill."

The *Daily Telegraph* devoted two long articles to *Babil and Bijou*, and went further than *The Times* in its appreciation and in its description of the scenic display. It is interesting to compare the full-blooded, roaring prose of this mid-Victorian dramatic critic with the more staid and anaemic productions of his descendants of today. In the first notice, it will be observed that the *Daily Telegraph* pillories a wretched dissentient, a conscientious objector, as it were, to the general run of applause and of fulsome first-night compliments.

"The first question to be asked this morning by many lips will be 'Was *Babil and Bijou* a success?' We doubt if there will be one hand held up antagonistic to the popular verdict declaring the fantastic fairy drama to be one of the most gorgeous and elaborate stage spectacles witnessed by any playgoer, old or young. We question if a single individual would attempt to combat the decision emphatically pronounced by an overwhelming house patiently remaining from seven o'clock until midnight to be dazzled by scene after scene of splendour, to be amazed with such properties and decorations as have never before been produced, to be delighted with a fanciful legend, pleasant music and elaborate costume, and to marvel how such a work could have been brought to such a point of elaborate beauty. We said there would be no dissentient voice. We beg pardon, there will be just one. It will be raised by an isolated and thoroughly eccentric individual who planted himself in the very centre of the front row of the pit, and made himself so obnoxious during the evening by hissing in the wrong place,[1] by conducting himself foolishly, and by making uncalled-for remarks, that the major part of the stalls and pit, waiting quietly and courteously till the curtain had finally fallen, turned round like enraged lions on the obstinate offender, and threatened to break him into little pieces if he did not instantly quit the theatre and get home. The isolated and childish hostility of this silly young man, coupled with the threatening attitude of the audience towards him, proves that *Babil and Bijou* had gained the popular ear; and that, whatever might be thought of the occasional mystification of the story, of the length of many scenes, and of the almost nauseating excess of splendour, still such a bold and spirited undertaking as this was not to be hounded down and insulted by some very insignificant and obstinate personage. . . . And now, perhaps, will come the question, 'Well, and what was best? What was the finest sight and most original scene in the whole play?' It would be as well to ask a *bon vivant* to select his pet dish after a dinner of countless delicacies, or to make a child select a toy from the Lowther Arcade or Soho Bazaar. Some will vote for the quaint elf-like mystery, all king-cups and fairy-bells, of the prologuial scene: some will be describing the daring notion of the River of Life, with the history of costume from Jemima Ann, in 1872, to the pre-Adamite ape: some will be telling the children of the stage lobsters, the property oysters, the man octopus, the shrimps, the soles—all unequalled properties—to be seen in the coral grove underneath the sea. And then again there will be a rush and chatter of voices to tell the best news and most authentic intelligence of the Grand Ballet of the Seasons—how Spring was represented by a chorus of fresh-voiced lads, who sang with such exquisite freshness and innocence that the audience would have encored them three times over had not Mr. Boucicault come forward and pleaded. . . .

"Spring melted into Summer, not only by means of delicately graduating tints, but the whole landscape changed at the command of some hidden fairy: . . . Autumn brought out Mdlle. Henriette Dor [sic], such a dancer, not of the vulgar modern class, but of the old-fashioned poetry of motion, graceful and expressive style, such as has not been seen for many a long year: and . . . Autumn's wane produced a grand burst of effective colour, lighting up the stage with the colours of the rainbow, and producing an exciting finale of brilliancy, and . . . the curtain fell upon a fantastic winter scene making the house gasp with astonishment, and causing confidential neighbours to ask one another what now could possibly be coming. But the triumph was not quite complete even then. There was yet a scene which for magnificence and taste has never been equalled. Passing by some most clever cloud effects, we came at last to the Mountains of the Moon, and then saw the Princess Fortinbrasse reviewing her

[1] A curious comment on the prevailing habit of hissing the villain, whose appearance would constitute the *right place* in which to hiss.

Amazonian troops. This was the scene *par excellence* of the play, and will no doubt soon become the talk of the town. Such a glitter of gold, such burnished armour, such tossing plumes and jewelled head-dresses, such tunics of brown and blue, and black and scarlet, such lavish wealth, such fringes of bullion, such lances and swords gleaming in the limelight, such drummers and bandsmen in Royal apparel, such comely faces, and such superb specimens of womanhood, have never surely yet been combined with such scenes, and the isolated individual in the pit longing to applaud, looked supremely miserable, knowing at this moment he would have been a rash man to hiss."

At last the entertainment had ended, applause swept through the auditorium. Yet the *Féerie's* vogue was short. Burlesque had won. By one of those ironic strokes of fortune to which life accustoms us, this form of comedy, apparently moribund in 1873, was in reality on the verge of its most popular and enchanting period. Four years later the inimitable Kate Vaughan made her appearance as Maritana in Byron's[1] extravaganza *Little Don Caesar de Bazan*, and, with the other three members of a famous quartette—Edward Terry, Nellie Farren and E. W. Royce—, inaugurated that sequence of burlesques at the Gaiety, still so greatly celebrated in the annals of English Low Comedy.

But, at the time, this was not suspected. The future of the *Féerie*, as exemplified in *Babil and Bijou*, seemed bright enough. The false atmosphere of the first night continued for a little to cast its spell of intoxication. And in a second notice of the piece, a week later, the critic of the *Daily Telegraph* goes further, even, than in the first. Often, not until many years have passed, he writes, do the most favourable impressions of so complicated an entertainment stand out clearly in the mind. The prose has, this time, an almost Dickensian ring and gusto. "Then," he proceeds, "if we mistake not, will come back to us the happy idea of the half spirit, half mortal Bijou wandering through space to regain the lost regalia, and in regaining them to release her mother from captivity in the ruby, and to win her Babil, whose love were death unless the search is successful. Then we shall trace a delicate satirical meaning in many a scene, and perceive somehow that the author had a mind to show how poetry and art and taste and feeling are exposed to the attacks of coarse unrefined people and to the influence of brutal minds. Bijou is half of earth and half of fairyland. She is art, cheered on her way by delicate minds, by Mistigris, by the fairies, by the flowers, by sweet music, by all that is enthusiastic and beautiful in life. She is art, hunted down by the gnomes and the imps, by Skepsis and Pragma, by the uninteresting fish, by the coarse vegetables of the earth, by revolutionists and egotists, by all that is vulgar and unrefined in the world. Then, when the unrecognised impressions assert themselves, we shall remember

---

[1] Henry James Byron (1834–1884), actor and dramatist. He produced a number of farces, comedies and extravaganzas, a complete list of which, says the *D.N.B.*, "can scarcely be attempted". "He revelled", we are told, "in pun and pleasantry, and in a certain Cockney smartness of repartee."

possibly that there was something approaching to the dramatic when war is first declared between Melusine and Skepsis, when the regalia are confided to the spirits of air and water, subsequently to be discovered by the half-enchanted Bijou—that there was something bold, original and humorous in the exhibition of the River of Life, with its history of costume and interview between the Darwinian ape and Lord Dundreary—that the essence of true poetry is contained in that charming notion of the vegetables and fruits rebelling against the aristocracy of flowers because they contained sweet essences and were royally clothed, because they were loved by beautiful women and refined men—that poetry emphatically declared itself when the flowers, hard pressed by their coarser antagonists, summon to their aid the bees, the wasps, the butterflies, and the dragon flies, lovers and champions of the inhabitants of the garden—that, somehow or other, there was something inexpressibly sweet when the innocent boys burst upon us with their rare young voices, and carolled their delightful madrigal of spring . . . that there was a prettiness in the suggestion of Bijou's journey to the moon, a happy thought in the life in the lunar regions not altogether unworthy of Swift, and obviously imitated from the idea of *Gulliver's Travels*, a magnificent extravaganza in the display of the army of the Princess Fortinbrasse, and on the whole a not unwelcome termination to a not unpleasant allegory."

APPENDIX D

Louisa Lady Sitwell

By DAME ETHEL SMYTH

Letter to Osbert Sitwell about his Grandmother

My DEAR OSBERT,

You ask me to tell you anything I remember about my all too brief connection with your extremely unforgettable grandmother, Louisa Lady Sitwell. My impressions of her personality—so gentle yet so clean-cut—were heaped up with rapidity and violence during a period of relative calm in the epoch I tried to describe in my first volume of *Impressions that Remained*.

Four or five years before we met, I had conceived an iron determination to go to Germany and study music as first step to becoming a professional musician, an intention my father considered equivalent to "going on the streets" and vetoed with the vehemence such a conviction naturally engendered. Sometimes opposition took the form of cutting off my allowance, whereupon one borrowed small sums of the postman or the grocer "to be put down to the General"; and at one moment through the splintered panel of my locked bedroom door appeared a military jackboot—spur and all!

Eventually it was decided to pack me and my sister Mary off to school. Like most girls of that epoch I was deeply religious, lost in the raptures of Confirmation and all that goes with a first Communion. My chief school friend was your cousin Lucy Thomas, a girl of my own age, who never wearied of describing the charms and the fervent piety of her aunt Louisa Lady Sitwell. Indeed by degrees this lady came to loom in my imagination as a sort of Anglican "Blessed Virgin", regardless of the fact that she was a widow with two nearly grown-up children.

What at last brought her and me together was the sad death of one of Lucy's brothers. This gifted and saintly youth was at Liverpool, training for the Navy on board the *Conway*, and one of his favourite hymns was "I need Thee, precious Jesu". But both he and his aunt "Loo", who was specially attached to him, considered the tune so unsatisfactory, that she sent me a message by Lucy suggesting that I should write another for it. Which of course I did, but I never knew what the boy thought of it, for he died while Lucy and I were still at Miss Darke's school. His aunt, however, liked it so much that she wrote to me, sending me a long religious poem called "Coming" which she greatly admired, and asked me whether I felt tempted to set it to music.

I think it was in that connection that I was asked to go and stay at Wood End, the house she lived in at Scarborough, and talk matters over. As you probably know the finances of Renishaw, the family property, were not in a brilliant condition when your grandfather died, and to pull them together against the coming of age of your father was her chief preoccupation. I knew that her family considered her not only a fine woman of business, but also very musical, and needless to say, after possessing myself of two photos of her, which lived (as inspiration) on my writing-table, I rapturously fell in with her idea, and soon after departed for Wood End.

My first action there was to prove that the admirable French saying "Toute vérité n'est pas bonne à dire" did not yet form part of my worldly equipment, for when she sang to me, I appear to have said, "What a sweet voice you must have had when you were young, Lady Sitwell." And the nieces agreed that this compliment must have given their aunt a pang. True, she no longer sang habitually, but not because she realised that her voice was no longer what it had been.

Oh, shall I ever forget that visit! Of all the flaming passions that in my time have consumed my spiritual substance none raged more fiercely than the one kindled by your grandmother! I was too infatuated to ask myself whether she was really as beautiful as the vision that haunted me for the next few years; but, of one thing I am certain: when Nature set herself to create an ideal Victorian *grande dame* with a pronounced religious bent, she can never have done better!

I remember two instances in which she left a mark, so to speak, that went all through life with me. You never heard her talking about herself; her conversation always centred on the affairs of the people she was talking to. I well knew this was not my own habit, for my mother had told me often it was bad manners to talk so much of myself, but I found the subject so absorbing that I never cultivated the opposite art—the very essence of good breeding. Still I did think it very wonderful and attractive, and occasionally tried, rapidly as the effort broke down, to emulate it!

The second instance I have never forgotten, and to this day I have often checked impatience by recalling the scene! To me it was, and still is, torture to hang about, and I fear it must have been my habit to bully my girl friends and establish a certain funk if they kept me waiting. On this occasion I was going out with Lady Sitwell, and stood waiting at the foot of the stairs, gazing—no doubt impatiently— up at her door. Presently Edda Thomas (who was my fellow visitor at Wood End—not Lucy) shot past me, knocked at the half-open bedroom door of the lady of the house, and said, with a slight touch of trepidation in her voice, "*Ethel is ready!*" Whereupon a calm voice remarked, "*Then Ethel must wait.*" I really believe that in Scarborough, for the first time in my life, it dawned upon me that Miss Ethel Smyth was not the only person in the world, and I believe too that my idol meant me to take a hint and follow her example.

She had most amusing ways of conveying certain lessons. For instance Edda, who worshipped her and, in the end, almost lived with her, could not refrain from envying my power of giving Lady Sitwell intense musical joy and at last her aunt took her to her doctor to "treat" her for "*unreasonableness*"! I do not know what he did about it; very likely prescribed, at her aunt's private suggestion, something so nauseating that this "unreasonableness" died a natural death!

After Scarborough followed a few stray meetings. Your father came of age in 1881, and in '81 and '82 there were various parties at Renishaw, to one or two of which I was bidden. On one occasion George MacDonald and his family performed his dramatised version of *Pilgrim's Progress*. Crowds of relatives and friends were billeted about the county; my religious fervour had cooled down in Germany, but I heard the performance was very moving. (I should add that by now my father's opposition had also cooled down—chiefly, I fancy, because I had not exceeded my allowance!)

It has always seemed strange to me that one who evidently was an authoritative parent should have tolerated the presence in her home of such a thorough-paced rebel, but—she did! The nieces have since told me she was really interested in and genuinely fond of me; and I remember that their cousin, Goring Thomas, then a quite well-known musician, said mine was a case of a "real vocation". . . .

I don't think my infatuations ever blinded me to little weaknesses in those who inspired them. I well remember, for instance, an absurd little incident which for some obscure reason smuggled itself into my collection of Sitwell impressions. Lady Sitwell was more than rigid on the evil of joking on sacred subjects—(not, by the by, a fault of mine)—and one day, I am sure by sheer inadvertence—having referred before me, *a stranger*, to one of her great friends, Tait—the then Archbishop of Canterbury—as "*the ABC*", she instantly shot an arch glance in my direction which said as clearly as a spoken word: "Yes! I know this is next door to joking on sacred subjects, but for once *we will let it pass!*" I was not apt to take an extra reverential view of high Church dignitaries—not at that time, at least—and was rather . . . well, not exactly "provoked" but . . . a little *resentful* of that glance! But I held my peace.

The fact is I did feel at times rather a wolf in sheep's clothing—a feeling entertained, I am certain, by Florence Sitwell, my idol's only daughter, who I don't think approved of her mother's new adorer! But I was not particularly drawn to her either, so "here was naught for tears".

In the same way I retained next to no impression of George Sitwell, but for that there was another reason. I was rather insanely afraid that nine out of ten eligible young men were likely to fancy penniless girls wanted to "catch" them; still more painful thought, sometimes their Mamas might share this belief! ! I thought, and still believe, that this young man's mama was far too comprehending to think anything of the sort in my case, but it was as well to be on the safe side; not difficult if his mother possesses your whole heart!

It used to amuse and yet annoy me (for I think I must have been always what they call a feminist) to hear certain old ladies of both sexes, all in professing warm admiration for the way his mother was managing the regeneration of the Sitwell finances, sometimes talk of "*Poor George*", and pity him for being ridden on so tight a rein. So much so that to one of these I once said, "I do believe you would rather he should come in for Renishaw with nothing but the husks of wild oats in his pockets rather than enjoy a comfortable income thanks to his mother!" I don't remember what the reply was but I felt the shot *hit the target* and did not endear me to it! . . .

But now, dear Osbert, it is time to have done with these desultory attempts to give some idea of the impression made on one who was really a callow schoolgirl by a most remarkable and lovable woman. I will only add that the break-up of my own life took place in 1885 and during the ensuing years only one idea possessed me—the desperate and never-to-be-realised hope that time might bring back to me the chief treasure that had been swept away in the storm—the friendship of Elizabeth von Herzogenberg, who for seven years had been my all in all.

Strange that now, writing one by one these pages, the subject of them has come back into my consciousness with something of the same overwhelming force with which she entered it more than sixty years ago! I cannot even recall her appearance as I do that of others who had little or no real place in my life. But whereas at first it was sheer joy to feel her coming alive again in my memory, it is now something very like pain to reflect, that but for the story told in those autobiographical volumes I might have been near her to the last! But life is like that—what it gives you with one hand it takes away with the other!—Yours ever, E.

INDEX